UTILITARIANISM AND THE
NEW LIBERALISM

In this groundbreaking study, David Weinstein argues that nineteenth-century English New Liberalism was considerably more indebted to classical English utilitarianism than the received view holds. T. H. Green, L. T. Hobhouse, D. G. Ritchie and J. A. Hobson were liberal consequentialists who followed J. S. Mill in trying to accommodate robust, liberal moral rights with the normative goal of promoting self-realization. Through careful interpretation of each, Weinstein shows how these theorists brought together themes from idealism, perfectionism and especially utilitarianism to create the new liberalism. Like Mill, they were committed to liberalizing consequentialism and systematizing liberalism. Because they were no less consequentialists than they were liberals, they constitute a greatly undervalued resource, Mill notwithstanding, for contemporary moral philosophers who remain dedicated to defending a coherent form of liberal consequentialism. The New Liberals had already travelled much of the philosophical ground that contemporary liberal consequentialists are unknowingly retraveling.

DAVID WEINSTEIN is professor of political science at Wake Forest University, North Carolina. His previous publications include *Equal Freedom and Utility* (Cambridge, 1998) and *The New Liberalism* (co-edited with Avital Simhony, Cambridge, 2001).

IDEAS IN CONTEXT 83

Utilitarianism and the New Liberalism

IDEAS IN CONTEXT

Edited by Quentin Skinner and James Tully

The books in this series will discuss the emergence of intellectual traditions and of related new disciplines. The procedures, aims and vocabularies that were generated will be set in the context of the alternatives available within the contemporary frameworks of ideas and institutions. Through detailed studies of the evolution of such traditions, and their modification by different audiences, it is hoped that a new picture will form of the development of ideas in their concrete contexts. By this means, artificial distinctions between the history of philosophy, of the various sciences, of society and politics, and of literature may be seen to dissolve.

The series is published with the support of the Exxon Foundation.

A list of books in the series will be found at the end of the volume.

UTILITARIANISM AND THE NEW LIBERALISM

D. WEINSTEIN

Wake Forest University, Winston-Salem

CAMBRIDGE
UNIVERSITY PRESS

CAMBRIDGE UNIVERSITY PRESS

Cambridge, New York, Melbourne, Madrid, Cape Town, Singapore, São Paulo

Cambridge University Press
The Edinburgh Building, Cambridge CB2 8RU, UK

Published in the United States of America by Cambridge University Press, New York

www.cambridge.org
Information on this title: www.cambridge.org/9780521875288

First published 2007

Printed in the United Kingdom at the University Press, Cambridge

A catalogue record for this book is available from the British Library

ISBN 978-0-521-87528-8 hardback

For Kiddo

Contents

Preface

I would like to thank Gale Sigal, Peter Nicholson, Michael Freeden, Fred Rosen, Avital Simhony, Jerry Gaus, Robert Audi, Roger Crisp, Bart Schultz, David Brink, Avihu Zakai, Leah Hochman, Win-Chiat Lee, Lee Overton, Tom Brooks and Colin Tyler for their willingness to comment on parts of this manuscript over recent years.

I would also like to thank the National Endowment for the Humanities for a 1998 Summer Stipend; the Hebrew University of Jerusalem for awarding me a 1999 Visiting Professorship and Mansfield College, Oxford University for hosting me as 2003 Visiting Fellow. Many thanks, in addition, are owed to the Master and Fellows of Balliol College, Oxford University for allowing me to examine the T. H. Green Papers held at Balliol and to the Warden and Fellows of Merton College, Oxford University for granting me permission to examine the F. H. Bradley Papers held at Merton. Finally, I owe special debts of gratitude to Wake Forest University for providing me with a 2001 Reynolds Research Leave and to Dean Paul Escott and Dean Deborah Best for being flexible and generous by allowing me to take advantage of the other fellowship opportunities that I have had. Lastly, I am especially grateful to Kathy Smith, Chair of Political Science at Wake Forest, for being no less flexible and supportive.

Parts of this book have been published in *Political Studies, The Journal of the History of Ideas* and *Utilitas*. Segments have also been presented at international conferences of The International Society for Utilitarian Studies; annual meetings of the American Political Science Association; the 2003 Idealism Today conference, Manchester College, Oxford University and the Centre for the Study of Political Ideologies, Oxford University. I am grateful to the participants and commentators for their queries, criticisms and suggestions about how to make my account of the new liberals more compelling.

I have always viewed writing as a collective enterprise in which authors depend upon their critics to assist them in refining and clarifying what they are trying to say. Without sympathetic critics, and even unsympathetic ones, the practice of philosophy and intellectual history might produce better or worse results but it would certainly be lonelier and thus much less gratifying. Reading is equally collective rewriting. My text now begins life on its own.

CHAPTER I

Introduction

ANALYTICAL POLITICAL PHILOSOPHY AND THE HISTORY OF POLITICAL THOUGHT

The converging currents of Anglo-American political theory have swept away much of English political theory's distinctiveness including the latter's greater sensitiveness to its own historical past. For all its many virtues, contemporary Anglo-American political theory has become an impoverished history of ideas, having substituted a truncated eulogized canon for the richness of its predominantly English historical tradition.

This historical amnesia stems, in large part, from the legacy of logico-positivism, which discredited normative political theorizing as just another variety of emotivist venting and unmeaning metaphysical gibberish. Fortunately, Hart's *The Concept of Law* (1961) and Barry's *Political Argument* (1965) resurrected normative political theory. Rawls followed with *A Theory of Justice* (1971), which, in turn, unleashed an industry of criticism that shows no signs of abating.[1] Ironically, then, English analytical philosophy eviscerated English-speaking political theory early on in the last century only to redeem it fifty years later. And what it redeemed quickly spread elsewhere, becoming what we now know as Anglo-American political theory.

Whereas English political theory may have lost much of its identity in its confluence with Anglo-American political theory, the latter remains robustly at odds with the continental philosophical tradition. Whatever English political theory has become, its analytical rigor and empiricism extensively immunized it from the counter-Enlightenment preoccupations of continental theory. This is not to say that Anglo-American political

---

[1] I am following Philip Pettit, "The Contribution of Analytical Political Philosophy" in *A Companion to Contemporary Political Philosophy*, ed. Robert Goodin and Philip Pettit (Oxford: Blackwell, 1993), who provides a compelling account of the impact of analytical philosophy on modern political theory. Also see Richard Tuck's contribution, "The Contribution of History," in the same volume.

theory has been uninfluenced by continental theorizing, especially recently. Continental motifs have also informed late nineteenth-century English idealism, Berlin's value pluralism and even, as we shall momentarily see, the Cambridge School of textual interpretation.

Despite Anglo-American political theory's homogenizing interpolation, English theorists have resisted forsaking intellectual history more than their American counterparts. The triumph of conceptual analysis caused American political theorists to lose interest in the history of political thought except as a way of certifying their current theoretical positions. Canonical theorists were typically invoked (Nozick's use of Locke) as remarkably prescient in purportedly anticipating – or at least identifying – solutions to current conceptual disputes.

By the 1970s, the Cambridge School of political thought, led by Skinner, Pocock, Dunn and later Tuck, began challenging such interpretative strategies, countering that the meanings of past political philosophical texts could only be recovered with difficulty by historically contextualizing them. Contemporary English political theory has struggled to resist marginalizing the history of political thought in face of the ascendancy of philosophical analysis. Indeed, the parochialism of analysis has rejuvenated the former, which has, in turn, rebounded to the practice of analysis itself. For the Cambridge School, intellectual history remains a veiled analytic exercise. Both its method and purpose are fundamentally linguistic. What words formerly meant can help us refine our own meanings and consequently improve our own philosophical thinking. Intellectual history, when not rational reconstruction, can be analytically provocative and therefore "educationally mandatory."[2]

Pocock is less vexed than Skinner about the dangers of parochialism, which may partially account for the similarities between his method of doing intellectual history and continental political theory. For instance, his emphasis on the determining roles played by discursive paradigms makes his interpretative methodology structuralist. Yet, his interpretative methodology is equally post-structuralist insofar as meanings are unstable since he claims that every textual interpretation invariably spins, recasts and multiplies meanings in ways unintended by the author. As one post-structuralist insists, "our meaning always escapes any unitary conscious grasp we may have of it, for language, as 'writing,' inevitably harbors the

[2] John Dunn, *The History of Political Theory and other Essays* (Cambridge: Cambridge University Press, 1996), 1.

possibility of ... an indefinite multiplicity of recontextualizations and reinterpretations."[3]

Contemporary Oxford political theory has not been entirely swept aside by the vogue of philosophical analysis either. Isaiah Berlin early on abandoned analytical theorizing for Herderian-inspired history of ideas. Like Pocock, he affirms that the "history not only of thought, but of consciousness, opinion, action too, of morals, politics, aesthetics, is to a large degree a history of dominant models." In examining any civilization, "you will find that its most characteristic writings ... reflect a particular pattern of life which those who are responsible for these writings ... are dominated by."[4] Echoing Skinner, he writes that "unless you try by some act of imagination to reconstruct within yourself the form of life which these people led ... your chances of truly understanding ... their writings and really knowing what Plato meant ... are small."[5] In short, in order to interpret Plato properly, we must contextualize him as best we possibly can by re-imagining the form of life in which he lived and philosophized.

More recently, Oxford's Freeden has championed conceptual political theory but also without forsaking the value of the history of political thought. Following Gallie, Freeden agrees that conceptual disputes are unavoidable but locates the source of these disputes in the underlying ideological structure of political theorizing. For Freeden, political ideologies are distinct systems of interrelated conceptual interpretations. The disagreements between liberalism and socialism about liberty are tethered, for example, to their respective disagreements about the meaning of equality. Hence, conceptual disputes are always disputes about a host of interconnected political ideas. Political ideas come in distinctive conceptual packages. Diligent intellectual history is crucial in sensitizing us to the nuanced variety of these conceptual packages, reminding us of the contested nature of all normative political concepts and thus commemorating the always unfinished nature of political theory.[6]

In sum, analytical English political theory has never forsworn the history of political thought as much as its American counterpart. It has not relegated intellectual history to the margins of scholarship despite the

---

[3] T. McCarthy, "The Politics of the Ineffable," *Philosophical Forum*, 21 (1989–90), 148.

[4] Isaiah Berlin, *The Roots of Romanticism* (Princeton: Princeton University Press, 1999), 2.

[5] *Ibid.*, 62.

[6] See Michael Freeden, *Ideologies and Political Theory* (Oxford: Oxford University Press, 1996). Also see John Plamenatz and W. L. Weinstein for earlier Oxford combinations of conceptual analysis and the history of political thought. See especially John Plamenatz, *Consent, Freedom and Political Obligation* (Oxford: Oxford University Press, 1968) and W. L. Weinstein, "The Concept of Liberty in Nineteenth Century English Political Thought," *Political Studies*, 13 (1965).

ascendance of Anglo-American philosophical analysis. And in taking intellectual history seriously, English political theory has been less historically nearsighted and less prone to mistake its purported discoveries for unwitting duplications of past debates.[7]

Nevertheless, for all its greater historical sensitivity to its own past, contemporary English political theory has not entirely avoided following American political theory in dichotomizing this past, reducing varieties of liberalism, utilitarianism, communitarianism and socialism to mutually exclusive, rival discourses. Dichotomizing conceptual analysis has encouraged contemporary analytic liberals to reconstruct rationally their own very uncertain tradition in accordance with their analytical preoccupations, compressing the history of liberalism into a slim and convenient canonical tale full of pregnant anticipations. This study will try to renarrate an undervalued piece of this history, hoping to restore it to prominence in the liberal canon.

More particularly, this study examines two historical versions of two purportedly rival theoretical discourses, namely nineteenth-century English utilitarianism and turn-of-the-century, English new liberalism. I suggest, first of all, that new liberals borrowed more from nineteenth-century English utilitarianism than they rejected. In my view, the new liberalism, including Green's new liberalism, was fundamentally consequentialist if not always straightforwardly and traditionally utilitarian. Secondly, I insist that precisely because the new liberalism absorbed more utilitarianism than the received view acknowledges, contemporary critics of utilitarianism should proceed more judiciously in condemning utilitarianism as fundamentally incompatible with liberalism. In other words, the new liberalism's *actual* historical debts to nineteenth-century utilitarianism reinforces the cogency and promise of recent analytical attempts to liberalize utilitarianism by investing it with respect for strong moral rights and robustly celebrating individuality.[8]

---

[7] For the way that contemporary liberals and communitarians replay unknowingly new liberal political theory in their efforts to accommodate their positions, see Avital Simhony and D. Weinstein, "Introduction" in *The New Liberalism: Reconciling Liberty and Community*, ed. Avital Simhony and D. Weinstein (Cambridge: Cambridge University Press, 2001).

[8] My study assumes that the reader is sufficiently familiar with several basic terms of contemporary moral theory. These include liberal utilitarianism, consequentialism and perfectionism. For readers wishing to familiarize themselves with these concepts more adequately, I suggest they consult the following: for liberal utilitarianism, see Jonathan Riley, *Liberal Utilitarianism: Social Choice Theory and J. S. Mill's Philosophy* (Cambridge: Cambridge University Press, 1988) and see the "Introduction" to my *Equal Freedom and Utility: Herbert Spencer's Liberal Utilitarianism* (Cambridge: Cambridge University Press, 1998); for consequentialism, see *Consequentialism*, ed. Stephen Darwall (Oxford:

IDEALISM, UTILITARIANISM AND THE NEW LIBERALISM

Utilitarianism reigned in England during the nineteenth century, gradually giving way to analytical egalitarian liberalism during the twentieth. As English political theory lost its distinctively utilitarian identity, it also lost its distinctively English identity, becoming just another comforting voice in the homogenizing discourse of Anglo-American, egalitarian liberalism.

Egalitarian liberalism's pedigree emerged in the late nineteenth and early twentieth centuries via English new liberals such as Green, Hobhouse, Hobson and Ritchie who were, in turn, powerfully influenced by the British idealists.[9] Hence, the history of the triumph of Anglo-American egalitarian liberalism requires taking account of its undervalued indebtedness to the new liberalism. And insofar as the new liberalism borrowed heavily from idealism, including especially the latter's criticisms of Benthamite utilitarianism, we must reach back into idealism too if we wish to understand properly the emergence of egalitarian liberalism. So the history of Anglo-American liberalism should include the legacy of the new liberalism and idealism much better than it does. As we shall see, this legacy is, in turn, considerably more indebted to nineteenth-century utilitarianism than we have otherwise been misled to expect. This study makes a sustained and extensive effort to substantiate these much underrated debts.

British idealists combined a coherence theory of truth with neo-Hegelian historical teleology. For them, thinking partially constitutes whatever we describe, explain or interpret. Facts are never simply discovered nor just speak for themselves but are mediated by cognition. When we theorize, we make and organize facts according to our systems of value, interpretative perspectives and preoccupations. Hence, the more

---

Blackwell, 2003); for perfectionism, see Thomas Hurka, *Perfectionism* (Oxford: Oxford University Press, 1993); and for a comprehensive historical and conceptual introduction to utilitarianism, see Geoffrey Scarre, *Utilitarianism* (London and New York: Routledge, 1996).

[9] Some scholars consider Green and Ritchie idealists as much as new liberals. For Peter Nicholson, *The Political Philosophy of the British Idealists* (Cambridge: Cambridge University Press, 1990), Green is a quintessential idealist as much as Bradley and Bosanquet. For David Boucher and Andrew Vincent, *British Idealism and Political Theory* (Edinburgh: Edinburgh University Press, 2001), 12–13, Green, Bosanquet and Ritchie are idealists in addition to Bradley, Caird, Jones, Haldane, Collingwood and Oakeshott. By contrast, Hobhouse and Hobson are new liberals. Boucher and Vincent nevertheless claim that idealists and new liberals "shared the same general moral and political ideals." But Boucher calls Green, Caird, Ritchie, Bosanquet, Jones and Haldane "Idealist New Liberals" in his "Introduction," *The British Idealists*, ed. David Boucher (Cambridge: Cambridge University Press, 1997), xxiii. Also see 182–3, n34, where Boucher and Vincent claim that the new liberalism fractured into three major strands (left, center and right) after 1914. For them, Hobson is a left new liberal whereas Hobhouse is a centrist new liberal.

coherently we theoretically mediate and organize the world, the more truthful our understanding becomes. And as we theorize the world with increasing sophistication, we realize universal history more completely.

British idealists like Bradley and Bosanquet were as much indebted to Hegel for their social ontology and moral and political theory as for their conception of history. Bradley argues that individuals are socially consti-tuted, making morality deeply social in the sense that acting morally requires acting *for* others rather than simply leaving them alone. Hence, insofar as Bradley regards good as self-realization, acting morally means promoting everyone's self-realization, not merely one's own. Being so interdependently constituted, we best promote our own self-realization by simultaneously promoting our fellow citizens' and they best promote theirs by promoting ours.[10] Moreover, because our identities are socially encum-bered, rationalistic moral theories like utilitarianism and Kantianism are misconceived and self-defeating. Both theories share the misguided pre-Hegelian delusion that we can somehow detach ourselves from our social milieu when determining how to act. Acting morally primarily entails embracing one's socially constituted identity by fulfilling "one's station and its duties." Nonetheless, fulfilling the duties of one's station is not the whole of morality since the kind of society in which one lives also matters. For Bradley, conventional morality must not be taken uncritically.

Bosanquet's *The Philosophical Theory of the State* (1899) takes up polit-ically where Bradley's *Ethical Studies* (1876) leaves off. Bosanquet agrees with Bradley that, insofar as our identities are socially constituted, others are not merely external constraints on our self-realization. Societies are free according to how well they manipulate social relations so that everyone flourishes. For Bosanquet, and for new liberals as well, freedom consists in being empowered by meaningful opportunities ("positive or political . . . liberty") as well as being left alone ("negative or juristic liberty"). "It . . . must be maintained . . . that the 'higher' liberty is also . . . the 'larger' liberty, presenting the greater area to activity and the more extensive choice to self-determination."[11] For Bosanquet, higher freedom *also* entails

---

[10] F. H. Bradley [1927], *Ethical Studies* (Oxford: Oxford University Press, 1988), 116. According to Nicholson, *The Political Philosophy of the British Idealists*, 14, Bradley's conception of self-realization, though difficult to understand, is crucially important because it underlies "the whole political philosophy of the British Idealists." And since Nicholson regards Green as a British idealist, we can assume that Nicholson believes that Bradley's notion of self-realization grounds Green's political theory. For Nicholson's subtle analysis of Bradley's conception of self-realization, see 12–17. Also see Richard Wollheim's briefer discussion in *F. H. Bradley* (London: Penguin, 1959), 236–9.

[11] Bernard Bosanquet [1899], *The Philosophical Theory of the State*, eds. Gerald F. Gaus and William Sweet (South Bend, IN: St. Augustine's, 2001), 147.

mastering oneself in the sense of giving "effect to the self as a whole, or remov[ing] its contradictions and so mak[ing] it most fully what it is able to be."[12] Being fully free is therefore being autonomous.

Moreover, being positively free entails juridical security: Our "liberty . . . may be identified with such a system [of rights] considered as the condition and guarantee of our becoming the best that we have it in us to be."[13] Self-realization is most effectively promoted indirectly by a system of strong, though not indefeasible, rights. As with liberal utilitarianism, rights function as ready-made decision procedures. Like habitual bodily activities such as walking or even just breathing, acting justly by respecting other's rights usually demands "no effort of attention" enabling citizens to devote themselves to "problems which demand . . . intenser efforts."[14] And whenever citizens lose their justice habit, liberal states swiftly reeducate them through punishment. While states can never make citizens just, they can encourage just behavior indirectly by maintaining a system of rights. By enforcing rights, they "clear the road to true volition" thus securing the conditions of self-realization.[15] And insofar as states restrict themselves to hindering "hindrances of the good life," they warrant our loyalty.[16]

As we shall shortly see, new liberals theorized self-realization, freedom and rights much like idealists such as Bradley and Bosanquet. Few readers will find this similarity surprising. But what many might find surprising are their similar criticisms of Benthamite utilitarianism (or at least what they took Benthamite utilitarianism to be) and, even more remarkably, their similar receptivity to improved Millian utilitarianism. Idealists famously attacked utilitarianism on many fronts, which new liberals mimicked without explicitly acknowledging. However, like new liberals, they were

---

[12] *Ibid.*, 149–50. Bosanquet's theory of freedom complements Gerald MacCallum's later celebrated analysis of the over-inflated distinction between negative and positive freedom. For MacCallum, see Gerald C. MacCallum, "Negative and Positive Freedom," *Philosophical Review*, 76 (1967). For Bosanquet, see, *The Philosophical Theory of the State*, 148.

[13] *Ibid.*, 139   [14] *Ibid.*, 201–2.

[15] *Ibid.*, 216. According to Nicholson, Bosanquet follows Green insisting that the state should limit itself primarily to enforcing rights as conditions of individual self-realization though he differs from Green somewhat regarding the content of social rights. Hence, Bosanquet did not "radically and dangerously" depart from Green contrary to the "myth" created by Hobhouse in his 1918 *The Metaphysical Theory of the State: A Criticism*. In particular, for Nicholson, Hobhouse's account of Bosanquet's conception of the general will as literally a corporate independent will is a misplaced "caricature." See Nicholson, *The Political Philosophy of the British Idealists*, 199 and 207. Also see S. Panagakou, "Defending Bosanquet's Philosophical Theory of the State: A Reassessment of the 'Bosanquet–Hobhouse Controversy'," *British Journal of Politics and International Relations*, 7 (2005), 29–47.

[16] Bosanquet, *The Philosophical Theory of the State*, 21. Also see 155–6 for more on Bosanquet's account of political obligation.

not unambiguously anti-consequentialist. Furthermore, though they were clearly more hostile to *utilitarian* consequentialism than new liberals, they never rejected utilitarianism *in toto*. They followed Green, conceding that utilitarianism possessed at least some practical value. The story of the relationship between idealism, utilitarianism and the new liberalism is complicated and nuanced.

Bosanquet was much less preoccupied with utilitarianism than Bradley though he criticized Bentham, Mill and Spencer especially in Chapter III of *The Philosophical Theory of the State*. Mostly, Bosanquet took issue with what he regarded as Bentham, Mill and Spencer's excessive individualism, which he felt their respective theories of liberty presupposed. Nevertheless, Bosanquet treats utilitarianism briefly on occasion such as where he discusses Sidgwick critically in the "Introduction to the Second Edition" of *The Philosophical Theory of the State*. For instance, there, Bosanquet says that every person and organization "must take account of the consequences" of their actions, which entails that "limitations on veracity, justice, and good faith (I take Sidgwick's cases) become more and more imperative."[17] For Bosanquet, in other words, utilitarian considerations matter for determining right action. They also matter because "taking perfection as our criterion we are not barred from recognizing pleasure as an evidence . . . of certain elements in it."[18]

According to Nicholson, Bradley and Bosanquet admired each other greatly. In Nicholson's view, Bradley's *Ethical Studies* especially influenced Bosanquet, causing him to describe Bradley as his "master." Bradley, in turn, wrote Bosanquet that he valued his opinion most of all. However, Nicholson believes that neither Bradley nor Green knew one another particularly well nor seem to have directly influenced each other much, which is surprising.[19] Moreover, unlike Green as well as unlike Bosanquet, Bradley avoided political philosophy. Whereas as one might say that *Ethical Studies* complements Green's *Prolegomena to Ethics*, Bradley never explored the political implications of his moral theory as Green did in *Lectures on the Principles of Political Obligation* or as Bosanquet did in *The Philosophical Theory of the State*.

---

[17] *Ibid.*, 37–8, n53.

[18] Bernard Bosanquet, "Hedonism among the Idealists," *Mind*, n.s., 12 (1903), 213.

[19] Nicholson, *The Political Philosophy of the British Idealists*, 50–3. Nicholson claims that Bradley (*Ethical Studies*, 96, note 1) only once referred to Green explicitly. Nicholson also holds that Bosanquet viewed hedonism and utilitarianism more favorably than Bradley. I have been arguing that Bradley, like new liberals after him, was much less adverse to utilitarianism than most scholars have recognized. Nicholson's assessment may therefore be overstated.

Nevertheless, as we are about to see in the chapters that follow, Bradley's ambivalence towards utilitarianism not only matched Green's in crucial respects but also reappeared in Hobhouse, Ritchie and Hobson. Though Bradley may not have influenced Green directly (and vice versa) nor Hobhouse, Ritchie and Hobson, still much in the new liberalism resembles Bradley's idealism, including their respective assessments of the then dominant utilitarianism. But my concern here is principally with the new liberalism and its philosophical debts to utilitarianism. British idealism shared some of these debts but not nearly so extensively.

New liberals, then, shared some of Bradley's ambivalence about utilitarianism. And they also followed Bradley and Bosanquet in combining a moralized theory of freedom and strong rights with a communitarian social ontology. For Green, Ritchie, Hobhouse and Hobson, moral self-realization was unconditionally good. Realizing oneself morally meant being fully free by being both "outward[ly]" and "inward[ly]" free. Such freedom meant, as Green famously said, having the enabling "positive power or capacity of doing ... something worth doing" *and* actually "doing ... something worth doing."[20] Or as Hobhouse put it, morally realizing oneself meant being "moral[ly]" as well as "social[ly]" free.[21]

For new liberals as well, rights indirectly promoted everyone's self-realization by enabling each with opportunities to flourish. And to the extent that each flourished morally, each, in turn, promoted common good by respecting the rights of others. Thus, for Hobhouse, common good was "the foundation of all personal rights."[22] In Green's words, rights realize our moral capacity negatively by "securing the treatment of one man by another as equally free with himself, but they do not realise it positively, because their possession does not imply that ... the individual makes a common good his own."[23]

In addition, new liberals invoked strong rights in defense of robust equal opportunity. Although they concurred with politically cautious idealists like Bosanquet that possessing property was a potent means of "self-utterance" and therefore crucial to externalizing and realizing ourselves successfully, they also stipulated that private property was

---

[20] T. H. Green [1881], "Lecture on 'Liberal Legislation and Freedom of Contract'," *Collected Works of T. H. Green*, ed. Peter Nicholson (Bristol: Thoemmes Press, 1997), Vol. III, 371.

[21] L. T. Hobhouse [1922], *The Elements of Social Justice* (London: Allen and Unwin, 1949), 57.

[22] L. T. Hobhouse [1911], *Social Evolution and Political Theory* (Port Washington, DC: Kennikat Press, 1968), 198.

[23] T. H. Green [1886], *Lectures on the Principles of Political Obligation*, *Collected Works of T. H. Green*, Vol. II, Sect. 25.

legitimate only as long as it did not subvert equal opportunity.[24] In Hobson's words, "A man is not really free for purposes of self-development ... who is not adequately provided" with equal and easy access to land, a home, capital and credit.[25] New liberals, therefore, transformed English liberalism by making social welfare, and the state's role in promoting it, pivotal. But this story is a slightly more familiar one. Much less familiar, if not entirely unfamiliar, is the extent to which they also transformed utilitarianism.

Regrettably, contemporary Anglo-American political theory has under-appreciated the new liberalism both for the way in which it accommodates liberalism with what we now call communitarianism and for the way in which it additionally accommodates liberalism with utilitarianism. No doubt the new liberalism has gone undervalued partly because it makes these accommodations and partly because it constitutes an idiosyncratic medley of neo-Kantianism, consequentialism and perfectionism.[26] Rather than creating an interconnected, legitimizing narrative, these mixed allegiances have caused contemporary liberals and communitarians to disable themselves, due to their historical insensitivity, in their struggle for theoretical accommodation.[27] Contemporary liberals

---

[24] Of course, not all idealists favored limited government like Bosanquet. Some, like Jones and Collingwood, favored vigorously expanding equal opportunities through government like the new liberals.

[25] J. A. Hobson [1909], *The Crisis of Liberalism*, ed. P. F. Clarke (Brighton: Barnes and Noble, 1974), xii. Also see L. T. Hobhouse [1911], *Liberalism* (Oxford: Oxford University Press, 1964), 87, where Hobhouse labels his new liberalism, "Liberal Socialism."

[26] See D. Weinstein, "The New Liberalism and the Rejection of Utilitarianism" in *The New Liberalism*.

[27] See especially Simhony and Weinstein, "Introduction" in *The New Liberalism*. Contemporary political theory's historical myopia has consequently made Raz's perfectionist liberalism seem more anomalous than it is in fact. Though Mulhall and Swift are correct in concluding that Raz "transcends" the rivalry between liberalism and communitarianism, they overemphasize his originality (Stephen Mulhall and Adam Swift, *Liberals and Communitarians* (Oxford: Blackwell, 1996), 250). Raz's perfectionist liberalism is refurbished new liberalism with some differences. For instance, Raz distinguishes autonomy, a seminal value requiring serious political attention, from self-realization, which he holds is merely one variety of autonomy. Whereas a self-realizing person develops all of his capacities to their full potential, an autonomous person merely develops "a conception of himself, and his actions are sensitive to his past." In "embracing goals and commitments, in coming to care about one thing or another," such persons "give[s] shape" to their lives though not necessarily according to a unified plan as we shall see Hobhouse claims (Joseph Raz, *The Morality of Freedom* [Oxford: Clarendon Press, 1986, 375 and 387]). Notwithstanding such differences, for Raz, autonomous agents nevertheless "identify" with their choices and remain "loyal" to them just like new liberal self-realizing agents. Secondly, in shaping their lives, autonomous agents, like new liberal, self-realizing agents, do not arbitrarily re-create themselves in spite of their social circumstances. Brute Nietzschean self-creation is impossible, for we are all born into communities presupposing our values. At best, acting autonomously transforms slightly, or reconfirms, these values selectively (382 and 387–8). But more than anything, Raz echoes new liberals because of the thoroughly liberal nature of his perfectionism. For Raz, following the new liberals, rights equalize opportunities for

and utilitarians have likewise handicapped themselves just as much, if not more, in their parallel attempts at accommodation. Again, the latter project of accommodation concerns me primarily in this study.

KANT AND HEGEL

[W]oe to him who crawls through the windings of eudaemonism in order to discover something that releases the criminal from punishment or even reduces its amount by the advantage it promises, in accordance with the Pharisaical saying, "It is better for *one* man to die than for an entire people to perish."[28]

The preceding from *The Metaphysics of Morals* reinforces the view that Kant was no less anti-hedonistic than he was anti-utilitarian. For instance, Thomas Hill, Jr. insists rather typically that much of Kant's ethics was "devoted to putting happiness in its place."[29] And although Hill admits that, for Kant, acting for the sake of happiness is permissible as long as doing so is compatible with duty, Hill nevertheless reads him as devaluing happiness as an essentially unworthy pursuit. By splitting happiness off from virtue, he thus parts company with perfectionists going back to Aristotle for whom both virtue and happiness constitute human flourishing.

Contrary to views of Kant typified by Hill, Paul Guyer has insisted that Kant never irrecoverably divorced happiness from virtue. For Guyer's Kant, virtue and happiness were always inseparable both in Kant's early unpublished notes and fragments on moral philosophy and in his mature published writings. They were permanently and ineluctably "joined at the

---

acting autonomously. Rights are necessary though insufficient conditions for achieving autonomy. Furthermore, these conditions must be redistributively robust if citizens are to enjoy *meaningful* opportunities to make the best of themselves. Hence, as with new liberals, rights indirectly promote good. Governments cannot make citizens good but governments should indirectly encourage them to make themselves good by providing appropriate opportunities. Hence, politics can, and should be, perfectionist: "The autonomy principle permits and even requires governments to create morally valuable opportunities, and to eliminate repugnant ones. In other words, we are duty bound to provide fellow citizens with the conditions of autonomy as long as we do not harm them. Coercing citizens into leading valuable lives harms them whereas providing valuable options for all harms no one. For more on how contemporary theorists, including Miller especially, unwittingly renegotiate new liberal efforts to fuse liberalism and communitarianism, see D. Weinstein, "English Political Theory in the Nineteenth and Twentieth Centuries" in *Handbook of Political Theory*, ed. Gerald Gaus and Chandran Kukathas (London: Sage, 2004).

[28] Immanuel Kant [1797], *The Metaphysics of Morals*, trans. Mary Gregor (Cambridge: Cambridge University Press, 1991), 183. Leah Hochman has suggested to me that Kant misreads the Pharisaical tradition of Rabbinic Judaism according to which killing one person kills an entire people because when one kills a single individual, one also kills that individual's innumerable descendants. Hence, one is really not just sacrificing one to save many but sacrificing perhaps just as many to save many.

[29] Thomas E. Hill, Jr., "Happiness and Human Flourishing" in *Human Welfare and Moral Worth* (Oxford: Clarendon Press, 2002), 168–9.

hip."[30] Whereas in earlier, unpublished material, Kant valued virtue instrumentally as necessary for realizing happiness qua a flourishing, harmonious life (what I shall call H1), which alone had intrinsic value, in his post-1781 "critical" writings he began characterizing virtue as being intrinsically valuable. That is, early on, Kant deemed human flourishing (H1) intrinsically good (much as Hobhouse later did as we shall see soon enough). Later on, however, he *privileged* virtue's intrinsic goodness without denying that flourishing (H1) partially constituted it.[31] Moreover, and even more importantly for my present purpose, Kant subsequently began championing another, more nuanced happiness that he often referred to as self-contentment (what I shall call H2). Happiness not only meant a well-ordered, flourishing life in Aristotle's sense. Such a life, as constituting a virtuous, autonomous life in part, also generated self-contentment as its *accompanying* contingent attribute. To make his point, Guyer quotes *The Critique of Practical Reason* (*CPracR*) (1787):

Does one not have a word that designates not a pleasure [*Genuß*] like that of happiness but yet a delight in one's own existence, an analog of happiness, which must necessarily accompany the consciousness of virtue? Yes! This word is *self-contentment* ... Freedom and the consciousness of it as a capacity to follow the moral law with an overpowering disposition is *independence from inclinations*, at least as determining (if not *affecting*) grounds of our desire, and, so far as I am conscious of it in following my moral maxims, the sole source of an unalterable contentment connected with it and resting on no particular feeling. (*CPracR*, 5: 117–18)[32]

Here virtue produces a different kind of happiness (H2), namely "self-contentment," as its contingent accompaniment. Wherever virtue flourishes, this kind of happiness thrives as well, testifying to virtue's presence. As Guyer puts it, happiness (H2) makes moral conduct "intelligible."[33]

---

[30] Paul Guyer, "Nature, Freedom and Happiness: The Third Proposition of Kant's *Idea for a Universal History*" in Paul Guyer, *Kant on Freedom, Law, and Happiness* (Cambridge: Cambridge University Press, 2000), 379. Guyer also writes that "the traditional assumptions that Kant's moral philosophy concerns solely the purity of intentions without regard to their realization in nature, and that it prescribes as the object of moral willing solely virtue and not happiness, are misleading" (378).

[31] Regarding Kant's earlier position about happiness' intrinsic value, see especially page 116 where Guyer suggests: "Rather, what Kant appears to be arguing is that although our pleasures considered separately are merely natural, the principle of their unity is intellectual, therefore a product of freedom rather than nature, but also itself a source of pleasure even greater than that of our particular sensory gratifications."

[32] Cited in Guyer, "Kant's Morality of Law and Morality of Freedom" in *Kant on Freedom, Law, and Happiness*, 165.

[33] Guyer, "Nature, Freedom, and Happiness: The Third Proposition of Kant's Idea for a Universal History," 386.

Another passage from Kant's later *The Metaphysics of Morals* makes Guyer's point about the relationship between virtue and happiness (H2) more clearly and more forcefully:

When a thoughtful man has overcome incentives to vice and is aware of having done his often bitter duty, he finds himself in a state that could well be called happiness, a state of contentment and peace of soul in which virtue is its own reward. Now a eudaemonist says: This delight, this happiness is really his motive for acting virtuously. The concept of duty does not determine his will *directly*, he is moved to do his duty only *by means of* the happiness he anticipates. But since he can expect this *reward* [my italics] of virtue only from consciousness of having done his duty, it is clear that the latter must have come first, that is, he must find himself under obligation to do his duty before he thinks that happiness will result from his observance of duty and without thinking of this. A eudaemonist's *etiology* involves him in a *circle*; that is to say, he can hope to be *happy* (or inwardly blessed) only if he is conscious of having fulfilled his duty, but he can be moved to fulfill his duty only if he foresees that he will be made happy by it. But there is also a *contradiction* in this reasoning. For on the one hand he ought to fulfill his duty without first asking what effect this will have on his happiness, and so on *moral* grounds; but on the other hand he can *recognize* [my italics] that something is his duty only by whether he can count on gaining happiness by doing it, and so in accordance with a *sensibly dependent* principle, which is the direct opposite of the moral principle.[34]

Happiness, in short, helps us to "recognize" whenever we are doing our duty because a certain kind of happiness (H2) invariably accompanies doing one's duty. Wherever virtue goes, "self-contentment" is sure to follow, making "self-contentment" virtue's sign. Acting from duty satisfies, signaling dutiful behavior's presence. As we saw above, Bradley's account of the relationship between virtue and happiness was remarkably similar. And as we shall see subsequently, Green's account of the relationship between virtue and happiness was equally nearly identical. But Green went further than Bradley, concluding that a suitably refined utilitarianism could substitute practically in place of his moral theory. In sum, then, we will see how Kant's earlier account of virtue and happiness (H1) resembled Hobhouse's view while Bradley and Green's account of this relationship resembled Kant's mature view of virtue and happiness (H2). And though

---

[34] Kant, *The Metaphysics of Morals*, 183. Kant continues: "Pleasure that must precede one's observance of the law in order for one to act in conformity with the law is sensibly dependent and one's conduct follows the *order of nature*, but pleasure that must be *preceded* by the law in order to be felt is in the *moral order*. If this distinction is not observed, if eudaemonism (the principle of happiness) is set up as the basic principle instead of *eleutheronomy* (the principle of the freedom of internal lawgiving), the result is the *euthanasia* (easy death) of all morals." In other words, eleutheronomous pleasure accompanying virtue is "in" morality and is therefore worthy. It attaches to morality as a marker of it.

Bradley and Green's views are nearly identical, Green nevertheless goes beyond Bradley, conceding utilitarianism's considerable practical value, especially in politics. Green's concession is, in all likelihood, driven by his greater interest in political theory.

In his obituary notice about Bradley, A. E. Taylor writes that Bradley believed that "Green's work would have been of more permanent value if he had selected Hegel rather than Kant as the thinker whom he should either follow, or desert only when he was absolutely clear about his reasons for disagreement."[35] Indeed, we have seen how Green plainly owed much to Kant, at least with respect to the relationship between virtue and happiness. But new liberals, including Green, owed much to Hegel despite Bradley's assessment of Green and Hobhouse's infamous criticisms of the sinister Hegelianism infecting Bosanquet's theory of state.

Recent interpreters of Hegel have stressed that Hegel follows Kant more closely than has too often been assumed. For instance, Franco maintains that sympathetic Hegel scholars like Avineri, Pelczynski and Taylor have rescued Hegel as a genuinely liberal communitarian though ironically at the cost of understating his continuity with Kant.[36] Likewise, Patten insists that Hegel followed Kant more closely than is usually granted particularly with respect to how both understood freedom. While, according to Patten, Hegel denies that reason or duty *alone* can motivate, he nevertheless holds that the "objectively free agent" is motivated by "a desire or disposition that it is reasonable or appropriate for him to have in the circumstances."[37] This

---

[35] A. E. Taylor, "F. H. Bradley," *Mind*, n.s., 34 (January, 1925), 8. Also see Nicholson, *The Political Philosophy of the British Idealists*, 51. Nicholson also contends that it is wrong to assume that Bradley was primarily Hegelian while Green was Kantian inasmuch as Bradley neither swallows Hegel wholesale nor rejects Kant entirely. Moreover, Green often criticizes Kant as well as partially affirms Hegel. (30). This assessment seems exactly right and is hardly surprising insofar as Kant and Hegel were not, as revisionists correctly contend, so antagonistic.

[36] Paul Franco, *Hegel's Philosophy of Freedom* (New Haven and London: Yale University Press, 1999), xi.

[37] Alan Patten, *Hegel's Idea of Freedom* (Oxford: Oxford University Press, 1999), 57. Therefore, for Hegel, desires profitably reinforce moral behavior as long as they are reasonable. The desire for happiness, in particular, can boost moral action most effectively when it is reasonable, namely when it is endorsed by reason. Also see Robert Pippin, "Hegel's Practical Philosophy: The Realization of Freedom" in *The Cambridge Companion to German Idealism*, ed. Karl Ameriks (Cambridge: Cambridge University Press, 2000), 194, where Pippin notes that, for Kant, the desire for happiness is one among several "'helping' elements, useful and motivationally helpful" toward acting rightly. By contrast, Hegel's helping consideration is a "more Aristotelian consideration of the original, indispensable role of the ethical community in the formation and very being of individuals." In other words, reasonableness is always communally situated in institutional practices, customs and habits, making the vitality of the latter a source of moral reinforcement. Finally, for an example of Hegel's argument that "subjective satisfaction" (presumably pleasure) is contingently "present" in acting rightly, see *Hegel's Philosophy of Right*, trans. T. M. Knox (Oxford: Oxford University Press, 1952), Sect.124.

disposition constitutes rational freedom for Hegel, which Patten maintains is not inimical to Kant's conception of rational freedom. Reflective freedom, by contrast for Hegel, consists in harmoniously integrating one's desires whether doing so is reasonable or not even though doing so generates happiness.[38] Hegel, then, neither breaks with Kant entirely regarding rational freedom nor regarding happiness qua reflective freedom. Though Patten does not make clear the relationship between happiness qua reflective freedom and rational freedom in Hegel, clearly, for Patten, happiness is not some marginally distracting pursuit. If reflective freedom constitutes happiness, and if higher rational freedom combines reasonableness with reflectively harmonized desires, then rational freedom incorporates happiness for Hegel.[39]

THE ARGUMENT

Chapter 2, "Between Kantianism and Utilitarianism: T. H. Green," examines Green's assessment of nineteenth-century English utilitarianism, particularly Mill's version of utilitarianism in comparison to Bentham's (or at least what he takes to be Mill's version compared to what he takes to be Bentham's). Since Green's assessment of Bentham and his praise for Mill correspond with Bradley's estimation of both, I also discuss Bradley at length. Furthermore, I examine Green's critical exchange with Sidgwick. Both Green's assessment of Mill as having improved Bentham and Sidgwick's account of Green justify reading Green as what we would term an indirect consequentialist. For Green, as we shall see, freedom and moral rights were indirect strategies for promoting the good of

---

[38] Patten, *Hegel's Idea of Freedom*, 51.

[39] Despite sharing Patten's concern that Hegel's continuity with Kant has been understated, Franco thinks that they nevertheless diverged over the worth of happiness. For Franco, Hegel links happiness and rational freedom (unlike Kant). For Kant, "happiness is merely indeterminate and shares little with the moral or autonomous will; and this reflects the larger dualism running through his practical philosophy between freedom and nature, reason and sense" (Franco, *Hegel's Philosophy of Freedom*, 168). But as we have seen for Kant, happiness shares more than a little with duty, suggesting that he was not the dualist Franco thinks he was. Neuhouser also overstates how much Kant and Hegel diverge on the union between morality and happiness despite how much their moral theories otherwise share (Frederick Neuhouser, *Foundations of Hegel's Social Theory* [Cambridge, Mass: Harvard University Press, 2000], 238–40). By contrast, see Kenneth Westphal, "The Basic Context and Structure of Hegel's *Philosophy of Right*" in *The Cambridge Companion to Hegel*, ed. Frederick C. Beiser (Cambridge: Cambridge University Press, 1993), 243, where Westphal claims that Kant and Hegel indeed agreed about *utilitarianism* insofar as they both flatly rejected it. But they did not reject it out of hand. And they could not have had nineteenth-century English *utilitarianism* in mind in any case even though they may have had in mind something that subsequently came to resemble Bentham and Mill.

moral self-realization. Moreover, Green not only concedes that his moral theory resembles Mill's liberal utilitarianism in crucial *justificatory* respects even if it diverges significantly from Bentham's utilitarianism, he further concedes that, notwithstanding the *justificatory* similarities between Mill and himself, their complementary versions of consequentialism also converge *practically*. That is, Green and Mill's versions of liberal justice are fundamentally the same. Green even concedes how closely his version of liberalism mimics Mill's. Finally, I discuss Kant's legacy to Green, suggesting that Green was indeed neo-Kantian but in David Cummiskey's controversial consequentialist sense. In my view, Green exemplifies historically the kind of Kantian consequentialism that Cummiskey defends.

In Chapter 3, "Between Utilitarianism and Perfectionism: L. T. Hobhouse," I contend that Hobhouse's new liberalism was even more quintessentially consequentialist than Green's. Indeed, Hobhouse's new liberalism was a form of consequentialist perfectionism, making him strongly evocative of Mill. Like Green, he criticized traditional utilitarianism for equating good with pleasure, which he likewise regarded as an incoherent maximizing goal. And like Green, he therefore equated good with self-realization. But following Mill, he equated self-realization with individual flourishing and happiness. Moreover, following Mill, he argued that self-realization ought to be promoted universally though indirectly via the sanctity and respect for strong moral rights. In sum, Hobhouse maneuvered between Green and Mill; in the end, however, he looked back more to Mill than he did to Green.

Chapter 4, "Excursus: Green, Hobhouse and Contemporary Moral Philosophy," is much less intellectual history and more contemporary moral theory insofar as it suggests that Green and Hobhouse are considerably undervalued resources for those still struggling to accommodate consequentialism with liberalism. Chapter 4, then, is a philosophical interlude that aims to exploit intellectual history in order to address contemporary philosophical concerns all the while keeping in mind that using intellectual history to fight our analytical battles risks misusing it.[40] Accordingly, in this chapter, I begin by showing how much Green and Hobhouse's alternative versions of new liberalism foreshadow recent efforts

---

[40] I will not devote a separate chapter to suggesting how we might similarly exploit Ritchie and Hobson for contemporary philosophical purposes because neither Ritchie nor Hobson are as philosophically fertile as Green and Hobhouse. I do not mean to deny, of course, that Ritchie and Hobson have much to offer contemporary economists, for example. However, in discussing Ritchie and Hobson, I will not eschew appropriating them for their contributions to making liberal consequentialism plausible.

by contemporary liberals and communitarians to find common philosophical ground. In notable respects, contemporary liberals and communitarians have been retracing unwittingly much of the same journey that new
liberals such as Green and Hobhouse already took roughly a century ago.
The accommodation that contemporary liberals and communitarians
imagine themselves to be discovering is mostly just rediscovery analytically
refined and reshaped.

Even contemporary perfectionist liberals such as Raz, Frankfurt and
Hurka retrace Green and Hobhouse though they do not do so entirely
unawares. While perfectionist liberals have been preoccupied with other
concerns than just accommodating liberalism and communitarianism,
their respective accounts of perfectionist liberalism nevertheless reiterate
Green and Hobhouse more than they recognize.

But however much contemporary perfectionist liberals unknowingly
echo seminal facets of the new liberal predecessors, this very echoing helps
us appreciate the kind of perfectionist new liberals Green and Hobhouse
were. And not surprisingly, given my intentions in this current work, they
proved to be consequentialist perfectionists. Green and Hobhouse not only
instruct us in how best to go about accommodating liberalism and communitarianism, but they also instruct us, perhaps more surprisingly and just
as importantly, on how we might better proceed in liberalizing consequentialism. This chapter, then, illustrates just how instructive the history of
political thought can be for us as we struggle to liberate ourselves from
various debilitating conceptual dichotomies that oppress and immobilize
too much of our contemporary philosophical thinking. In particular, it
aims to instruct us how we can use the history of liberal political thought to
grapple more expeditiously with the seeming incompatibility between
liberalism and consequentialism that some of us are committed to refuting.
Whether we succeed or not does not depend on how much we refamiliarize
ourselves with Green and Hobhouse obviously. After all, what is at stake is a
matter of logical compatibility. Still, greater familiarity with Green and
Hobhouse would have, in my view, at least speeded up recent analytical
efforts to resolve once and for all this important logical issue.

Chapter 5, "Vindicating Utilitarianism: D. G. Ritchie," reverts to the
approach utilized in Chapters 2 and 3 about Green and Hobhouse respectively. As in those chapters, Chapter 5 mostly aims at showing just how
much another new liberal owed to nineteenth-century English utilitarianism. Similar to my reading of Green and Hobhouse, I am keen to disclose
the extent to which Ritchie's new liberalism was likewise consequentialist
in some sense if not unambiguously in the utilitarian sense.

The chapter opens by examining the kind of utilitarianism Ritchie insists natural selection "vindicate[s]." I argue that Ritchie, like Hobhouse, looks to Mill for guidance and inspiration. Like Hobhouse, he sees himself as repairing and fortifying Mill by invoking a more robust and more nuanced account of happiness as self-realization. As with Hobhouse, Ritchie holds that we ought to promote happiness qua self-realization universally. And as with Hobhouse following Mill, he holds that strong moral rights constitute the best happiness-promoting juridical strategy.

Unlike other new liberals (with the partial exception of Hobhouse), however, Ritchie deployed evolutionary theory in order to bolster his underlying liberal utilitarian commitments. For all his animus towards Spencer, he followed Spencer in arguing that "rational" utilitarian calculation was gradually and inexorably replacing the haphazard inefficiency of natural selection as the mechanism of moral progress. Ritchie's disguised similarities with Spencer further disclose the extent to which his new liberalism was fundamentally liberal utilitarian. As I have argued at length elsewhere, Spencer was a liberal utilitarian too, contrary to the received view that erroneously regards him as a meretricious social Darwinist.[41] Finally, we shall also see how Ritchie's undervalued similarities with Hume no less than with Spencer further attest to his underlying utilitarian, or more properly, consequentialist allegiances. For Hume, Spencer and Ritchie, morality is conventional and ultimately grounded in utility though only more recently has this grounding become self-conscious and deliberate. Hence, taking Mackie seriously leads back to taking Spencer and Ritchie no less seriously than Hume.

Chapter 6, "Utilitarian Socialism: J. A. Hobson," concludes my account of the new liberalism's indebtedness to utilitarianism. I argue that, of all new liberals, Hobson was unquestionably the most conventionally utilitarian. Hobson frequently identified himself as a "new" utilitarian, making his new liberalism effectively new utilitarianism. Like English idealists and fellow new liberals, he criticized "old" utilitarianism for its narrow hedonism, which made it incoherent. Whereas promoting good qua maximizing pleasures was nonsensically futile, promoting "social utility" was not. "Social utility" was new liberal self-realization fortified by Ruskin's qualitative conception of wealth. For Hobson, inspired by Ruskin, self-realizing happiness entailed satisfying informed preferences

---

[41] See Weinstein, *Equal Freedom and Utility.* Also see D. Weinstein, "Herbert Spencer," *Stanford Encyclopedia of Philosophy,* Center for the Study of Language and Information, Stanford University, online hypertext: plato.stanford.edu (December, 2002).

primarily, making self-realization for him more straightforwardly hedonic and much less perfectionist than it was for Green, Hobhouse or Ritchie. In any case, however we regard Hobson's consequentialism whether as a form of utilitarian or perfectionist consequentialism, Hobson followed other new liberals in defending robust moral rights as good-promoting conditions. But he more than followed fellow new liberals insofar as he was as much a self-described socialist as he was a self-described liberal. Consequently, Hobson endorsed a more full-bodied system of equal opportunity, positive rights. Hobson's new liberalism was just as much a new socialism as it was a new utilitarianism.

My study's Conclusion is brief and returns to what I regard as the troubled heritage of analytical philosophy for the history of political thought. Contemporary, Anglo-American political philosophy deserves many accolades; its impact on intellectual history in general, and the history of political thought in particular, is not the best of them. Regrettably, analytical political philosophy has telescoped the history of political thought into a purportedly forward-looking narrative that is really just backward-looking from the present. Past philosophic greatness is measured by its relevance to current analytical preoccupations, causing us to ignore too much of the history of political thought as misguided and dreary. Consequently, we have blinded ourselves to some of the liberal tradition's more provocative discoveries, setting ourselves up to rediscover them again as if they were novelties. While I agree with Dunn that studying the history of political thought "is not to finger gloatingly over the jewels of an intellectual treasury which offers, in the luminous phrase of the Greek historian Thucydides 'a possession for ever,'" I hesitate to go as far as concluding that studying past texts constitutes "a struggle to win from often inaccessible and refractory seams, the materials for grasping the possibilities and dangers of the human world as this still confronts us."[42] I doubt that the history of political thought is so politically fecund. But I am convinced that it has great bearing on how imaginatively we practice contemporary political philosophy.

CONCLUSION

Contemporary liberal utilitarianism is often criticized in much the same way Mill's contemporary opponents assailed him for trying to reconcile the irreconcilable. For instance, Gray has recanted his earlier enthusiasm for

---

[42] Dunn, *The History of Political Theory*, 27.

liberal utilitarianism, agreeing with the critics of liberal utilitarianism that it futilely seeks to join multiple *ultimate* normative criteria, namely utility and indefeasible moral rights. For Gray, either maximizing utility logically trumps rights or rights trump maximizing utility (insofar as they possess authentic moral weight). Liberal utilitarianism fails logically because it pulls in opposite normative directions, instructing us to maximize utility when doing so violates rights and to respect rights when doing so fails to maximize utility. In other words, we sometimes must choose between our liberalism and our utilitarianism.[43]

Now if the new liberals were really masquerading liberal utilitarians, or at least liberal consequentialists, as I am contending, then surely we ought to defer to them as much as Mill insofar as liberal utilitarianism remains for us either promising or misbegotten. If Mill is seminal to our debate, then so are the new liberals. New liberals not only have much that is helpful to say to those attempting to reconcile liberalism with communitarianism but also they have just as much to say to those still struggling to accommodate liberalism with utilitarianism and perfectionism. Notwithstanding whether such accommodation succeeds and whether new liberals help us see why or why not, we should nevertheless judge the fact that they followed Mill in marrying robust liberal principles with utilitarianism, contrary to the received view of them as anti-utilitarian, as sufficiently meritorious intellectual history. At the very least, as revisionist history of political thought *only*, my study is distinctive. And even if it succeeds as just intellectual history, I would like to think that I will be grateful enough.

---

[43] John Gray, *Liberalisms* (London: Routledge, 1989), 218–24.

PART I

Consequentialist perfectionism

CHAPTER 2

Between Kantianism and utilitarianism: T. H. Green

INTRODUCTION

Most men, however, at least in their ordinary conduct, are neither voluptuaries nor saints; and we are falling into a false antithesis if, having admitted (as is true) that the quest of self-satisfaction is the form of all moral activity, we allow no alternative (as Kant in effect seems to allow none) between the quest for self-satisfaction in the enjoyment of pleasure, and the quest for it in the fulfilment of a universal practical law. Ordinary motives fall neither under the one head nor the other. They are interests in the attainment of objects, without which it seems to the man in his actual state that he cannot satisfy himself, and in attaining which, because he has desired them, he will find a certain pleasure, but only because he has previously desired them, not because pleasures are the objects desired.

(Green, *Prolegomena to Ethics*, Sect. 160.)[1]

In his study of L. T. Hobhouse's social and political thought, *Liberalism and Sociology*, Stefan Collini remarks that "men make their own theory but they do not do so in circumstances of their own making."[2] Following Pocock, Collini means that any innovative theoretical enterprise is ineluctably constrained and sculpted by its surrounding, authoritative conceptual discourse. This discourse, though never static, envelops new philosophical inquiry within established conceptual horizons. These conceptual horizons function hegemonically by structuring and framing subsequent theorizing. They subdue and tame philosophical innovation.

As the Introduction makes plain, I am deeply sympathetic towards this method of writing intellectual history. Though like Skinner more recently, I prefer deploying intellectual history for the sake of saying something germane, even if modestly germane, about problems preoccupying

---

[1] Also see T. H. Green [1886], "Lectures on the Philosophy of Kant," *Collected Works of T. H. Green*, Vol. II, 140 for a nearly identical, word-for-word claim.

[2] Stefan Collini, *Liberalism and Sociology* (Cambridge: Cambridge University Press, 1979), 50.

contemporary political philosophers. Anachronism for its own sake is, in any case, implausibly misadventurous.

T. H. Green made his moral theory in theoretical circumstances made by others and these circumstances were fundamentally utilitarian. Those who fashioned them were the great nineteenth-century English utilitarians like Jeremy Bentham, J. S. Mill and Henry Sidgwick. Utilitarianism suffused nineteenth-century English moral philosophy so pervasively and thoroughly that all who struggled against it and endeavored to transcend it were, in large measure, chastened by it. Hence, the discourse of Victorian utilitarianism disciplined even those who joined battle against it. In moral philosophy, this discourse permeated and tempered the best efforts of contemporary neo-Kantians, Spencerians and idealists alike.[3] Green's moral theory was no exception as it never escaped from some of the rudimentary motifs of the dominant utilitarian paradigm. Despite his generous criticisms of traditional utilitarianism, Green was a consequentialist who also, in a fashion not unlike that of Mill, took stringent moral rights seriously. Though no "liberal utilitarian" as Mill has come to be known, he was unquestionably a liberal consequentialist. His moral philosophy was, in short, plainly goal-based but not at the cost of devaluing basic moral rights. Unfortunately, recent interpreters of Green have not adequately appreciated the extent to which Green's liberalism was also consequentialist. The received view of Green sees him as neo-Kantian and therefore anti-consequentialist or, at least, anti-utilitarian. It tends to put him on the deontological side of the polarizing rivalry between neo-Kantians and utilitarians, which has indelibly scarred much modern moral and political philosophizing.[4]

This chapter's strategy for displaying Green's liberal consequentialism is six-fold. I begin by suggesting that his theories of freedom and moral rights were *indirect* strategies for promoting good, making Green a consequentialist for whom freedom and rights are instrumental. Second, I explore

---

[3] For interpretations of Spencer, which view him as fundamentally utilitarian, see M. W. Taylor, *Men Versus the State* (Oxford: Oxford University Press, 1992) and especially my *Equal Freedom and Utility*.

[4] In *The Political Philosophy of the British Idealists*, 294, n39, Nicholson lists contemporary studies of Green which view him as fundamentally anti-utilitarian as well as those few studies which acknowledge that his relationship to utilitarianism was more complex than outright and facile rejection. More recently, though he admits that Green's intellectual debts are often difficult to discern, David Brink generally treats Green as anti-utilitarian or, at least, as an avid anti-psychological hedonist. See, for instance, David O. Brink, "Introduction" in T. H. Green, *Prolegomena to Ethics*, ed. David O. Brink (Oxford: Oxford University Press, 2003), lxxvi.

Green's critical assessment of utilitarianism in general and Mill's liberal utilitarianism in particular. I focus on Green's treatment of Mill's notion of moral "self-development." Green was favorably impressed by this feature of Mill's moral theory and likened moral self-development in Mill to his own conception of moral self-realization. Third, I argue that insofar as Green held that moral self-realization was the good that we ought to promote, he was what I call a "dispositional consequentialist" for whom realizing oneself morally was no less than developing and exhibiting the disposition of good willing. Next, I demonstrate how the practical or prudential recommendations of Green's consequentialism mirror or mimic the practical strategies recommended by many of his utilitarian rivals, particularly Mill. Here again, the philosophical dissimilarities between Green and Mill prove remarkably narrow. (Chapter 4 shall return to some of these three themes but with the aim of showing how Green's consequentialism exemplifies remarkably well the kind of perfectionist extensionalism that Thomas Hurka has recently defended so aptly.)

Fifth, I show that despite Sidgwick's criticisms of Green, he clearly interpreted Green as being a non-utilitarian consequentialist. Once more, the distance between Green and some of his utilitarian opponents (especially one so preoccupied with him as Sidgwick was) proves smaller than many imagine. Finally, I discuss Kant's legacy to Green, whose critical treatment of Kant appears to distance him substantially enough from Kant to reveal once more the fundamentally consequentialist nature of his moral philosophy. But to suggest that Green was no Kantian is only to suggest that he was no traditional Kantian. David Cummiskey has controversially argued that Kantianism is not inherently deontological. Rather, Kant's moral law generates what Cummiskey calls Kantian consequentialism. Hence, though no traditional, deontological Kantian, Green arguably exemplifies the kind of non-traditional, neo-Kantianism that Cummiskey thinks is both coherent and appropriate.

Green, then, must be set firmly within his own intellectual context. When read as some of his principal opponents and proponents read him, he emerges weighted down with the conceptual baggage and ethos of Victorian utilitarianism.

BRADLEY

Not enough has been written about Bradley recently. And even less has been written specifically and in detail about his rejection of utilitarianism. While Bradley was highly critical of Bentham's utilitarianism, especially its hedonism, he nevertheless was not irrevocably hostile to utilitarianism as something devoid of redeeming value.

The 1927 "Preface" to the posthumous edition of *Ethical Studies* contends that Bradley wrote *Ethical Studies* in order to rebut the stagnating legacy of utilitarianism to nineteenth-century English philosophy. And in his "Introduction" to the 1962 paperback reissue of the 1927 edition, Wollheim observes that the sustained criticism of hedonism in Essay III has come to be considered a "*locus classicus* for arguments against Utilitarianism *at least in its more traditional form*" (my italics).[5] Wollheim is a very sensitive reader of Bradley, noting as well that Essay IV, "Duty For Duty's Sake," of *Ethical Studies* takes aim primarily at Kantianism while Essay V, "My Station and Its Duties," has wrongly been identified with Bradley's own position thanks mostly to Sidgwick's misinterpretation of him.[6]

Nonetheless, Wollheim's "Introduction" reinforces the thrust of the 1927 "Preface" that *Ethical Studies* was written, first and foremost, in criticism of utilitarianism. Wollheim thus unfortunately perpetuates the received view that nineteenth-century utilitarianism and British idealism were largely irreconcilable rivals. More generally, the "Preface" and Wollheim's "Introduction" also play to contemporary analytical philosophy's tendency to cast philosophical disputes as dichotomizing contests that pit, for instance, consequentialism against deontology. But this bad habit, too often encouraged out of pedagogical convenience, risks reducing philosophical dispute to polemic. Polemic, in turn, feeds on our complex, amorphous philosophical traditions, reifying them into canonical anticipations of mature contemporary concerns. Whatever fails to anticipate is consequently forgotten as dross and misdirection.

Bradley indeed criticized sharply what he took to be classical utilitarianism. Not unlike Rawls much later, he saw himself steering a middle course between utilitarianism and deontology. But unlike Rawls, his understanding of utilitarianism was more subtle and his attitude towards it more deferential. Bradley faulted hedonistic utilitarianism on many now familiar grounds. For instance, while hedonists (Bradley seems to be thinking of Bentham) concede that it is not possible to prove that my pleasure is the good, they wrongly hold that my pleasure's goodness is self-evident to me. On the contrary, "moral consciousness repudiates" such

---

[5] Richard Wollheim, "Introduction" in F. H. Bradley [1927], *Ethical Studies*, ed. Richard Wollheim (Oxford: The Clarendon Press, 1962), xiv.
[6] Wollheim, "Introduction," xv.

purported self-evidence.[7] Mill, by contrast, thinks that because each person desires his or her own pleasure, everybody therefore desires universal pleasure thus somehow proving, in addition, that universal pleasure is the good. But, according to Bradley, this line of reasoning is "not a good theoretical deduction" but instead a "pitiable sophism."[8] Or, more sarcastically: "If many pigs are fed at one trough, each desires his own food, and somehow as a consequence does seem to desire the food of all; and by parity of reasoning it should follow that each pig, desiring his own pleasure, desires also the pleasure of all."[9]

Moreover, Mill "throws over Hedonism altogether" insofar as he distinguishes between higher and lower pleasures. Hedonism is "made false to its principle and becomes incoherent" because if "you are to prefer a higher pleasure to a lower without reference to quantity," then you introduce a second quality, in addition to pleasure, as a decisive moral criterion.[10]

But more importantly and interestingly for the purposes of this study, Bradley goes to great lengths to discredit *hedonistic* utilitarianism, arguing that it makes moral rightness unintelligible and therefore utterly impractical. According to Bradley, pleasure is merely a term that "stands for a series of this, that, and other feelings, which are not except in the moment or moments that they are felt, which have as a series neither limitation of number, beginning nor end, nor in themselves any reference at all, any of them, beyond themselves."[11] To maximize pleasure, then, means trying "to realize this infinite perishing series," which is plainly nonsensical and futile.[12] In other words, pleasure cannot be maximized because "it can not be summed till we are dead, and then, if we have realized it, we, I suppose, do not know it, and we are not happy; and before death we can not have realized it, because there is always more to come, the series is always incomplete."[13] Hence, Bradley concludes that good must be

---

[7] Bradley, *Ethical Studies*, 112.   [8] *Ibid.*, 114.

[9] *Ibid.*, 113. Bradley fails to anticipate Moore's subsequent criticism of Mill's proof that intensely desiring something does not entail that what we intensely desire is desirable. Mill's infamous proof has generated considerable critical discussion ever since Moore's treatment of it in *Principia Ethica* ([1903] Cambridge: Cambridge University Press, 1986). See my *Equal Freedom and Utility* for a more detailed analysis of Moore's account of how Mill and Spencer supposedly committed the naturalistic fallacy. Bradley also criticizes Sidgwick's utilitarianism in a lengthy footnote in *Ethical Studies* added just subsequent to the 1877 publication of *The Methods of Ethics*. There, Bradley interprets Sidgwick's utilitarianism essentially egoistically as well as hedonistically. For Bradley, both attributes render Sidgwick's utilitarianism objectionable. See my unpublished "British Idealism and the Refutation of Utilitarianism," *Idealism Today*, Harris Manchester College, Oxford University, Oxford, July 2005, for the striking parallels between Bradley and Green's respective criticisms of Sidgwick. Also see Vincent and Boucher, *British Idealism and Political Theory*, ch. 2, which details Bradley's critical exchange with Sidgwick.

[10] Bradley, *Ethical Studies*, 116–20.   [11] *Ibid.*, 95.   [12] *Ibid.*   [13] *Ibid.*, 97.

something other than pleasure. It must at least be *something stable* that it is possible to experience practically and therefore cultivate. As we shall soon see, new liberals deployed versions of this same incoherence argument against hedonistic utilitarianism. And furthermore, though rejecting hedonistic utilitarianism, they never abandoned utilitarianism entirely. Even Green never fully rejected utilitarianism, the received view of his having done so notwithstanding.[14]

Bradley nevertheless readily conceded that "modern" utilitarianism, by contrast to hedonistic utilitarianism, had much to recommend for it. It has the "same object in view" that his moral theory has though it understood that object differently. Modern utilitarians agree with him that the "standard of virtue" must be "palpable and objective" in the sense of being something that we can meaningfully and consistently apply rigorously. Both agree that "happiness is the end; and therefore we say pleasure is not the end." Both "agree that pleasure is *a* good" and not "*the* good." Finally, modern utilitarians concur with him that "the test of higher and lower can not lie in a feeling which accompanies the exercise of every function, but is to be found in the quality of the function itself." That is, like Bradley, they effectively acknowledge that "the end and the standard is self-realization, and is not the *feeling* of self-realizedness" (my italics).[15]

Bradley's distinction between "self-realization" and the "feeling of self-realizedness" is especially significant for understanding how new liberals theorized the relationship between self-realization and happiness. For him, good is both self-realization and the "feeling of self-realizedness" that invariably accompanies self-realization. Though Bradley does not specify here what constitutes this accompanying feeling, he does elsewhere in *Ethical Studies* and in his unpublished notebooks. For instance, in "Note to Essay III," *Ethical Studies*, Bradley clarifies the relationship between self-realization and its accompanying feeling though not without introducing new complicating ambiguities. Bradley now insists flatly that pleasure is "felt-realizedness." Hence, pleasure is unquestionably good but only *insofar* as "it accompanies and makes a whole with good activity, because it goes with that self-realization which is good; or secondly, because it heightens the general assertion of self, which is the condition of realizing the good

---

[14] While new liberals never explicitly acknowledge Bradley's influence on their anti-hedonism, Bradley, for his part, recommends Green's assessment of utilitarianism as complementing his own. See Bradley, *Ethical Studies*, 96, n1.

[15] *Ibid.*, 124–5.

in self."[16] In other words, pleasure is "included in" and "belongs to" self-realizing activities.[17] However, not *all* pleasures are good because, although pleasure always accompanies self-realization, it sometimes accompanies non-self-realizing activities as well. Moral action is always pleasurable but not all pleasurable actions are moral. Hence:

Since pleasure and life are inseparable, can we say that to aim at the realization of life is to aim at pleasure? No, in the sense of making it an object, it is not to aim at pleasure; and this distinction is a vital difference, which we must never slur. Function carries pleasure with it as its psychical accompaniment, but what determines, makes, and is good or bad, is in the end function. Function, moreover, is something comparatively definite. It gives something you can aim at, something you can do. Not so the pleasure. Further, so far as function and pleasure are separable objects of choice, we must, if we are moral, choose the former. If they are inseparable, are one whole, why are we to aim at the indefinite side, at the subjective psychical sequent and accompaniment, when we have an objective act which we can see before us and perform, and which is the prius of the feeling? It is the act that carries with it the pleasure, not the pleasure the act.[18]

Nevertheless, because pleasure, though more indefinite, generally accompanies self-realizing activities, aiming at pleasure usually can safely substitute in place of aiming at self-realization. Bradley writes, "And again, when we are doubtful what is higher in progress, it may be a safe course to increase pleasure and diminish pain, because that heightens the good function we have."[19] Or again, "Of course one sees quite clearly that, generally speaking, it is a good thing to aim at the increasing of pleasure and diminishing pain; but it is a good thing because it increases the actuality and possibility of life."[20] Still, he warns, "to propose [pleasure] as the end to which the act or objective event is the means, and nothing but the means, is simply to turn the moral point of view upside down."[21] That is:

The coincidence of the two [pleasure and self-realization] is an extremely general truth; it need not (*presumably,* that is) be true for this man or generation; and, if so, how is it possible to aim at progress except by aiming at function? The function must (on the whole and in the end) carry the pleasure with it, and it is surely a more definite mark. Is it not preposterous to think of aiming at more pleasure, in the end and on the whole (not in any future that we can see), in order, by making this the end, to get along with it some higher function which we know nothing about? ... Must we not say that this going together of function and pleasure is a

---

[16] *Ibid.,* 131–2.   [17] *Ibid.,* 133.   [18] *Ibid.,* 136.   [19] *Ibid.,* 137.   [20] *Ibid..*   [21] *Ibid.,* 93.

mere general faith, which we can not verify by experience in every case, and so can not use to determine our particular course?[22]

At the end of the day, then, Bradley seems ambivalent about how effectively promoting pleasure qua "felt-realizedness" can stand in as a substitute for promoting self-realization as the ultimate good. On the one hand, promoting the former in place of the latter may well be a "safe course." On the other hand, promoting pleasure is not an especially true "test" for promoting self-realizing function. By pleasure, "you can not tell higher from lower function; and, if you go by it, you must prefer a lower state of harmony to a higher state of self-contradiction."[23]

Bradley's ambivalence about the probity of deploying promoting pleasure as a substitute strategy is surely rooted in his admission, noted earlier, that while all moral actions are pleasurable, not all pleasurable actions are moral.[24] And no doubt, his ambivalence was further exacerbated by his occasional worry that moral actions were not always necessarily pleasant. Moreover, Bradley sometimes seemed uncertain whether or not moral actions were always necessarily pleasurable. For instance, in "Whether Pleasure is Good and in What Sense – Is Pain Evil?" the unpublished version of "Note To Essay III," Bradley writes: "If you say more pleasure & higher function are inseparable on the whole – I will not deny it as I said though I do not see how it can be proved – though I have a right to refuse to

---

[22] *Ibid.*, 137. Bradley's doubts about moral actions necessarily being pleasant and therefore his doubts about whether aiming at pleasure could reliably substitute for aiming at self-realization are just as, if not more, pronounced in his unpublished notebooks. For instance, see "Morality," in which Bradley writes "This is a false assumption that the two sides of good (call them virtue and happiness) coincide in the individual man – or in the individual race – & even in the history of our planet is so . . . baseless assumption though not proved false." F. H. Bradley, *Red Notebook, Related to ETR* in Bradley Collection, IIB2, Merton College, Oxford University. Also see *Red Notebook* in *Collected Works of F. H. Bradley*, ed. Carol A. Keene (Bristol: Thoemmes Press, 1999), Vol. III, 129, for the same quote.

[23] Bradley, *Ethical Studies*, 138. Also see F. H. Bradley, "Utility as (1) an End or (2) Standard of Morality," *Multi-Colored Notebook* in Bradley Collection, IA12. Bradley writes "Whether apart from such knowledge, utility in any shape can be adopted as an index in order to give a content to the formal moral law, seems at least very doubtful." Bradley could be referring to the relationship between utility and morality in Kant and not so much himself here. Also note that this essay is an undergraduate essay mostly devoted to criticizing Mill. Also see *Collected Works of F. H. Bradley*, ed. Carol A. Keene, Vol. 1, 56, for the same quote.

[24] Also see Bradley, *Ethical Studies*, 138 where Bradley explains: "But, leaving this subject, we must observe that we have no right to assume that higher function [self-realization] and more pleasure do on the whole go together. We have bitter proof that in particular cases and stages of progress this is not the case, and so are forced to separate the two in our minds." Yet see his 1927 note where he says ambiguously "I have modified my opinion here" (138, n1). Also see his 1927 note, 126, where he admits, "I should now assert it [that self-realization 'means always greater surplus' pleasure]."

allow you to assume it & if so then *more* pleasure is not an end."[25] In other words, promoting pleasure may not always be an effective substitute strategy because we should not assume that pleasure invariably accompanies higher, self-realizing functions.

Notwithstanding Bradley's ambivalence about pleasure's contingent dependency on self-realization and about how well promoting pleasure could therefore effectively substitute for promoting self-realization, Bradley nevertheless was willing to be considered a utilitarian (albeit emphatically not a *hedonistic* utilitarian). Bradley was opposed to hedonism as such and not to utilitarianism and certainly not to what we now call consequentialism. Utilitarianism has never been equivalent to hedonism. Rather, hedonism has always been simply a variety of utilitarianism. Hence:

> If 'happiness' means well-being or perfections of life, then I am content to say that, with Plato and Aristotle, I hold happiness to be the end; and, although virtue is not a *mere* means, yet it can be regarded as a means, and so is 'useful'. In this sense we, who reject Hedonism, can call ourselves Utilitarians, and the man who thinks he is pushing some counter view by emphasizing 'happiness' and 'usefulness' does not touch us with his phrases, but rather perhaps confirms us.[26]

Bradley, then, was not indifferent to pleasure but merely to *pleasure for pleasure's sake* (which is the title of Essay III). As we have seen, he held, but not without ambivalence, that pleasure generally accompanies self-realization like a loyal companion. Though Bradley never adequately worked out in detail the nature of this contingent dependency, he never repudiated its potency. Bradley was therefore an *extensional* consequentialist much like Green. Reading Bradley and Green as consequentialists is controversial. I will vigorously defend my view that Green was an *extensional* consequentialist in Chapter 4. But for now, I prefer to discuss Bradley's extensionalism only a little more since a major focus of this study is the legacy of

---

[25] F. H. Bradley, "Whether Pleasure is Good and in What Sense – Is Pain Evil?", *Black Notebook, Related Chiefly to ES*, Bradley Collection, IB11. Otherwise, the unpublished text more or less follows the "Note"; both unpublished text and Note discuss the relationship of pleasure to self-realizing moral action. For instance, see "Note to Essay III," in which Bradley is emphatic: "When the activity is good the pleasure is good, because the two are a psychical whole. You can not have the function without the pleasure" (133). See, too, 135, where Bradley writes that "the pleasures pronounced desirable are so because they are inseparable from and heighten life." Bradley's ambivalence about pleasure's connectedness to self-realization may be related to his deeper lack of clarity about whether self-realization and pleasure were contingently or constitutively related. Whereas sometimes pleasure constitutively "belongs" to goodness as one of its elements, sometimes pleasure is merely a "felt affirmation" of goodness, which generally "accompanies" it contingently. The latter, obviously, entails that moral action is not necessarily pleasurable.

[26] Bradley, *Ethical Studies*, 140–1.

utilitarianism to the new liberalism and not its legacy to British idealism. Still, the legacy of utilitarianism to both is noticeably similar.

In Essay IV, "Duty For Duty's Sake," Bradley depicts Kantianism (though not Kant explicitly) as failing where utilitarianism succeeds and succeeding where utilitarianism fails. Kantians over-exaggerate the shortcomings of hedonistic utilitarianism and overcorrect as a consequence.[27] Where utilitarianism provides little practical guidance because, as we have seen, maximizing pleasure is fundamentally incoherent, Kantianism likewise provides limited practical guidance because it is overly abstract. Taking good will as good "tells us nothing." It merely stipulates that "will is the end." It fails to "say *what* will is the end; and we want to know what the good will is."[28] Kantianism is therefore empty. To act at all, including acting morally, one must at least will something "definite." At most, acting morally for Kantians requires simply acting self-consistently, which even the most vicious might agree to do.[29] Moreover, Bradley adds that Kantianism falls down insofar as it fails to take consequences into account at all, though Bradley couches taking consequences into account in terms of the importance of always considering "circumstances." Circumstances decide when duties conflict insofar as they "determine the manner in which the overruling duty must be realized."[30]

Several of Bradley's interpreters agree that he tried to synthesize the best in utilitarianism with the best in Kantianism while rejecting what he regarded as the worst in both though too many interpreters have wrongly taken him to be utterly hostile to utilitarianism.[31] But only a few of his interpreters, particularly Wollheim (as noted previously) and Nicholson,

---

[27] See especially, *ibid.*, 142, where Bradley explains: "In Hedonism we have criticized a onesided view; we shall have to do here with an opposite extremity of onesidedness . . . Its fault is the opposite, since for mere particular it substitutes mere universal; we have not to do with feelings, as this and that, but with a form which is thought of as not this or that. Its fault is the same fault, the failing to see things as a whole, . . . In a word, we find in both [hedonism and Kantianism] a onesided view, and their common vice may be called abstractness."

[28] *Ibid.*, 143–4. See, as well, Wollheim, *F. H. Bradley*, 244: "Each doctrine [hedonistic utilitarianism and Kantianism] is wrong not in what it asserts but in what it denies, and this is the fault of their common vice, 'abstractness' (ES p. 142)."

[29] Bradley readily acknowledges that his criticisms of Kantianism are drawn from Hegel's critique of Kant. See Bradley, *Ethical Studies*, 148, n1.

[30] *Ibid.*, 158.

[31] For an example of someone who sees Bradley as synthesizing utilitarianism and Kantianism, see Crispin Wright, "The Moral Organism" in *The Philosophy of F. H. Bradley*, ed. Anthony Manser and Guy Stock (Oxford: Clarendon Press, 1984), 77. For a typical instance of the received interpretation of Bradley, see the back cover of the 1988 reissue of the Oxford University Press 1962 edition of *Ethical Studies*, which declares that Bradley wrote the text "as a counterblast to the Utilitarianism which then dominated English moral philosophy."

have warned that too often others have overemphasized the synthesizing function of Essay V, "My Station and Its Duties." Nicholson cautions, for instance, that "it is a serious error to isolate this essay from the rest of the book, as is frequently done."[32]

For Wollheim and Nicholson, Essay VI, "Ideal Morality," constitutes Bradley's preferred synthesis of rival, moral philosophical approaches. Moreover, for both Wollheim and Nicholson, properly appreciating Essay VI's synthetic function betrays the error of those who condemn Bradley's moral theory for being politically conservative. Instead, Essay VI clearly argues that ideal morality, though grounded in the everyday morality of each person's station and its duties, nevertheless requires going beyond these. Ideally realizing oneself morally means refining and realizing more fully the moral demands of one's social station. In addition, it entails realizing purely self-regarding, moral demands, such as promoting and appreciating truth and beauty, that have nothing whatsoever to do with one's social station and its concomitant obligations.[33]

Nevertheless, for all their astute grasp of how ideal morality constitutes the dialectical confluence of hedonistic utilitarianism, Kantianism and conventional morality, neither Wollheim nor Nicholson emphasize enough the extent to which Bradley's moral ideal is arguably a variant of non-hedonistic utilitarianism (as we saw above that Bradley himself conceded). Earlier, in discussing Essay III, "Pleasure For Pleasure's Sake," I suggested that Bradley was what we might be tempted to characterize as an *extensional* consequentialist. British idealists like Bradley concurred with Green and subsequent new liberals in exhibiting much greater respect for consequentialism, including its utilitarian variant, than the received view acknowledges. In a critical passage of Essay VII, Bradley says:

The good self is the self which is identified with, and takes pleasure in, the morally good; which is interested in and bound up with pursuits, activities, in a word, with ends that realize the good will. The good will is the will to realize the ideal self; and the ideal self we saw had a three-fold content, the social reality, the social ideal, and

---

[32] Nicholson, *The Political Philosophy of the British Idealists*, 23. Also, see Wollheim, *F. H. Bradley*, 233.

[33] See, for instance, Bradley, *Ethical Studies*, 224–5, especially Bradley's summary of ideal morality: "Our result at present is as follows. Morality is co-extensive with self-realization, as the affirmation of the self which is one with the ideal; and the content of this self is furnished (1) by the objective world of my station and its duties, (2) by the ideal of social, and (3) of non-social perfection." For Wollheim and Nicholson's parallel accounts of Bradley's theory of ideal morality, see Wollheim, *F. H. Bradley*, 249–51 and Nicholson, *The Political Philosophy of the British Idealists*, 33–9 respectively. Also note Wollheim's claim that ideal self-realization requires harmonizing one's desires throughout a complete life. (265). I mention this claim here because, for new liberals and for Hobhouse especially, desire harmony was constitutively essential to self-realization.

the non-social ideal. We need say no more, then, but that the good self is the self whose end and pleasure is the realization of the ideal self.[34]

Notwithstanding the circularity of equating morally good with realizing good will and with realizing the will to realize the ideal self, plainly pleasure *attends* to moral goodness. Moral goodness generates pleasure contingently as an accompanying feeling. Pleasure "has to do with the outer results" of what transpires in the "heart."[35] And these "outer" pleasures tend to reflect inner moral goodness in some kind of rough one-to-one correspondence. Hence, pleasures are an "index, but an index that must be used with caution."[36]

Bradley's distinction between being moved and having a motive helps clarify his account of the relationship between pleasure and moral goodness. Whereas a "pleasant thought" typically moves us to act, it never motivates us. To think otherwise is to confuse a "pleasant thought" with the "thought of pleasure" or, more fundamentally, to confuse an "idea of an objective act or event, contemplation of which is [also] pleasant, and of which I desire the realization, and the idea of myself as the subject of a feeling of satisfaction which is to be."[37] Only *thinking about* myself as an objective state worth realizing can motivate me to act even though actually realizing this objective state will also happen to cause me pleasure. Anticipating this concomitant pleasure may also well move me by reinforcing my motive, but anticipating pleasure can never, of itself, motivate me. In sum, pleasure is the "feeling of self-realizedness; it is affirmative self-feeling, or the feeling in the self" of realizing oneself. As a contingent feeling, it can additionally "excite" my self-realizing motivations and thus move me with supervening desires, but, once again, it cannot motivate me.[38] As we shall see, especially with Green, pleasure plays a very similar extensionalist role.

FREEDOM, MORAL RIGHTS AND SELF-REALIZATION

Alan Gewirth has recently observed that, "to many moderns self-fulfillment has seemed a murky and confused concept that should not be invoked by serious-minded analytic philosophers."[39] For Gewirth, Green, among

---

[34] Bradley, *Ethical Studies*, 279.   [35] *Ibid.*, 229.   [36] *Ibid.*   [37] *Ibid.*, 258.
[38] *Ibid.*, 261. Bradley seems to admit, however, that pleasure can indeed motivate insofar as we make the idea or thought of pleasure itself the objective of our actions, if we think of, and aim at, realizing our lives exclusively hedonically (259).
[39] Alan Gewirth, *Self-Fulfillment* (Princeton, NJ: Princeton University Press, 1998), 4.

others, exemplifies the kind of muddled thinking about self-fulfillment that analytic critics have targeted. Setting aside until Chapter 4 Gewirth's efforts to rehabilitate the ethics of self-fulfillment analytically as well as the accuracy of his passing references to how Green typifies a version of this ethics, it will suffice to say Gewirth correctly appreciates its centrality for Green.

For Green, each of us ought to promote self-realization, including especially moral self-realization, in ourselves and in others. And for Green, freedom and moral rights are necessary conditions for promoting both. For instance, in becoming morally self-realizing, we must cultivate our "moral capacity." Cultivating this capacity successfully, in turn, requires that we "exercise" this capacity "freely." If each is to have the opportunity or power to do this, then each also needs the sanctuary of basic moral rights. Hence, moral rights are just as crucial and as *instrumental* as freedom. They shelter each individual's "moral capacity" so that each can safely "exercise" and refine it, thereby promoting common good. As Green succinctly declares in *Lectures on the Principles of Political Obligation*:

The moral capacity implies a consciousness on the part of the subject of the capacity that its realisation is an *end* desirable in itself, and rights are the *conditions* of realising it. Only through the possession of rights can the power of the individual freely to make a common good his own have reality given to it. Rights are what may be called the negative realisation of this power. That is, they realise it in the sense of providing for its free exercise, of securing the treatment of one man by another as *equally free* with himself, but they do not realise it positively, because their possession does not imply that in any active way the individual makes a common good his own. [my italics][40]

Plainly, basic moral rights (and the freedom that they secure), empower moral self-realization. They empower individuals with the equal opportunity to develop themselves morally, to exercise and cultivate their moral capacities and thereby realize such capacities to the fullest. Moral rights, then, indirectly promote moral self-realization by ensuring that all individuals enjoy the safety of the same necessary baseline conditions from which to contribute freely to the common good as they best see fit.

Common good, and not merely moral self-realization, thus justifies moral rights as well. To claim moral rights is to recognize them, which, in turn, depends upon recognizing how they promote common

---

[40] Green, *Lectures on the Principles of Political Obligation*, Sect. 25.

good: "A right is a power claimed and recognized as contributory to a common good."[41]

Recognition and common good play significant roles in Green's theory of moral rights. Both conceptions are problematically vague and discussing both is best postponed, except for the bearing that recognition has for his rejection of natural rights.[42] Understanding why Green rejected natural rights helps us, in turn, appreciate how he regarded moral rights as indefeasibly instrumental.

Again, much like Ritchie subsequently, Green rejected natural rights theorizing for its superficiality. Traditional natural rights theorists who claim to derive legal and political rights from underlying natural rights must still explain *why* we should abide by the latter in the first instance assuming that we could somehow establish their reality. Simply positing their existence is no justification for them.

Green nevertheless concedes, much like Ritchie as we shall see later, that we may deem rights as natural but only in the unconventional sense of them being necessary conditions for effectively promoting self-realization.[43] And this necessity only becomes plain very gradually as societies develop. We slowly recognize the essentiality of certain powers as conditions for realizing ourselves, which we then secure by valorizing as basic rights. That is, "in any sense in which there can be truly said to be natural rights, the question has to be asked, how it is that certain powers are recognized by men in their intercourse with each other as powers that *should be* exercised, or of which the possible exercise *should be* secured."[44] Recognizing rights, moreover, is simply appreciating their vital instrumentality: "A power on the part of anyone is so recognized by others, as one which should be exercised, when these others regard it as in some way a means to that ideal good of themselves which they alike conceive: and the possessor of the

[41] *Ibid.*, Sect. 99. Also, see Sect. 207, where Green says: "A right is a power (of acting for his own ends – for what he conceives to be his good) secured to an individual by the community, on the supposition, that its exercise contributes to the good of the community. But the exercise of such a power cannot be so contributory unless the individual, in acting for his own ends, is at least affected by the conception of a good as common to himself with others."

[42] For Green's rights-recognition thesis, see especially Rex Martin, "T. H. Green on Individual Rights and the Common Good" in *The New Liberalism*, ed. Avital Simhony and D. Weinstein. Also see Darin Nesbitt, "Recognising Rights: Social Recognition in T. H. Green's System of Rights," *Polity*, 33 (2001).

[43] "'Natural rights', so far as there are such things, are themselves relative to the moral end to which perfect law is relative ... We only discover what rights are natural by considering what powers must be secured to a man in order to the attainment of this end." Green, *Lectures on the Principles of Political Obligation*, Sect. 20.

[44] *Ibid.*, Sect. 24.

power comes to regard it as a right through consciousness of its being thus recognized as contributory to a good in which he too is interested."[45]

Now Green also concedes that utilitarianism has at least "one negative point in common" with his theory insofar as utilitarians likewise ground fundamental rights in recognition. They too justify rights in terms of recognizing them as powers necessary to achieving some end. But unlike him, they conceive our end differently and therefore wrongly. They mistakenly see our end hedonically as pleasure rather than self-realization. But their theory of rights is nonetheless on the mark to a large extent: "They do not seek the ground of actual rights in a prior natural right, but in an end to which the maintenance of the rights contributes. They avoid the mistake of identifying the inquiry into the ultimate justifiability of actual rights with the question whether there is a prior right to the possession of them."[46] In other words, utilitarians correctly ground rights in recognition too. And they pretty much recognize many of the same rights justified by Green's theory. They just misrecognize the end that justifies them.

Moral rights, then, primarily enhance choices by opening opportunities for promoting moral self-realization though they also promote common good simultaneously. They position citizens to make choices of which choosing to cultivate our moral faculties as best as we can is the most important. This is what makes them "conditions" to moral self-realization.

But ensuring that all enjoy the same baseline opportunities does not entail that individuals will necessarily make the most of them. This is why moral rights merely constitute the "negative" (and not the "positive") realization of each person's "moral capacity." They make its realization possible and even probable but they do not "positively" guarantee that it will occur.

For Green, having basic moral rights is more than being empowered by having the opportunity to develop and perfect one's "moral capacity," more than just being free to act morally. Having them also means being

---

[45] *Ibid.*, Sect. 25. Also see Sect. 31 where Green says "'Natural right', as = right in a state of nature which is not a state of society, is a contradiction. There can be no right without a consciousness of common interest on the part of members of a society. Without this there might be certain powers on the part of individuals, but no recognition of these powers by others as powers of which they allow the exercise, nor any claim to such recognition; and without this recognition or claim to recognition there can be no right." Unless others acknowledge, qua allowing the exercise of certain powers as conditions for achieving self-realization, such powers cannot be claimed as rights. Such powers remain merely assertions of power rather than legitimate claims. In Sect. 138, Green explains recognition somewhat differently. Powers become rights insofar as each recognizes that the free exercise of his or her power depends on allowing others the same free exercise and insofar as each "recognizes the other as an originator of action" like himself.

[46] *Ibid.*, Sect. 23.

equally free because, as we saw above, they ensure the "treatment of one man by another as equally free with himself." Having them means each person "is capable of bearing his part in a society in which the free exercise of his powers is secured to each member through the recognition by each of the others as entitled to the same freedom with himself."[47]

So if enjoying fundamental moral rights also means being equally free besides being empowered to realize one's "moral capacity," then being equally free means being empowered in this way too. That is, being equally free amounts to being empowered, or having the equal enabling power, to develop a moral personality. It is having the like enabling power, or like opportunities, to do what is morally worth doing. Plainly, then, Green's celebrated and much misunderstood definition of positive freedom in "Liberal Legislation and Freedom of Contract" (1881) is nothing less than a principle of equal freedom: "When we speak of freedom as something to be so highly prized, we mean a positive *power* or capacity of doing or enjoying something *worth doing or enjoying*, and that, too, something that we do or enjoy in common with others" (my italics).[48]

Now Green's famous definition of positive freedom is ambiguous and even problematic but not in the way that his ideological critics, like Berlin, have unfairly claimed. Very significantly, Green is unclear whether being positively free means having (1) *enabling opportunities* to do what is worth doing (and enjoying) as well as (2) *actually doing* (and enjoying) what is worth doing. Whereas the famed definition above implies quite clearly that being positively free means both having opportunities and actually doing what is worth doing, Green also says more vaguely soon after that freedom of contract (a form of negative freedom) is valuable only as a means to positive freedom, namely the "liberation of the powers of all men equally for contributions to a common good." So long as the freedom of possession of each does not interfere with the like freedom on the part of others, such "freedom contributes to that equal development of the faculties of all which is the highest good for all."[49]

This second rendering of positive freedom seems to suggest that it consists primarily of having equal enabling opportunities to do what is worth doing and not actually doing what is worth doing in addition. One has all the positive freedom one needs or can possibly have when one is sufficiently and equally empowered to self-realize. Self-realizing activity

[47] *Ibid.*, Sect. 25.
[48] T. H. Green, "Lecture on 'Liberal Legislation and Freedom of Contract'," 199.
[49] *Ibid.*, 201.

itself, whether of the narrow moral kind or wider more generic, is not seemingly constitutive of positive freedom at all.[50]

In Sects. 5 and 8 of "On the Different Senses of 'Freedom' as Applied to Will and the Moral Progress of Man" (1879), Green distinguishes "outward" from "inner" freedom, which he also sometimes characterizes as the distinction between "juristic" or "civil" freedom and "autonomy of will." Whereas the former consists in doing as one likes or being free to act, the latter consists in having the "power to prefer" or being free to will. Whereas someone free in the former sense is able to "assert himself against others," someone free in the latter sense also "distinguishes himself from his preferences" and determines them rather than permits them to determine him.[51] Such fortunate individuals are able to make themselves objects to themselves. They enjoy the "possibility" of being determined by "objects conceived as desirable in distinction from objects momentarily desired."[52]

These distinctions, then, match Green's subsequent and confusing elaboration of positive freedom in "Liberal Legislation and Freedom of Contract" that being positively free means simply being *empowered* to determine one's preferences rather than *actually* determining them. And one is suitably empowered insofar as one's will is not just determined externally by others but also not determined internally by passing desires, momentary fancies and overwhelming and disabling compulsions, etc.

But Green also contends in Sect. 7 that, whereas according to the "primary [presumably negative] meaning" of the term, freedom means having the power to do what one prefers secured from compulsion, Kantian, Hegelian and Stoic conceptions of freedom also appeal to the "nature of the will or preference." For their proponents, freedom is "not constituted by the mere fact of acting upon preference, but depends wholly on the nature of the preference, upon the kind of object willed or preferred."[53] Hence, being fully free is not only a matter of being sufficiently *empowered* with meaningful opportunities, contrary to the previous discussion, but also a matter of how one *actually* makes use of these opportunities. So we are back to the two-pronged, considerably enriched definition of positive freedom from the later "Liberal Legislation and Freedom of

---

[50] Also see Green, *Lectures on the Principles of Political Obligation*, Sect. 248, where Green says being "really free" is "being enabled to make the most of [one's] capabilities."

[51] T. H. Green [1886], "On the Different Senses of 'Freedom' as Applied to Will and the Moral Progress of Man," *Collected Works of T. H. Green*, Vol. 11, Sect. 8

[52] *Ibid.*, Sect. 5. I shall explore the relationship between Green's conceptions of willing, good willing and freedom more extensively in Chapter 4.

[53] *Ibid.*, Sect. 7.

Contract." One might nevertheless resist concluding that Green is endorsing the enriched, narrower definition in this later essay because he is merely attributing it to other thinkers without explicitly endorsing it himself. However, Sect. 8 opens by embracing this very "extension" of freedom's meaning before backtracking by conceptualizing full freedom more narrowly as having the "power to prefer" as noted above.

We have little choice but to conclude that Green's theory of positive freedom was confused in not being adequately thought through with sufficient analytical care. He nevertheless seems to have been moving towards a theory of ascending degrees of freedom. Accordingly, externally enforced "outward" freedom (freedom as rights-protected non-interference and as rights-protected enabling power) promotes, without assuring, full "inner" freedom (freedom as exhibiting a good will, as actually doing what is worth doing, as realizing one's "moral capacity"). As rights-protected non-interference, "outward" freedom is negative freedom. As rights-protected enabling power, it constitutes a form of external positive freedom, which is not fully moralized positive freedom of the highest most sublime kind. Only morally self-realizing "inner" freedom comprises the finest, most inspiring positive freedom.[54] Both the second kind of "outward" freedom and "inner" freedom are positive "senses" of freedom though the former merely opens doors to complete positive freedom in the latter sense. The former complements and reinforces negative "outward" freedom by increasing everyone's chances of making the best of themselves morally. As I have argued elsewhere, the relationship between "outward" and "inner" freedom is dynamically symbiotic.[55] Both kinds of rights-secured "outward" freedom indirectly foster moral "inner" freedom, which, as it develops, leads to greater spontaneously upheld "outward" freedom including especially respect for moral rights. This heightened respect for moral rights, in turn, fosters yet deeper degrees of "inner"

---

[54] One might also say that, for Green, self-realizing "inner" freedom consists of two kinds just as "outward" freedom consists of two kinds. We might say that non-moral self-realization is a lower kind of "inner" freedom while narrower, *moral* self-realization (good willing) is the highest kind. Brink likewise distinguishes three types of freedom in Green, namely juridical, moral and real freedom. According to Brink, "juridical" freedom is simply freedom from compulsion. "Moral" freedom is freedom of the will or being able to assess and choose desires. "Real" freedom is self-realization. Though Brink is unclear whether "real" freedom is generic or moral self-realization, he seems to imply that it is the latter. While Brink's depiction of Green's three kinds of freedom obviously overlaps with mine in part, Brink's account differs principally from mine both because he doesn't emphasize empowerment and because he doesn't find Green's theory of freedom especially ambiguous or confusing. See Brink, "Introduction," lxix–lxxiii.

[55] D. Weinstein, "The Discourse of Freedom, Rights and Good in Nineteenth Century English Liberalism," *Utilitas*, 3 (1991).

freedom. In short, moral progress accelerates as both "senses" of positive freedom continually fortify each other.

Both kinds of "outward" freedom thus indirectly encourage the realization of full "inner" freedom. Developing the latter depends upon being guaranteed the former though the latter itself is never guaranteed. Enjoying rights-secured "outward" freedom merely guarantees everyone the opportunity to become more moral, to become fully and inwardly free. Enjoying rights-secured "outward" freedom merely ensures that everyone has the equal juridical chance to become good by developing a good will.[56]

Notwithstanding the ambiguities swirling about Green's conception of positive freedom, his politics are clearly perfectionist. By enforcing negative and positive rights, the state removes obstacles blocking moral development. For instance, because illiteracy and ignorance constitute such formidable obstacles of this kind, elementary education is a basic moral right contrary to appearances. Forcing parents to educate their children might seem like futilely trying to make parents act from duty. However, being uneducated incapacitates citizens from beneficially exercising their rights, effectively eviscerating rights in practice.[57] Being uneducated means being irreparably and brutally disempowered from having any real chance whatsoever of developing one's capacities including especially one's moral capacities.

Likewise, unrestricted freedom of contract disempowers citizens from exercising their rights in the name of developing themselves properly. Unregulated contract impoverishes citizens, crippling them just as much, or even more, than ignorance. It denies the proletariat adequate property essential to carrying out a "plan of life." Anyone "who possesses nothing but his powers of labour and who has to sell these to a capitalist for bare daily maintenance, might as well, in respect of the ethical purposes which the possession of property should serve, be denied rights of property altogether."[58] He is "practically excluded from such ownership as is needed to moralize man."[59] Mere labor power, in short, empowers

---

[56] In this regard, see Ritchie's observation in *The Principles of State Interference* [1902] in *Collected Works of D. G. Ritchie*, ed. Peter P. Nicholson (Bristol: Thoemmes Press, 1998), Vol. 1, 147, that, for Green, the "*direct* legal enforcement of morality cannot be considered expedient or inexpedient: it is impossible. The morality of an act depends on the state of the will of the agent, and therefore the act done under compulsion ceases to have the character of a moral act" [my italics]. As we shall see in Chapter 5, Ritchie shared this conviction.

[57] Green, *Lectures on the Principles of Political Obligation*, Sect. 209.

[58] *Ibid.*, Sect. 220.   [59] *Ibid.*, Sect. 222.

insufficiently and is therefore immoral, making genuine liberalism unavoidably regulatory.[60]

However fuzzily Green conceptualized moral rights and freedom, he nonetheless unquestionably justified them *instrumentally*. In short, his theories of rights and freedom demonstrate why his moral theory is fundamentally goal-based and not rights-based, why good is decidedly prior to right for him. As Green observes in *Lectures on the Principles of Political Obligation*, full moral freedom (moral goodness) is "not the same thing as a control over the outward circumstances and appliances of life. It is the *end* to which such control is a generally necessary *means* and which gives it value" (my italics).[61] But if good is decidedly prior, what precisely does Green mean by good and how does his conception of good differ from that of his contemporary utilitarian rivals, particularly J. S. Mill?

UTILITARIANISM PROPER AND IMPROVED UTILITARIANISM

Though the anti-utilitarian, Kantian features of Green's moral philosophy are well known, much less is known of the extensive reservations that he nevertheless harbored towards Kantianism. Neither crude utilitarian nor inviolate Kantian, Green was nonetheless a consequentialist who enshrined moral self-realization on the altar of good requiring that we revere it by promoting it. In Green's view, Mill often enshrined something similar on this altar to the same normative effect.

---

[60] Besides wage and other contracts, Green favors regulating the sale and distribution of land. Because land is "no ordinary" commodity, the value of its unearned increment, as opposed to the value added to it by labor, rightfully belongs to society and therefore should be nationalized. But like other land nationalizers of the same era, including even Spencer, he balks at putting land reform into practice because it would be too complicated to administer and because it would dissuade landowners from using land productively (*ibid.*, Sects. 231–2). While Spencer surprisingly agreed with Green and others by endorsing land nationalization in theory but not in practice, he otherwise differed from Green in ways the received view of him would lead us to expect. While Spencer worried that liberalism was losing its way by over-legislating, Green, no doubt thinking of Spencer, adamantly denied the "danger of over-legislation." See especially, Green, "Lecture on 'Liberal Legislation and Freedom of Contract'," 202. For Spencer on land nationalization, see my *Equal Freedom and Utility*, ch. VII.

[61] Green, *Lectures on the Principles of Political Obligation*, Sect. 219. Though primarily instrumental in the juridical "outward" sense, rights and freedom are also constitutive of moral self-realization in the "inner" sense of freedom. See, for instance, Green's observation that by habitually respecting the rights of others, an individual "has in him at least the negative principle of virtue; a principle that will effectually restrain him from doing all that he ought not, if it does not move him to do all that he ought." T. H. Green [1883], *Prolegomena to Ethics, Collected Works of T. H. Green*, Vol. IV, Sect. 212. I am indebted to Peter Nicholson for encouraging me to develop this point, which I do more fully in Chapter 4.

Many of Green's criticisms of Benthamite utilitarianism, or "utilitarianism proper" as he referred to it, have become commonplace even if they arguably do not do justice to Bentham's own thinking. For instance, Green faults unsophisticated utilitarians for devaluing humans insofar as they implicitly commit themselves to including animals' pleasures and pains in their utilitarian calculations; for failing to respect the integrity, sanctity and separateness of persons; for requiring complex computations beyond the intellectual capabilities of most humans; and for impoverishing our understanding of freedom by restricting its meaning exclusively to non-interference.[62]

Green also criticizes as illogical rule utilitarian maneuvers to salvage utilitarianism from the charge that it justifies sacrificing some for the good of the rest. Echoing Whewell and James Fitzjames Stephen, and more recently repeated by David Lyons and John Gray, Green observes that notwithstanding the rule utilitarianian's obligation to follow general rules, he or she is nevertheless also obligated to consider every possible action according to its "own merits."[63] Or as Stephen asks rhetorically, "Why should [anyone] prefer obedience to a rule to a specific calculation in a specific case, when . . . the only reason for obeying the rule is the advantage to be got by it, which by the hypothesis is . . . a loss in the particular case?"[64] Why, in short, should we follow any rule when doing so happens not to be for the utilitarian best in a given situation? Why should I be a mindless, rule-worshipping sucker? Hence, rule utilitarianism fails logically because it pulls in opposite normative directions, instructing us to maximize utility when doing so violates rules and to respect rules when doing so fails to maximize utility. We have no choice but to be act utilitarians if we insist on being utilitarians at all. Benthamism, then for Green, is clumsy and ignoble. Rule utilitarian attempts (presumably Mill's) to rescue it are ultimately illogical. Nevertheless, Benthamism was not without considerable redeeming virtues. For example and as noted above, crude

---

[62] See, for example, Green's remark in *Lectures on the Principles of Political Obligation* that "if it is pleasure, as such, and not the person enjoying it, that has intrinsic value, all pleasures alike, by whatever beings enjoyed, must be considered in making up the main account" (Sect. 339). William Whewell earlier and similarly criticized Bentham for having to take into account, when calculating effects on utility, the pleasure and pains of animals and insects. Regarding how utilitarianism devalues persons, see Green's assertion in *Prolegomena to Ethics* that Benthamites "would repudiate or pronounce unintelligible the notion of an absolute value in the individual person." According to them, "not every person" but rather merely "every pleasure" has value in itself (Sect. 214).

[63] Green, *Prolegomena to Ethics*, Sect. 343.

[64] James Fitzjames Stephen [1874], *Liberty, Equality and Fraternity* (Chicago: University of Chicago Press, 1991), 277. For Gray's version of this criticism, see Gray, *Liberalisms*, 218–24. For Lyons, see David Lyons, "Utility and Rights" in *Ethics, Economics and the Law*, Nomos 24, ed. John W. Chapman and J. Roland Pennock (New York: New York University Press, 1982).

utilitarians properly deny the existence of natural rights. More importantly, Benthamite utilitarianism also deserves our respect for rationalizing
morality by encouraging us to extend our sense of moral impartiality to a
wider range of persons.[65]

Green's overall assessment of "utilitarianism proper" was, then, mostly
though not entirely negative. This did not mean that utilitarianism could
not be improved in an appealing way. Indeed, it already had. Improved
Millian utilitarianism was much like his own moral theory and therefore
deserved our esteem. Like his theory, it took stringent moral rights seriously because it correctly viewed them as indispensable powers for promoting moral individuality indirectly. As Green admits in *Lectures on the
Principles of Political Obligation*, "utilitarianism may be presented in a
form in which it would scarcely be distinguishable from the doctrine just
now stated, viz., that the ground of political obligation, the reason why
certain powers should be recognized as belonging to the state and certain
other powers [rights, in other words] as secured by the state to individuals,
lies in the fact that these powers are necessary to the fulfilment of man's
moral vocation as a moral being, to an effectual self-devotion to the work of
developing the perfect character in himself and others."[66]

Green, then, applauds Mill's improved utilitarianism not only for its
juridical strategy for promoting good. Just as importantly for our purposes
here, he further approves of Mill's notion of good itself (or the notion of
good that he thinks Mill sometimes deploys). Mill, in his more enlightened
moments, rightly construes good as developing perfect moral character.
That is, Mill's notion of moral "self-development" is not unlike Green's
own notion of moral self-realization as far as Green was concerned.
Nevertheless, for Green, Mill stubbornly and inconsistently refuses to
abandon general utility as the ultimate criterion of right. He refuses to
do this despite admitting that "higher" pleasures were qualitatively more
valuable than "lower" ones. In admitting this, Mill should have discerned
that he was thereby defining good as something else besides pleasure; that

---

[65] Green, *Prolegomena to Ethics*, Sect. 331. Also see Sect. 333 where Green says: "Impartiality of reference
to human well-being has been the great lesson which the Utilitarian has had to teach." Utilitarians
simply go wrong in their hedonistic conception of well-being, which renders it a potentially counterproductive consequentialism. Only a "truer analysis" of human well-being can deliver consequentialism from error and bad practical effect. Later in this chapter and in Chapter 4, we will explore more
fully Green's assessment of utilitarianism's practical political merit despite its hedonic mischaracter-
ization of ultimate good. As we shall see, in contrast to his worries here, Green often endorses
utilitarian practical reasoning as a handy substitute for his own more cumbersome perfectionist
reasoning.
[66] Green, *Lectures on the Principles of Political Obligation*, Sect. 23.

he had virtually surrendered his hedonism. He should have seen that "this is to give up the doctrine that pleasure is ultimate good, and to find such good in some object, the attainment of which of course is pleasant but which is not itself pleasure."[67] He should have conceded that good was no less than the "attainment of a certain type of character or some realization of the possibilities of man, not pleasure, as the end by relation to which goodness or value is to be measured."[68] Mill, in effect according to Green, is confused about good though he should not have been and though he sometimes came close to getting it right when he extolled the "higher" pleasures of self-development. The latter clearly implies for Green that good cannot possibly be pleasure but rather must be some sort of deeper or abiding self-satisfaction of which pleasure is merely incidental and contingent.

As far as Green was concerned, Mill's confusion about good was rooted in another deeper confusion about what individuals actually can and do desire. Mill, that is, also confused our actual overriding desire for self-satisfaction with our imagined and unfounded desire for greatest pleasure.[69] He mistook the latter for the former though he should have recognized that the latter could never be a legitimate object of desire. Indeed, all utilitarians were misguided in thinking that the *summum bonum*, as the greatest possible sum of pleasures, was something "definite and intelligible."[70] All utilitarians failed to see that the desire for greatest pleasure was simply psychologically and empirically incoherent. Its satisfaction simply could not be experienced for pleasures could only be experienced disjunctively and serially. There was no such experience as aggregate or summed pleasure. In Green's words:

Hedonism, in short, logically leaves no chief good at all, but as Hedonistic ethics cannot do without it, an attempt is made to find it in a greatest possible collection or sum of pleasures, ... which altogether must be better than any one or any less sum of them, and thus altogether, form the chief good. This I call an absurdity because for the consciousness of the pleased person, in relation to which alone

---

[67] T. H. Green, "Lecture E. T. 78," unnumbered MSS, T. H. Green Papers, Balliol College, Oxford University. Also see Green, *Prolegomena to Ethics*, Sect. 162. And see Sect. 170 where Green continues: "But this [Mill's underlying real position], as we have seen, is no more than saying that they [desires for higher pleasures] are desired by a self-conscious subject, who in all desire, or at any rate in all that amounts to will, is seeking self-satisfaction, and who, so far as he reflects on any desire, reflects also on the pleasure of its possible fulfillment." So, according to Green, Mill's improved utilitarianism is no authentic utilitarianism at all. Mill simply says that acting morally, which is not acting to promote pleasure, tends to be contingently pleasant. Acting as we should fortunately just happens to be pleasant. But Mill didn't always fully appreciate the real implications of what he was saying.

[68] Green, *Prolegomena to Ethics*, Sect. 164.

[69] See, for instance, Green's comments in *ibid.*, Sect. 167.   [70] *Ibid.*, Sect. 358.

pleasures are called good, they cannot form a sum. Each is over before the other begins and it is only as *counted and not as enjoyed* that they coexist, and when we speak of them as together constituting the chief good we are confusing a *sum of numeration* with a *sum of existence or enjoyment.* [my italics][71]

As Raz has recently put it more clearly, the pursuit of pleasure is "insatiable and non-diminishing," making maximum pleasure an illusory object of desire. By contrast, for Raz, happiness is a legitimate object of desire because it is "not the accumulation of many happy experiences." Understood as a "quality of a person's life or of periods of his life, the pursuit of happiness is diminishing and satiable" and thus empirically possible to desire.[72]

Green admits that some utilitarian might respond by asserting that though, strictly speaking, it is not possible to have the experience of greatest aggregate pleasure, it is nevertheless possible to fill up one's life with ever larger amounts of discrete moments of pleasure. They might, he suggests, reply: "Everyone knows the difference between enjoying a longer succession of pleasures and a shorter one, a succession of more intense and a succession of less intense pleasures, a succession of pleasures less interrupted by pain and one more interrupted. In this sense every one knows the difference between enjoying a larger sum of pleasures and enjoying a smaller sum."[73]

But this response fails as far as Green is concerned because: "It seems, indeed, to be intrinsically as unmeaning as it would be to speak of a greatest possible quantity of time or space. The sum of pleasures plainly admits of indefinite increase, with the continued existence of sentient beings capable of pleasure."[74] It fails, Green seems to think, because the number of serial pleasures that one can pack into one's life is infinite. Hence, just as it is nonsensical to speak of the greatest amount of infinite space and time, so it is equally nonsensical to speak of the greatest amount of infinite pleasures. But the real failure would appear to lie with Green's attempt to dismiss

---

[71] Green, "Lecture E. T. 78." Also see Green, *Prolegomena to Ethics*, Sects. 221 and 227.
[72] Raz, *The Morality of Freedom*, 241.   [73] Green, *Prolegomena to Ethics*, Sect. 358.
[74] *Ibid.*, Sect. 359. In *The Moral Philosophy of T. H. Green* (Oxford: Oxford University Press, 1987), Geoffrey Thomas invokes Sidgwick's notion of a "continually renascent satisfaction" and suggests that hedonists could defend themselves against Green in the way that Green admits they might futilely try. Thomas, unfortunately, does not address Green's "time and space" counter-reply. Equally germane is Kant's remark (which may be the source of inspiration for Green's position) that "happiness is not an idea of reason but of imagination, resting solely on empirical grounds and it is vain to expect that these should define an action by which one could attain the totality of a series of consequences which is really endless." Immanuel Kant [1785], *Fundamental Principles of the Metaphysics of Morals*, trans. [1873], T. K. Abbott (Buffalo: Prometheus, 1987), 46. Also see *ibid.*, 24. And recall, from Chapter 1, Bradley and Bosanquet's similar claims about the incoherence of seeking greatest pleasure.

the above utilitarian maneuver. Thoughtful utilitarians need not foolishly maintain that one should futilely chase after phantom aggregates of *total* pleasure since pleasures are, after all, experientially infinite. They need not fall victim to regarding pleasure as some sort of limited experiential meal, which we ought to consume in its entirety. Rather, sober utilitarians simply need to hold that one ought to try to get as much pleasure as one can. There is no absolute aggregate of greatest pleasure. There are only lesser and greater amounts of pleasure. The more of it one gets in during one's life, the better. So the utilitarian maneuver anticipated by Green is not "intrinsically unmeaning" and most utilitarians might readily embrace it.

Notwithstanding this issue, Mill's principal shortcoming stems from his confusing good as pleasure with good as self-satisfaction. This confusion stems from the way in which he confuses, as do all utilitarians, desire for greatest pleasure with desire for self-satisfaction. The former is an experiential fiction. Hence, it cannot be desired and therefore, it cannot be desirable (good).[75] Mill nevertheless avoids this confusion to the extent that he privileges self-development and its higher pleasures. By invoking both, Mill virtually concedes that ultimate good is a particular "state of existence" or a certain "sort of social life." He effectively implies that the good "which he has before him is not an aggregate of pleasure but a pleasant life" instead.[76]

So it seems that Mill's moral theory, as far as Green was concerned, is quite similar to his own. In its better moments, it is remarkably similar. The good that it cherishes resembles that which his own theory recommends. In its weaker moments, Mill's theory misidentifies good in the more typical utilitarian way. Hence, the issue between Mill and himself was simply a matter of how consistently and appropriately Mill defined or understood good. The difference between them did not lie in the fact that Mill was a consequentialist and Green was not: both were consequentialists. The difference was merely one of properly *depicting* the good to be maximized.[77] Mill depicted good hedonically whereas Green depicted it non-hedonically.

---

[75] Of course, if each individual's greatest pleasure is a fictive end, then the greatest pleasure of the greatest number is no less fictive and incoherent.

[76] Green, *Prolegomena to Ethics*, Sect. 360.

[77] See especially Green's contention: "It will have appeared from the foregoing discussion that primary differences between the view here advanced and that of 'Hedonistic' philosophers relates to the generic definition of the good – not only of the morally good, but of good in the wider sense. Whereas with them the good generically is the pleasant, in this treatise the common characteristic of the good is that it satisfies some desire. In all satisfaction of desire there is pleasure, and thus

DISPOSITIONAL CONSEQUENTIALISM AND COMMON GOOD

Green, as we are now beginning to see, was a consequentialist, but certainly not of the utilitarian variety. He advocated a consequentialism of self-realization. Self-realization, however, admits wider and narrower meanings. Yet only the narrower meaning moralizes freedom in the full "inner" sense. Only the latter, then, is always to everyone's benefit. Only the latter constitutes the purest and most invaluable form of common good. In *Prolegomena to Ethics*, Green asserts quite candidly and unambiguously:

When from the nature of the case, however, a consideration of effects can alone enter into the moral valuation of an act, the effects to be considered, according to our view, will be different from those of which the Utilitarian, according to his principles, would take account. They will be effects, not in the way of producing pleasure, but in the way of contributing to that perfection of mankind, of which the essence is a *good will* on the part of *all* persons. [my italics][78]

Here especially, Green's consequentialism is striking and unmistakable (though it is plainly a non-aggregating kind of consequentialism insofar as *everyone's* moral self-realization constitutes the ultimate criterion of right). Whereas utilitarians evaluate actions in terms of their pleasure-maximizing results, Green proposes to evaluate them in terms of their virtue or good will-promoting results. Promoting virtue or moral self-realization among all citizens ought to be our standard of right and wrong. That is, the "rectitude" of actions is a function of their "tendency to produce rectitude in others" rather than their "tendency to produce general or individual happiness."[79] As Green also says in an unpublished manuscript:

Moral goodness and badness are attributes of character – of action only as a relation to character, either as flowing from it or contributing to its formation. (See bearing of this on question whether action morally good in virtue of motives or results. Neither one nor other absolutely. Not good in virtue of any *except* results in way of production of good character, nor good in virtue of

---

pleasantness in an object is a necessary incident of its being good." *Prolegomena to Ethics*, Sect. 171. For Brink, by sometimes taking pleasure as good instead of properly seeing it as merely accompanying good qua desire satisfaction, Mill fell victim to Butler's fallacy. According to this fallacy, supposing that we aim at pleasure because pleasure happens to accompany desire satisfaction is wrongheaded. Brink also suggests that Green failed to appreciate just how similar his and Mill's moral theories were especially insofar as Mill was a perfectionist, which Brink thinks he was. See Brink, "Introduction," xxxiii and c.

[78] Green, *Prolegomena to Ethics*, Sect. 294.

[79] T. H. Green, "Utility as a Principle of Art and Morality," unnumbered MSS, T. H. Green Papers. Also see *Collected Works of T. H. Green*, Vol. V, 51, for same quote. In addition, see Bradley's claim in *Ethical Studies*, 125 that he disagrees with utilitarians primarily because they make pleasure, and not self-realization, their normative criterion.

these unless proceeding from a character interested in production of such results.) [my italics][80]

Green's moral theory, as we should concede at least at this juncture, is a (non-aggregating) good-promoting theory with true good defined as moral self-realization. Hence, we can also profitably call it a form of "dispositional" consequentialism because moral self-realization or good will is, for Green, a dispositional quality. The disposition to be morally good, so widely prized and yet so precious and ennobling, endows us with dignity and commands our best maximizing efforts. It is "the only good in the pursuit of which there can be no competition of interests, the only good which is really common to all who may pursue it ... which consists in the universal will to be good – in the *settled disposition* on each man's part to make the most and best of humanity in his own person and in the persons of others" (my italics).[81]

Moral self-realization as the pure disposition to be good, then, ought to be encouraged in all citizens, or at least in as many as possible. Precisely because this loftiest form of good, this most worthy "inner" freedom, is naturally of "mutual service" to others, it is equally a "common good." It is a common good because those enlivened by this disposition invariably treat others with the unconditional respect, kindness, and even magnanimity, that they deserve. At the very least, they treat them with rights-respecting self-restraint. They exhibit, at a minimum, the kind of "self-denying will" that entails respecting the moral rights (both negative and positive) of others, thereby assuring others a measure of opportunity to make the most of their respective talents and capacities. And at a maximum, they additionally act beneficently. They not only feel *obliged* to forbear but equally *duty bound* to assist others for both obligation and duty constitute the "outer and inner side of the same spiritual development."[82] Again, both obligation and duty fill the conceptual space of

---

[80] T. H Green, "Note D on Pleasure and Kant's Moral Philosophy" in "Notes A–F," unnumbered MSS, T. H. Green Papers. See, in addition, *Prolegomena to Ethics*, Sect. 377, where Green observes, "the statement that the act of self-sacrifice has its value in itself is not to be understood as denying that it has its value in its consequences, but as implying that those consequences, to be of intrinsic value, must be of a kind with the act itself, as an exercise of a character having its dominant interest in some form of human perfection."

[81] Green, *Prolegomena to Ethics*, Sect. 244.

[82] Green, *Lectures on the Principles of Political Obligation*, Sect. 251. Green's distinction between obligation and duty mirrors Kant and Mill's distinction between perfect and imperfect duty. Whereas being obligated for Green means respecting the moral rights of others, being duty bound means helping them but not unconditionally. *Lectures on the Principles of Political Obligation*, as the full title suggests, focuses on obligation or justice primarily while *Prolegomena to Ethics* also treats duties and therefore morality more widely.

moral self-realization for Green. But, as should be plain by now, moral self-realization is not the only variety of self-realization. Self-realization, in its wider and more generic sense, is a matter of cultivating and developing the full plethora of one's other special talents and not just one's moral talents.

This wider kind of self-realization is as much a common good as its narrower moral variety because, in achieving it, each tends to contribute to everyone else's self-realization. By developing one's particular talents and capacities, each person becomes invaluable to others by enriching and complementing their lives. Each becomes a resource and boon to others.[83] But vicious talents are out because they violate moral rights and contravene beneficence.

Common good, therefore, is not some ironhanded despotic regimen that consumes and exhausts individual integrity as Green's critics, such as Berlin and Norman, typically charge.[84] Acting in a worthwhile way means, more generally, no more than making the most of one's rights-secured opportunities to develop one's interests and abilities as one sees fit. (More narrowly, it also means respecting the basic rights of others as well as aiding them in any way that one can so that they, in turn, can develop their respective interests and abilities as they see fit.[85]) Hence, Green can conclude: "Thus the ideal of virtue which our consciences acknowledge has come to be the devotion of character and life, in *whatever* channel the idiosyncrasy and circumstances of the individual may determine, to a perfecting of man, which is itself conceived not as an external end to be attained by goodness, but as consisting in such a life of self-devoted activity on the part of all persons" (my italics).[86]

---

[83] Also see Ritchie, *The Principles of State Interference*, 141–2, where Ritchie says that, for Green, common good is nothing less than "self-satisfaction" or "self-realisation."

[84] See Isaiah Berlin, "Two Concepts of Liberty" in *Four Essays on Liberty* (Oxford: Oxford University Press, 1982), 133 and Richard Norman, *Free and Equal* (Oxford: Oxford University Press, 1987), 32.

[85] At least one other interpreter of Green seems to hold that, by common good, Green means, in part, something like rights-respecting virtue. See W. D. Lamont, *Introduction to Green's Moral Philosophy* (London: George Allen and Unwin, 1934), 191. There, Lamont says that for Green, common good is the "disposition to balance and harmonize competing interests" by "keeping scrupulously within a balanced system of rights." Presumably, if being disposed to keep within a system of rights is a common good, then this system of rights itself is surely just as much a common good. For another and very recent perfectionist account of common good as comprising, in part, a "system of equal and mutually supporting rights and duties as contributory to each individual's self-fulfillment," see Gewirth, *Self-Fulfillment*, 189–99.

[86] Green, *Prolegomena to Ethics*, Sect. 286. For analysis of common good in Green that parallels my own in crucial respects, see Avital Simhony, "T. H. Green's Theory of the Morally Justified Society," *History of Political Thought*, 10 (1989), 496–7. I try to make further sense of Green's conception of common good again in Chapter 4 by analyzing it in terms of conceptions of will and good will.

Common good, then, is pluralistic. It displays, as Avital Simhony maintains, a "varied nature."[87] Moreover, though rich and diverse, it nonetheless
requires that, however individuals choose to conduct themselves, they do so
with rights-respecting virtuosity at a very minimum.

RETREAT TO THE CITADEL OF UTILITARIANISM

Regardless of the extent to which utilitarians fail to correctly identify good
as moral self-realization and despite their failure to appreciate how true
good is also a common good, Green concedes that utilitarianism ironically
prescribes much the same sort of thing as his own theory. That is,
he nevertheless allows that the practical implications of his own dispositional consequentialism may differ little from those of rival versions of
utilitarianism, especially improved versions. In *Prolegomena to Ethics*, he
acknowledges:

Again, in most cases where a man has to decide how he may best promote the
greatest good of others, it makes *little practical difference* in regard to the line of
action to be taken, whether he considers their greatest good to lie in the possession
of a certain character, as an end not a means, or in the enjoyment of the most
pleasure of which they are capable ... All that one man can do to make another
better is to remove obstacles, and supply conditions favourable to the formation of
a good character. Now, in a general way and up to a certain point, the line of action
directed to this removal of obstacles and supply of conditions favourable to
goodness, will also tend to make existence more pleasant for those whose good
is being sought. For instance, healthy houses and food, sound elementary education, the removal of temptations to drink, which are needed in order to supply
conditions favourable to good character, tend also to make life more pleasant on
the whole. The question at issue between Hedonistic Utilitarians and their
opponents [Green presumably] as to the nature of ultimate good cannot affect
their importance. [my italics][88]

Green, at least here it seems, is proposing that both utilitarianism (especially
its rights-oriented Millian variety) and his own moral theory nearly always

---

[87] Avital Simhony, "On Forcing Individuals to Be Free: T. H. Green's Liberal Theory of Positive
Freedom," *Political Studies*, 39 (1991), 308.

[88] Green, *Prolegomena to Ethics*, Sect. 332. Also see "Note D on Pleasure and Kant's Moral Philosophy"
where Green similarly contends: "In regard to most questions of political conduct, and many private,
different views as to the nature of the ultimate good do not affect judgement which if circumstances
were fully known should be formed as to the proper line to take ... Hence we often find political
agreement among those whose moral theories are antagonistic, because they agree in the *practical*
analysis of the social situation" (my italics). Unnumbered MSS, T. H. Green Papers. Also see Brink,
"Introduction," *Prolegomena to Ethics*, lxii–lxiv, for Brink's recognition of Green's concession that
utilitarianism and perfectionism may well generate the same practical recommendations.

generate the same practical moral rules. Notwithstanding the way in which these theories tend to conceptualize good differently, both advocate the same practical, rights-oriented strategies for maximizing it.[89]

Green repeats this same claim on several occasions sometimes even suggesting that utilitarianism may profitably substitute for his own theory. For instance, elsewhere in *Prolegomena to Ethics*, he concedes:

From the difficulty of presenting to ourselves in any positive form what a society, perfected in this sense [in the sense of all citizens self-realizing], would be, we may take *refuge* in describing the object of the devotion, which our consciences demand, as the greatest happiness of the greatest number; and until we puzzle ourselves with analysis, such an account may be *sufficient for practical purposes*. But our theory becomes false to the real demand of conscience, if it interprets this happiness except as including and dependent upon the unimpeded exercise by the *greatest number of a will*, the same in principle with that which conscience calls upon the individual to aim at in himself. [my italics][90]

In other words, given the imprecision and ambiguity of his own theory's rendering of morally good (though, in this case, a good to be maximized in terms of fostering it merely among the *greatest number* rather than among *all* individuals), and given the fact that utilitarianism (improved utilitarianism in particular) mirrors the practical recommendations of his own theory, utilitarianism emerges as an acceptable substitute strategy. (Green never expressly explains systematically why the practical counsel of utilitarianism imitates what his theory also recommends. However, as I try to show in greater detail in Chapter 4, because pleasure always accompanies or is always so closely incidental to moral self-realization, it can serve as a kind of marker or cipher for it. Hence, by

---

[89] Though by removing "obstacles" and supplying "conditions," Green does not explicitly mention moral rights, one can safely assume that he intends them. Recall that, for Green as with Mill, basic rights were second to none in terms of their good-promoting merit. Moreover, since Green's consequentialism mimics Mill's utilitarianism by embracing similar kinds of stringent moral rights because of their good-promoting worth, it is also a form of *indirect* consequentialism as well as a form of dispositional consequentialism. In other words, as in Mill's indirect utilitarianism, good in Green's consequentialism merely serves as a standard for evaluating individual actions and public policies. It never serves as a source of *direct* obligation as it does for act utilitarians. As with Mill, fundamental moral rights are the only sources of direct obligation. For both Mill and Green, diligently respecting them in most cases happens to be for the good-promoting best.

[90] Green, *Prolegomena to Ethics*, Sect. 286. See, by contrast, Colin Tyler, "The Metaethics of Pleasure: Jeremy Bentham and his Idealist Critics," *Contemporary Political Studies*, ed. Andrew Dobson and Jeffrey Stanyer (1998), 1, 266, for the received view that Green (as well as Bradley) held that Benthamite utilitarianism was "too vague to yield useful practical guidance." Chapter 4 will take up in detail the critical relationship among self-realization, utility and will in Green alluded to here. Also note that this quote immediately follows the sentence quoted as Note 86 above.

maximizing greatest pleasure in the world, you just happen to maximize moral self-realization as well.)[91]

Moreover, Green further concedes that normative utilitarianism, as opposed to utilitarianism merely as a psychological account of our motives, is inherently perfectionist in any case:

> But if the Utilitarian [presumably Mill especially] is committed to no more than a certain doctrine of the criterion of morality – the doctrine that the value of actions and institutions is to be measured in the last resort by their effect on the nett sum of pleasures enjoyable by *all* human, or perhaps by *all* sentient, beings, the difference between him and one who would substitute for this 'nett sum, etc.' 'the fulfilment of human capacities' may be *practically* small. A desire for the enjoyment of pleasure by others – whether in the largest quantity possible, or in some more positively conceivable form – is so entirely different from desire for *a* pleasure that, if the Utilitarian considers his "Summum Bonum," or any limited form of it, to be a possible object of desire to the individual, he clears himself practically, even though it be at the sacrifice of consistency, from chargeability with any such theory of motives as would exclude the possibility of a "pure heart". [my italics][92]

Now this passage from the *Prolegomena to Ethics* discloses and summarizes much. First, to the extent that utilitarians follow Mill in aiming at maximizing pleasures of *all* others, they forgo psychological hedonism in the name of universal hedonism. By making universal hedonism the *summum bonum*, they exhibit purity of heart and therefore implicitly good will as they should. By making *everyone's* well-being their moral end, they concede that acting morally means acting non-selfishly and therefore virtuously to some degree. They implicitly embrace perfectionist consequentialism thereby giving up utilitarianism or at least giving up utilitarianism understood simply as psychological hedonism.

The proceeding crucial passage occurs near the end of the *Prolegomena to Ethics* just before Green closes his study by answering his own rhetorical question whether utilitarianism, even with its perfectionist implications made explicit, is ultimately practically preferable to his ethics. But instead of addressing Mill's utilitarianism, as one might expect, he instead takes on

---

[91] Avital Simhony has suggested to me that Green's moral theory cannot possibly be genuinely consequentialist insofar as it is a non-aggregating theory. For her, Green champions moral self-realization among *all* citizens and not merely among their *greatest number*. In this regard, see Lamont's remark in *Introduction to Green's Moral Philosophy*, 164, that for Green (as well as himself), "the greatest perfection of the greatest number" was the ultimate criterion of right action.

[92] Green, *Prolegomena to Ethics*, Sect. 356. In Chapter 5, we will see that Ritchie likewise holds that utilitarianism is practically valuable notwithstanding its misconceived hedonic conception of good. And we shall also see how Ritchie regarded Green as mostly just improving Mill.

Sidgwick's more traditional variety. And though critical of Sidgwick, he nevertheless finds Sidgwick's utilitarianism not unpromising if not quite as promising as Mill's.

GREEN AND SIDGWICK

Of Green's contemporary utilitarian rivals, Sidgwick seems to have best understood the consequentialist nature of Green's moral theory.[93] He readily concurs that Green's moral theory is good-maximizing with "goodness of will in others" the good to be maximized.[94] In fact, Sidgwick holds that the only fundamental difference between himself and Green, as far as he can ascertain, lies in the fact that Green finds good as greatest pleasure psychologically unavailable. As Sidgwick concludes in a separate study of Green's *Prolegomena to Ethics*: "Such a doctrine indeed is indispensable as a basis to the intermittent controversy with Hedonism which Green carries on throughout the treatise; since, so far as I can see, his only substantial objection to the Hedonistic end relates to its transient quality; it is not a 'permanent' or 'abiding' good."[95]

Not surprisingly, Sidgwick rejects Green's contention that pleasure cannot constitute good because pleasures are of a serial and "perishing nature" and hence cannot be experienced as a sum. As Green anticipated some utilitarians might try to respond, Sidgwick asserts that utilitarianism remains cogent even if pleasures cannot be aggregatively experienced: "Certainly he [the utilitarian] cannot imagine the pleasures to be felt as a sum. But so far as they admit of being quantitatively compared at all ... pleasures can be summed in thought, i.e. they can be thought in the aggregate; and it is as so summed that they attract a man *qua* rational

[93] John Dewey, who was much influenced by Green in his earlier writings, also seems to have viewed Green as a consequentialist. See his "Self-Realization as the Moral Ideal," *Philosophical Review*, 2 (1893), 652. For Green's influence on Dewey, who Alan Ryan has called a "mid-western T. H. Green," see Alan Ryan, *John Dewey and the High Tide of American Liberalism* (New York: W. W. Norton, 1995), 12 and 89–97.

[94] Henry Sidgwick, *Lectures on the Ethics of T. H. Green, Mr. Herbert Spencer and J. Martineau* (London: Macmillan, 1902), 72. Sidgwick also uncharacteristically and correctly viewed Spencer as utilitarian. See my "Deductive Hedonism and the Anxiety of Influence," *Utilitas*, 12, special symposium on Henry Sidgwick (November, 2000).

[95] Henry Sidgwick, "Green's Ethics," *Mind*, o.s., 9 (1884), 174–6. Also see *Lectures on the Ethics of T. H. Green, Mr. Herbert Spencer and J. Martineau*, 38–42. By contrast, in "Introduction," *Prolegomena to Ethics*, Brink calls Sidgwick's attitude regarding Green "dismissive" and further suggests that Sidgwick's unnecessarily antagonistic attitude towards him constituted a "missed opportunity," whose effect continues to this day, for analytical ethical theory to engage perfectionism more seriously (xcix and cv). In his *Mind* essay, by the way, Sidgwick also views Green as advocating good-maximization. See 185 in particular.

being."[96] In short, all that matters for utilitarianism to go through is that it makes sense to talk about certain courses of action as tending to "make life more pleasant on the whole" in terms of generating a larger (rather than largest) sum of serial pleasures over the course of a lifetime.[97] In other words, a life filled with more pleasures, one after another, is both accessible and desirable.

So for Sidgwick, Green's disavowal of utilitarianism's handling of good fails. Utilitarianism's good is not vague at best and incoherent at worst. In fact, in Sidgwick's view, if vagueness lies anywhere, it lies with Green's notion of good. Sidgwick finds Green's concept of self-realization, especially where he describes it as some kind of permanent "abiding satisfaction," exceedingly obscure. Moreover, due to this elusive vagueness, Sidgwick also reproves Green's practical reasoning for being absolutely incapable of providing real practical guidance.[98]

Both Sidgwick and Green recognized each other's moral theories for what they were, namely good-promoting theories. Ironically, however, each accused the other of misidentifying good and each seemed to regard the other's mistaken version of good as being so shrouded in ambiguity that it unavoidably lapsed into incoherence. And as far as each was concerned, the other nonetheless sometimes verged on getting normative matters right. But insofar as Green conceded the *practical* high ground to utilitarianism, Green clearly moved closer to Sidgwick than Sidgwick did to him.

---

[96] Sidgwick, *Lectures on the Ethics of T. H. Green, Mr. Herbert Spencer and J. Martineau*, 109–10. Also see 111–12. For Green's anticipation of this kind of response, recall passages cited as notes 38 and 39.

[97] *Ibid.*, 110. For Green's response to such types of criticisms, see T. H. Green, "Hedonism and Ultimate Good," *Mind*, o.s., 2 (1877), 268–9. Also see Green, *Prolegomena to Ethics*, Sects. 364–369, for Green's favorable assessment of Sidgwick, notwithstanding his differences with him. For instance, Green praises Sidgwick for not confusing pleasure, which attends to desire satisfaction, with the desire for pleasure as many utilitarians supposedly do. (Brink, however, appears to think that Green faults Sidgwick for this kind of confusion. See Brink, "Introduction," *Prolegomena to Ethics*, c.) Green also commends Sidgwick for neither (1) holding that an agent should conclude that his or her own pleasure is desirable simply because he or she contingently desires it nor (2) holding that universal pleasure is desirable even if an individual could somehow establish that his or her own pleasure was desirable. Mill's critics typically accuse him of committing both fallacies in his famous proof of utility in ch. 4 of *Utilitarianism*. Sidgwick, of course, anticipated Moore's account of the naturalistic fallacy. See my *Equal Freedom and Utility*, 173–4 for Sidgwick's influence on Moore. Green's praise for Sidgwick suggests that he agreed with him in rejecting ethical naturalism. But note that Moore criticized Green, along with Kant, in ch. IV of *Principia Ethica* for exemplifying the "metaphysical" version of the naturalistic fallacy.

[98] Sidgwick, *Lectures on the Ethics of T. H. Green, Mr. Herbert Spencer and J. Martineau*, 73–4. Also see 107 where Sidgwick writes that the kind of good-maximizing calculations required by Green's theory would easily be "more difficult and more doubtful" than those required by utilitarianism.

GREEN, KANT AND KANTIAN CONSEQUENTIALISM

Green, as is widely known, was much influenced by Kant but this influence was not sufficient to make Green a traditional neo-Kantian. Green was also deeply critical of Kant. Indeed, his criticisms were so essential because they were so fundamentally consequentialist in spirit. Nowhere is this emphasis more evident than in his *Lectures on the Philosophy of Kant* (particularly chapter N entitled "The Good Will") as well as in some of his unpublished manuscripts. For instance, Green cautions that in adopting our normative commitments, our options are not simply limited to choosing between utilitarianism and deontology. We need not artificially confine ourselves to choosing between the degrading yet alluring heteronomy of utilitarianism or the saintly dignity of trying to live by the moral law exclusively. As the passage opening this chapter reminds us, we fall into a "false antithesis if, having admitted (as is true) that the quest of self-satisfaction is the form of all moral activity, we allow no alternative (as Kant in effect seems to allow none) between the quest for self-satisfaction in the enjoyment of pleasure, and the quest for it in the fulfilment of a universal practical law."[99] Instead, we ought to recognize and seek self-satisfaction in fulfillment of our talents including, especially, our moral talents.

Green also makes this same point against Kant in a more familiar way. More typical of Kant's critics, he complains that the moral law (the categorical imperative) is overly formalistic and empty, requiring "content" or an "object of which the reality is desired," namely certain kinds of consequences.[100] In other words,

There would be nothing against the spirit of Kant's doctrine in saying that an act of wise benevolence is good in virtue of its consequences so long as these consequences are other than the pleasure of the agent and being other than his pleasure, are the object for sake of which he does the act ... Kant, however, fell into the error of thinking that if the consequences were pleasant to an agent when attained, to do *y*, act for sake of its consequences, was to do it for pleasure, and hence pronounced that, in order to be morally good, it must be done not

---

[99] See also Green's unpublished "Note D on Pleasure and Kant's Moral Philosophy" where Green observes that the "notion that pleasure is ultimate good arises from the substitution for the true proposition that there is pleasure in all satisfaction of desire, of a false one that all desire is for pleasure – an error which Kant so far shared as to allow no alternatives between desire for fulfilment of the moral law and desire for pleasures."

[100] Green, "Lectures on the Philosophy of Kant," 130.

for sake of any consequences; but simply as enjoined by moral law – test of this being that it is done painfully.[101]

But *what* sorts of consequences might provide Kant's moral law with a legitimate "object?" *Which* consequences would furnish it with the "content" that it requires? Not surprisingly, self-realization, especially its moral variety, is the kind of consequence that Kant's moral law needs in order to escape its otherwise empty formalism. Moral self-realization gives it truly substantive "content," or an "object," and thereby invests the moral law with a point as well. That is, only those actions that promote good will in others, as well as exhibit good will, deserve being universalized.[102]

So in Green's view, Kant's moral law needs fleshing out with consequentialist content. It needs to be "relative" to something else:

But in fact the universal practical law on which Kant insists is unintelligible except as implying an object unconditionally good to which it is *relative*. It has no content, it prescribes nothing, except what is *relative* to this object … That which the exponents of Kant call "duty for duty's sake" is rather duty *for the sake of the attainment of that perfect will*, which in imperfection submits to duties, but in perfection supersedes them. [my italics][103]

Of course, relativizing Kant's moral law this way arguably instrumentalizes it by reducing it to a prudential strategy, that is, into what Kant calls a hypothetical or assertorial imperative. But if Green's improved Kant comes to this upshot, then Green's consequentialist commitments are clearer still.

Green drew generously from Kant's moral philosophy, but he also generously reworked it. He borrowed from Kant liberally and selectively while laboring to accommodate the moral law with the deeply consequentialist scope and temper of his own moral theory. In the end, consequentialist considerations were always overriding for Green: "When we find that actions to which we are constrained, as we believe, by the moral law, are tending to estrange us from our fellows – to make ourselves and mankind

---

[101] Green, "Lecture E. T. 78." If Green is right about Kant, then "neither being done painfully nor pleasurably," rather than the more stringent "being done painfully," would follow as a good enough test of moral action. I would like to thank Leah Hochman for bringing this implication to my attention.

[102] Kant might remind Green that such a "rule is simply heteronomy" for whether "the object determines the will by means of inclination, as in the principle of private happiness, or by means of reason directed to objects of our possible volition generally, as in the principle of perfection, in either case the will never determines itself *immediately* by the conception of the action, but only by the influence which the foreseen effect of the action has on the will; *I ought to do something, on this account, because I wish for something else*." Kant, *Fundamental Principles of the Metaphysics of Morals*, 74.

[103] Green, "Lectures on the Philosophy of Kant," III. Also see "Lecture E. T. 78" where Green tries several times to close the philosophical gap between Kant and improved, non-hedonistic utilitarianism.

miserable – we may naturally enquire whether they can be in accordance with any but a very strained interpretation of a law which is based, in part at least, on the considerations of human happiness."[104] In other words, as far as Green was concerned, Kantianism (when properly refurbished), turns out to be fundamentally perfectionist and consequentialist. It also dares not ignore concern for happiness. Whether Green's "improved" Kant is really much different from Kant properly interpreted is debatable. Guyer argues that Kant neither abjures consequentialist moral reasoning nor ignores considerations of human happiness as vital as the received view of him simplistically insists. For instance, regarding the importance of happiness for Kant, recall that Guyer claims emphatically that despite Kant's insistence that virtuous motivation excludes desiring one's own happiness, "virtue and happiness are far from being entirely separated, being joined at the hip."[105]

Green's reworking of Kant may also be less of a meaningful refurbishment even if Guyer's account of Kant is fundamentally misplaced (which I suspect is not the case). Interpreting Kant's intentions aside, the logical implications of Kant's moral law may not be necessarily narrowly deontological. In his suggestive *Kantian Consequentialism*, as well as in an earlier article by the same title, David Cummiskey argues that Kantianism, foundationally speaking, is not inconsistent with consequentialism. According to Cummiskey, a "conscientious moral agent acts from a sense of duty, not from self-interest or inclination, but for all that Kant says, she nonetheless may strive to maximally promote the good." That is, "even if a formal principle determines the normative content (or end) of moral principles, it may nonetheless be the case that the right action maximally promotes that content (or end)."[106] What matters for Kant, according to Cummiskey, is the reason *why* moral principles are adopted rather than their content. For Kant, the "question is not about whether a moral principle must presuppose a conception of the good; rather the question is about one's reason for adopting that conception of the good."[107] As long as consequentialists act dutifully rather than from natural inclination alone, they do not necessarily violate the moral law. As long as the "determining ground" of will is

---

[104] Green, "Utility as a Principle of Art and Morality."
[105] Guyer, "Nature, Freedom, and Happiness: Third Proposition of Kant's *Idea for a Universal History*," 378–9. Recall also from Chapter 1 how Guyer's account of Kant resembles Green's in crucial respects, making Green more faithfully neo-Kantian than Green perhaps fully realized. Also see ch. 3 ("Freedom as the Inner Value of the World") and ch. 4 ("Kant's Morality of Law and Morality of Freedom") in Guyer's *Kant on Freedom, Law and Happiness*.
[106] David Cummiskey, *Kantian Consequentialism* (Oxford: Oxford University Press, 1996), 10.
[107] *Ibid.*, 47.

formal and not material primarily, then good willing need not be anti-consequentialist. Cummiskey concludes:

It may be quite natural to conclude from this that a consequentialist principle is out of place in the Kantian scheme. What is actually out of place, however, are particular ways of *justifying* consequentialist principles. Specifically, Kant is arguing against all desire-based justifications of morality. The revolutionary idea that the determining ground of the moral will must be in some sense formal rather than material, however, does not have anything to do with the structure of the resulting normative principle.[108]

Now Cummiskey holds additionally that Kant's formula of humanity is best interpreted as a consequentialist principle. According to him:

How can a concern for the value of rational beings lead to a refusal to sacrifice rational beings even when this would prevent other more extensive losses of rational beings?... On this consequentialist interpretation of Kant's theory of the good, we are obligated to promote the conditions necessary for the existence of rational beings (unconditional value) and, in addition, we are obligated to promote the ends or happiness of rational beings (conditional value). It thus seems that in principle, a Kantian may have to sacrifice some rational beings in order to promote the existence of other rational beings or a Kantian may have to sacrifice the happiness of a few in order to further the happiness of many persons.[109]

Cummiskey, clearly, is suggesting that if persons are all equally valuable, then we cannot escape being consequentialist on some level. If all persons possess equal dignity and, hence, equal unconditional and incomparable value, then sacrificing some on behalf of others (especially if they are numerous) may sometimes be morally permissible if not morally obligatory. Otherwise, we simply risk *using* the former by our inaction and by our obsessive determination not to *use* the latter. Otherwise, we risk violating the second formula of humanity on a far grander scale. As Cummiskey contends, "By emphasizing solely the one who must bear the cost if we act, one fails to sufficiently respect and take account of the many separate persons, each with only one life, who will bear the cost of our inaction."[110]

Now Cummiskey's Kantian consequentialism trades on and elaborates considerably Peter Railton's crucial and somewhat earlier insight that both Kantianism and consequentialism take respect for persons equally seriously even if differently. Whereas neo-Kantians conceptualize respect in terms of

[108] *Ibid.*, 49–50.
[109] David Cummiskey, "Kantian Consequentialism," *Ethics*, 100 (1990), 597.
[110] *Ibid.*, 601. One might question whether Cummiskey's Kant is authentically accurate but this simply ignores the whole point of Cummiskey's thesis, namely that automatically equating Kantianism with deontology begs the question.

not using others in certain ways, consequentialists conceptualize respect in terms of everyone's good having an equal claim on us. For Railton, there is no non-question-begging way of determining which conception of respect for persons celebrates our separateness more seriously: "For every conse-quentially justified act of manipulation to which the deontologist can point with alarm there is a deontologically justified act that fails to promote the well-being of some person(s) as fully as possible to which the consequential-ist can point, appalled."[III]

Following Railton, respecting persons equally entails promoting their well-being *indirectly* by securing the necessary conditions for the flourish-ing of rational nature. As Cummiskey puts it:

The equal value of all rational beings implies that all rational beings are equally significant in deciding what to do . . . Clearly, the most straightforward way to do that involves striving as far as I can to promote the necessary conditions for, first, reflective rational choice, and, second, the effective realization of rationally chosen ends. The first part of this principle does not require us to maximize rational being or our rational capacities. Rational nature is not something that we are to max-imize in that sense. It does, however, require the maximal promotion of conditions that are necessary for the flourishing of rational agency.[112]

Moreover, for Cummiskey, securing the necessary conditions for the flour-ishing of rational nature commands certain positive duties. According to Cummiskey, this implication is precisely why Kant holds that everyone is entitled to basic sustenance and health care. Hence, those who are financially capable are "perfectly obligated" to provide sustenance and health care via the state to those too poor to provide for themselves.[113] (Kant distinguishes "duties of justice" from "duties of virtue." Whereas the former are subject to external legislation insofar as they are also "duties of perfect obligation," the latter are not subject to external legislation insofar as they are merely "duties

---

[III] Peter Railton, "Alienation, Consequentialism, and the Demands of Morality" in Darwall, *Con-sequentialism*, note 32, 193–4.
[112] Cummiskey, *Kantian Consequentialism*, 89.
[113] "Since these social goods provide the necessary conditions for the growth and exercise of our rational capacities, the priority of rational nature justifies their moral primacy." Hence, Kantian "consquen-tialism thus provides a justification for what seem to be the basic demands of social justice" (*ibid.*, 158). For an account of some of the liberal political implications of Kant's moral theory that complements Cummiskey's account, but without thoroughly consequentializing Kant, see Paul Guyer, "Kantian Foundations of Liberalism" in Guyer, *Kant on Freedom, Law and Happiness*. Guyer nevertheless artfully resists reducing Kant to the deontological fanatic that many have caricatured him to be. Again, for Guyer, Kant did not reject wholesale teleological practical reasoning nor did he, as noted previously in Chapter 1, deny that happiness and virtue were intricately intertwined. Moreover, my earlier suggestion that Guyer's Kant resembles my account of Green makes a similar point indirectly insofar as Green was a consequentialist for whom happiness was hardly irrelevant.

of imperfect obligation." Only in the former case, can we be compelled to act *according to* duty.)

Thus, in brief, the formula of humanity entails consequentialism and, hence, what may superficially seem like compulsory beneficence insofar as we are required to assist others positively. Negative rights, or rights to be left alone by not being subjected to force and fraud, are insufficiently potent. Respecting everyone equally requires, in addition, empowering them with meaningful equal opportunities which positive rights alone can secure. In short, in "the negative sense, we treat persons as ends when we do not interfere with their pursuit of their (legitimate) ends." In "the positive sense, we treat persons as ends when we endeavor to help them realize their (legitimate) ends."[114]

In sum, according to Cummiskey, Kant is implicitly committed to maximizing equal respect. Maximize equal respect and you optimize everyone's opportunities to flourish including cultivating a good will. You provide everyone with meaningful chances of exercising and developing "moral courage" or virtue: "Since the formula of the end-in-itself prescribes a moral goal, which we have a duty to advance, it does not provide a rationale for agent-centered constraints which limit what we can do in the pursuit of the moral goal. The imperative to respect persons thus generates a consequentialist normative theory, rather than the desired deontological normative theory."[115] And it generates a robustly redistributive consequentialist normative theory to boot.

Now the similarities between Cummiskey's Kantian consequentialism and Green's consequentialism are palpable. Like Cummiskey's Kant, Green conceives justice as comprising the conditions of acting virtuously though it can never make us virtuous. For both, behaving justly means, at the very least, acting *as if* one were virtuous. Just behavior means respecting others by being compelled to fulfill one's external negative and positive "perfect duties" to them. It means being compelled to respect their basic rights as opposed to respecting their rights out of an internal sense of "imperfect duty." One must act *as* the "duties of outer freedom" stipulate as opposed to acting *from* the "duties of inner freedom" (exhibiting a good will).[116] Behaving justly for Green as well as for Kant, then, is no less than

---

[114] Cummiskey, *Kantian Consequentialism*, 141.   [115] Cummiskey, "Kantian Consequentialism," 615.

[116] F. P. Harris draws similar parallels between improved utilitarianism and idealism and thus helps us to appreciate the juridical continuities between both of them and Kantianism. Harris writes, "The utilitarians said that government cannot by compulsion make men happy; the idealists said that government cannot by compulsion make men moral." F. P. Harris, *The Neo-Idealist Political Theory* (New York: King's Crown Press, 1944), 63.

conforming to what Kant calls his "universal Principle of Right," which states: "So act *externally* that the free use of your choice can coexist with the freedom of everyone in accordance with a universal law" (my italics).[117] Conforming to this juristic principle offers the best guarantee that as many others as possible will, of their own accord, find happiness and develop a virtuous will or, in Green's terminology, morally realize themselves.

The similarities between Cummiskey's Kantianism and Green extend further. Insofar as both Kant and Green were indeed Kantian consequential-ists, the moral theories of neither were rigidly juridical. For Green, no less than for Cummiskey, maximizing good invariably entails using people. For Cummiskey, promoting everyone's equal worth is necessarily redis-tributive. As Cummiskey insists, "the Kantian deontologist needs a non-consequentialist rationale for the intuitive priority of negative duties over positive duties, which prohibits the sacrifice of the innocent."[118] And for Cummiskey, he or she cannot possibly provide one. For Green, maximiz-ing moral self-realization requires nothing less as well, which explains why basic moral rights are ultimately defeasible for Green as they are for Cummiskey's Kantianism. As with Kantian consequentialism, negative rights in Green's theory share the juridical playing field with positive welfare rights. Hence, as with Kantian consequentialism, people must sometimes make sacrifices in terms of being compelled to assist others. That is, they sometimes need to forgo their negative rights to non-interference for the sake of fostering good.

Notwithstanding the cogency of Cummiskey's endeavor to consequenti-alize Kant's moral law, Green's moral philosophy seems to have embodied just this kind of unconventional (at least to many of us) amalgam, which is why Green can say,

Further, Kant's formula brings the account of the end, which is to serve as the criterion of what should be done, into conformity with that conception of *state of mind* in which it should be done ... which he and the non-hedonistic utilitarian practically share ... Thus, according to both Kant and *such a utilitarian*, a man is in the right state of mind, so far as he makes his 'higher self' – himself in the ideal or completely developed or rational personality, which is the absolute 'should be,' to which all other ends are relative, an absolute end.[119]

---

[117] Kant, *The Metaphysics of Morals*, 231. This principle also suggests that Kant's principle of justice is no less a principle of equal freedom than Green's conception of positive freedom.
[118] Cummiskey, *Kantian Consequentialism*, 142.   [119] Green, "Lecture E. T. 78."

And as we have already seen, and as we shall see in greater detail in Chapter 4, making one's "higher self" an "absolute end" means promoting this end, whether in oneself or in others, equally.

CONCLUSION

Green's moral philosophy was profoundly consequentialist insofar as it was genuinely good-promoting but because Green conceived good non-hedonistically, he was not a utilitarian consequentialist. Rather, by viewing good as self-realization and morally good as moral self-realization, Green was what I have called a "dispositional" consequentialist for now at least. The rightness or wrongness of actions and policies turned on whether or not they promoted this disposition in others, on whether they fostered the "unimpeded exercise by the greatest number of a [good] will."[120]

Though conceptualizing good differently than most of his utilitarian adversaries (Mill being something of an exception), Green nevertheless confessed that utilitarianism often mirrored his own theory by recommending the same practical, juridical strategies. Hence, *practically speaking*, Green might as well have been a utilitarian. At least he might as well have been an improved utilitarian for here again Mill's improved utilitarianism was remarkably close to his own theory. Like Mill's improved, liberal utilitarianism, Green's perfectionist consequentialism took moral rights seriously and like Mill's theory, Green's theory seems to have taken much the same moral rights seriously.

In sum, Green's consequentialism was more than just dispositional. It was also deeply juridical and therefore indirect. Hence, it was also liberal. Green, that is, combined a consequentialism of will and good will with a vigorous defense of strong moral rights. Thus, promoting goodness would seldom entail using people except in mildly redistributive, typically new liberal ways. Individuals would never be recklessly sacrificed in the pantheon of prioritizing good. Because of the protection provided by strong though defeasible moral rights, no one's integrity would ever be significantly and brazenly compromised. Nobody would ever be offered up to maximizing some fantastic, pooled good and, nevertheless, self-realization

---

[120] Now if morally good means good willing qua being disposed to promote good willing among the greatest number, then Green's moral theory risks circularity. That is, morally good amounts to nothing less than the disposition on behalf of the disposition of goodness among the greatest number and so on *ad infinitum*.

(including moral self-realization) might begin flourishing ubiquitously.[121] Each and all would at least enjoy equal opportunities for cultivating it. Many might actually succeed in achieving a fair measure of it. Now many uncompromising, battle-hardened, neo-Kantians might not find much especially inspiring in all this but contemporary, Millian liberal utilitarians like Jonathan Riley surely should. And such modest success is heartening enough for the rest of us who believe, following Riley, that a sufficiently liberal theory of consequentialist good is as compelling as it is plausible.

---

[121] Good will is probably not something that can be pooled or aggregated in any case. Thus, we have all the more reason not to worry that Green's perfectionist consequentialism would violate individual integrity meaningfully.

CHAPTER 3

Between utilitarianism and perfectionism: L. T. Hobhouse

INTRODUCTION

This chapter hopes to show that Hobhouse's new liberalism was unquestionably good-promoting but not good-aggregating. Hence, it was quintessentially consequentialist through and through. I will also contend, somewhat more controversially, that his new liberalism was unconventionally utilitarian; at least it was as unconventionally utilitarian as Mill's consequentialism was. Like Mill, who influenced him extensively, Hobhouse equated good with happiness though not with pleasure. And like Green, who influenced his thinking in equal degree, he theorized happiness in terms of self-realization, making his consequentialism perfectionist as least as much as Mill's if not as much as Green's. Though plainly consequentialist and perfectionist, if not obviously utilitarian in any more conventional sense, Hobhouse's new liberalism was equally firmly committed to strong moral rights and the flourishing of individuality. His new liberalism, then, was as robustly juridical and as authentically liberal as it was fundamentally consequentialist and perfectionist. And because it was perfectionist like Green's new liberalism, I prefer to take Hobhouse up after discussing Green. Although Ritchie follows Green chronologically rather than Hobhouse, Ritchie was not a perfectionist and was therefore more of a conventional utilitarian like Hobson. For this reason, and also because Ritchie and Hobson were less preoccupied with moral theory than either Green or Hobhouse, I discuss Ritchie and Hobson subsequently.

In sum, consequentialist practical reasoning infused Hobhouse's new liberalism as much as, or even more than, it infused Green's. Hence, we have all the more reason to conclude that the new liberalism was anything but a rejection of utilitarianism.

RATIONAL GOOD AND MORAL PERSONALITY

Self-realization is key to Hobhouse's new liberalism much as it is to Green's. Self-realization, in turn, can't be understood without examining

Hobhouse's notion of the rational good. Hence, *The Rational Good*, published later in his life in 1921, occupies a vital position in his thought, though recent scholarship has all but ignored this work.[1]

Hobhouse begins *The Rational Good* by asking "whether there is a Rational, and therefore demonstrable, standard of values to which the actions of man and the institutions of society may be referred for judgment."[2] For Hobhouse, such a standard exists and the remainder of the book endeavors to persuade us accordingly.

In a chapter entitled "The Good," Hobhouse claims that the proposition that something is good expresses a "disposition" and asserts a "fact." The disposition consists in a favorable "practical attitude" towards *pleasurable* feelings, which certain (self-realizing) experiences, as a matter of fact, invariably entail. In Hobhouse's words, "the judgment 'This is good' is not only the expression of an attitude, but also the assertion of a fact, and the fact which it asserts is a *harmony* between an experience and a feeling" (my italics).[3] In short, we deem good only those kinds of experiences that are harmonious in the sense of generating feelings of pleasure. (But Hobhouse also says, somewhat inconsistently, that in judging an experience good, we "express" towards it a favorable "mode of feeling" of pleasure. So whereas in the above, we judge favorably experiences that give off pleasure, here our very judgments seem to constitute pleasurable feelings. But perhaps Hobhouse also thinks that pleasures come in two basic kinds. Perhaps he thinks that in judging pleasure-producing experiences good, we simultaneously feel some kind of higher pleasure, which partially constitutes the very act of judging.[4])

---

[1] Together with *The Metaphysical Theory of the State* (1918), *The Elements of Social Justice* (1922) and *Social Development* (1924), *The Rational Good* comprises what Hobhouse called *The Principles of Sociology*. According to Ernest Barker, *The Principles of Sociology* belongs to the "third and last group of Hobhouse's writings" from his years as Martin White Professor of Sociology at the London School of Economics from 1907 until his death in 1929. For Barker, these post-war writings form the "central *corpus*" of Hobhouse's work. See Ernest Barker, "Leonard Trelawny Hobhouse 1864–1929," *Proceedings of the British Academy*, 15 (1929), 544–5. The relationship between *The Rational Good* and *The Elements of Social Justice* is particularly tight. The latter fleshes out the practical implications imbedded in the normative principles of the former.

[2] L. T. Hobhouse, *The Rational Good* (New York: Henry Holt, 1921), xxi.

[3] *Ibid.*, 96. In the same passage, Hobhouse notes that ethical "absolutist[s]" wrongly attribute good to certain kinds of actions exclusively whereas hedonists wrongly attribute it exclusively to the feelings certain actions happen to generate. Properly understood, good refers to certain actions and their pleasures as a package. This package is the harmonious "fact" that good "asserts."

[4] But see *ibid.*, 88, where Hobhouse muddies the waters of his conceptual apparatus further by claiming that pleasure is always an "equivalent in feeling" of asserting something good. Whether "equivalent in feeling" means that judging something good *is* a feeling of pleasure, or whether pleasure *is something separate* that accompanies evaluative judging, is unclear.

But feelings of pleasure are not identical to happiness though Hobhouse regards them as variants of the same "feeling tone." He writes: "Feeling in harmony with its objects is what we call Pleasure. The body of feeling in harmony with itself and the body of its objects is what we call happiness. Viewed as feeling, then, the Rational Good is happiness, viewed as the object of this feeling it is the fulfilment of vital capacity as a consistent whole."[5] Whereas pleasure is a "feeling tone" accompanying, or harmonizing with, certain individual experiences, happiness is a "feeling tone" accompanying, or harmonizing with, a body of experiences including life as a whole. Again, regarding just happiness, Hobhouse contends that the "end, as thus conceived, does not separate *happiness* from the *kind of life* in which it is sought, but treats them as two elements in the same whole, as the *experience* and the *feeling-tone* which qualifies the experience."[6]

Notwithstanding these many, sometimes confusing distinctions, Hobhouse holds much less ambiguously that pleasure-producing experiences are also harmonious insofar as they constitute actions in which results match intentions: "There is a harmony between the effort and its result, and the feeling involved in the harmony is one of pleasant tone, culminating in satisfaction."[7] When we achieve our aims, we thus experience double harmony, namely the harmony of successful action and the harmony of pleasurable feelings. And when we live this double harmony, we are disposed to pronounce it good. Lives replete with such double harmonies are self-realizing, culminating in the richer, enduring satisfaction of happiness. Again, self-realizing lives are simultaneously happy. We recognize them by the feeling tone of happiness that they steadily exude.

In *Morals in Evolution*, published some years prior to *The Rational Good*, Hobhouse similarly suggests that evaluative judgments are "expressions for feelings" that certain kinds of events provoke in us. Whatever they are, they

---

[5] *Ibid.*, 156–7. [6] *Ibid.*, 196–7.

[7] *Ibid.*, 84. Also see 83 where Hobhouse says: "In the psycho-physical process, then, of a baby trying to grasp a candle flame we suppose two essential characters. On the one hand there is effort broken off, frustrated in the moment of achievement. There is, that is to say, disharmony between the effort and its end. On the other hand there is pain felt in the moment of disharmony, and essential thereto. Pain characterizes the feeling involved in disharmony, and the mental attitude concerned in the process of checking and canceling effort." Hobhouse sometimes refers to feelings of pleasure and pain accompanying successful and unsuccessful action as feelings of approval and disapproval. For instance, see 93 where he says: "In judging an experience good, so far as the judgment is truly our own, and not a recognition of the judgment effectively passed by some one else, we express towards it a mode of feeling which may generically be called favourable; that is to say, it has the generic character of pleasure." Hobhouse also claims that experiences in harmony with pleasure (or in disharmony with pain) need not be active experiences. They can be passive as when we witness the actions "of others." Such an experience may also be a "sensation or an idea, it may be the experience of some outer object, of a beautiful scene, a bright warm fire, an event of public interest" (93).

are not the feelings themselves but are, instead, generated by the feelings we feel when witnessing certain events. So certain types of events elicit certain feelings that, in turn, spawn evaluative expressions about them. Unfortunately, according to Hobhouse, we wrongly attribute goodness or badness to the events themselves as if goodness or badness were objective qualities attaching to them. We mistakenly do this because we fail to see that goodness and badness do not inhere in events, let alone the feelings that events produce. Rather, to repeat, goodness and badness are evaluations that we make in response to events that are harmonious or disharmonious in the sense that they produce either pleasurable or painful feelings.[8]

However much Hobhouse equivocates about the relationship between evaluation, pleasure and happiness, he nevertheless argues consistently throughout his writings that separate harmonious experiences, unless *rationally* coordinated, will likely clash thereby generating overall disharmony and dissatisfaction. Experiences that are individually harmonious may conflict in a cacophony of frustrated intentions and unpleasantness. That is, experiences we separately judge as good may turn out to be bad on the whole. Good lives, as opposed to individual good actions, are satisfying coherent lives. Unless we coordinate our separately good actions, we will never become self-realizing personalities, never develop "character." And we will never feel happy *overall*. Hence, "strongly-marked," unified lives rich in personality are *also* effective, happy lives whose constituent experiences and projects are also separately gratifying. (Chapter 4 will explore the relationship between self-realization and happiness in Green and Hobhouse with greater nuance.) Only such lives are "intrinsically good" lives.[9] Only rationally coherent lives are fully self-realizing and constitute the "rational good." In short, "that what we reasonably call good or what is really [rationally] good must be a harmony of the totality of feeling with the totality of experience so far as it affects feeling."[10]

But if, for Hobhouse, practical reason is an ongoing "effort" in coordination, then the fully rational good is a formal ideal, which actual lives succeed more or less skillfully in realizing. Hence, Hobhouse also introduces the "realized good" as the practically possible good, and the distance

---

[8] But see 577 where Hobhouse says that good and bad refer to "objects of experience about which we feel." We find pleasure in good objects and therefore seek to "maintain" them. We might be tempted to explain away this anomaly, as those inclined to read Hobhouse as more idealist than empiricist, by insisting that Hobhouse really meant "experience" as opposed to its "objects." And see the extended note on 35 in *The Rational Good*, where Hobhouse says that pleasure and pain are not so much feelings as "tones" common to certain feelings.
[9] Hobhouse, *The Rational Good*, 139.   [10] *Ibid.*, 102.

one goes in realizing his or her own good is, as Hobhouse says, "what we call character."[11] To be rich in character is to live a full, unified life. But "fullness of life" is not merely an ordered life. That is, following Aristotle instead of Plato, we should avoid confusing "harmony and order" as merely *ordered* lives are flat, unsatisfying and, therefore, characterless.[12] Lives rich in character are vibrant, multi-faceted and not intoxicated with enthusiasm for any extreme:

Now personality itself, as we know, may be incomplete and onesided. It may starve itself of one meat and glut upon another. It may unify its life by ruthless repression. There is a "development" of the miser or the ascetic. But these are not developments of the personality as a whole, but of one part to the prejudice of others.[13]

For Hobhouse, then, the "realized good" is nothing less than the cultivation of pleasure-generating personality. It is the continual refining of personality which "by the continual interrelation of action and experience, gives to each man's active life whatever cohesion and whatever individuality it manifests."[14] Each personality, Hobhouse repeatedly reminds us, is equally a social nexus, a "transpersonal reference."[15] And because each self is so richly social, self-realization is therefore a matter of others realizing (and enjoying) themselves as well. Self-realization is other-regarding and other-realizing. Each of us achieves through the achievements of others, making true individuality a many-sided harmony. The "realized good," in other words, is socially dense and reciprocal.

---

[11] *Ibid.*, 133.   [12] *Ibid.*, 138.

[13] *Ibid.*, 142–3. And insofar as misers and ascetics lack multi-dimensional personalities, they are unhappy.

[14] *Ibid.*, 140–1.

[15] *Ibid.*, 145. See also Hobhouse's earlier *Social Evolution and Political Theory*, 85, where Hobhouse says "Each man is, so to say, the meeting point of a great number of social relations." And because each person's identity is so thickly, socially constituted, the development and flourishing of each entails the development and flourishing of all. See, too, L. T. Hobhouse, *The Labour Movement* (London: T. Fisher Unwin, 1912), 70–1, where Hobhouse chastises those who arrogantly believe that their success is self-made: "You think that you *made* yourself, and that we are a mere drag on you. But before you ever were we are. We sheltered and nourished your life. We are the order which made your path straight. We are the atmosphere of thought from which you took your ideas, which you imagined to be your own. We are the men and women whom you employ. We are the men and women who buy of you. Without us you are absolutely nothing . . . But grant, if you please, that this is a partnership, that we are partners whom you cannot dispense with, and that we may make our terms for the continuance of the association." Finally, see *Social Development*, 61, where Hobhouse says: "Men need society not merely to protect themselves, but as the field for their lives. We cannot be ourselves without others . . . If I am to be all that my capacities for the family affections would have me be, I must live in a family, and if I would be any of the things that would make me a man I must for their completeness live in a society."

Yet if self-realization is so thoroughly other-regarding and reciprocal, then others must have meaningful equal opportunities to realize themselves. Others must be free, and sometimes measurably helped, to cultivate and make the most of themselves. Hence, social "development 'as a moral being' will mean a development which harmonises with social life, and so *fits* in with and *contributes* to the development of others (my italics)."[16] And hence, and in sum, the self-realization (and happiness) of each entails the self-realization (and happiness) of all and the self-realization of all requires that each, in turn, develops him- or herself morally, that each becomes a *moral* and not just *a* personality.

Moral personality, then, is deeply moralized individuality. It means becoming a *specific* kind of person, a specific kind of "transpersonal reference." Moral persons realize themselves not in spite of others but in solidarity with others. For them, morality is not a burden but rather gratifying liberation.

COMMON GOOD AND SOCIAL MIND

Common good, like rational good, was a critical conceptual feature of Hobhouse's moral theory. Hobhouse, however, never discusses common good any less equivocally than Green, and it is hardly any less surprising that scholars have struggled to make sense of it. Collini seems to think that, for Hobhouse, common good consists principally of the "liberty for self-development."[17] For Morris Ginsberg, common good is "not a good distinct from the good of individuals" but is the "well-being actually shared by the members composing society."[18] Despite the fuzziness of Ginsberg's rendering of common good as shared well-being, it at least comes closer to Hobhouse's own terminology. As Hobhouse explains, common good is that which is "effectively shared by all members of the society to which we attribute it, as something entering into and enriching their personal

[16] L. T. Hobhouse [1904], *Democracy and Reaction* (New York: Barnes and Noble, 1973), 125. *Democracy and Reaction* was first published nearly twenty years before *The Rational Good* in 1904. According to Barker, "Hobhouse's *Democracy and Reaction* of 1904 found a natural complement in Hobson's *Crisis of Liberalism* of 1909." Barker, "Leonard Trelawny Hobhouse 1864–1929," 540. Also see *The Rational Good*, 147–8 where Hobhouse similarly remarks: "So far as the achievement of each man is truly social, it fits in with and advances the achievement of others, and the 'structure' so built up is a collective work, 'the general deed of man,' which grows from generation to generation."

[17] Collini, *Liberalism and Sociology*, 127. However, Collini explains this claim in a way that suggests that self-development itself, rather than the *liberty* of self-development, constitutes the essence of common good for Hobhouse.

[18] Morris Ginsberg, "Introduction" to L. T. Hobhouse, *Sociology and Philosophy* (Cambridge: Cambridge University Press, 1966), xv.

lives."[19] Common good is not an "abstraction floating above individual men and women," but a "life effectively shared by all, not repressive of personality, but opening for it a door to fuller and more harmonious development."[20]

But what does Hobhouse mean by a "life effectively shared by all?" He doesn't seem to mean some sort of metaphysical personality mysteriously transcending and yet exhibiting itself in and through individuals. Nor does he mean the mere aggregation for, as he insists in *The Rational Good*, common good is no "simple sum of self-realizations."[21] Hobhouse's classic study, *Liberalism* (1911), is helpful here. In the chapter, "The Heart of Liberalism," Hobhouse asserts that the common good is a good in which "each man has a share" and that share, in turn, "*consists in realizing* his capacities of feeling, of loving, of mental and physical energy, and in realizing these he plays his part in the social life, or, in Green's phrase, he finds his own good in the common good" (my italics).[22] Moreover, common good "*includes* every individual" and "postulates free scope for the development of personality in each member of the community" (my italics).[23] Apparently, then, common good is nothing less than the ideal of everyone jointly realizing themselves (or at the least having the equal wherewithal to realize themselves together), nothing less than the ideal of everyone living mutually reinforcing, happy lives together. The self-realization of some achieved at the expense of others is no common good.

Hobhouse returns to the question of common good in his later *The Elements of Social Justice*. There, he defines common good variously as the "harmony of which each individual good is a constituent," as "simply the total of all the lives that are in mutual harmony," and as the "realized harmony of these elements [talents and capacities] in all members of the community."[24] Thus, common good seems equivalent to everyone achieving self-realization in harmony, to society itself as a harmonious and harmonizing ideal arena of mutual self-development and satisfaction. So in contrast to earlier formulations, common good now means something richer and more nuanced than everyone simply achieving self-realization. Rather, it now means the interactive communal *concord* of everyone pursuing self-realizing happiness together. As Hobhouse aptly characterizes it elsewhere in a later work, common good is a "fellowship."[25]

---

[19] For instance, see L. T. Hobhouse, "Industry and State" reprinted in *Sociology and Philosophy*, 213.
[20] *Ibid.*, 233.   [21] Hobhouse, *The Rational Good*, 206.   [22] Hobhouse, *Liberalism*, 68–9.
[23] *Ibid.*, 70.   [24] Hobhouse, *The Elements of Social Justice*, 30 and 108–9.
[25] L. T. Hobhouse, *Development and Purpose* (London: Macmillan and Co., 1927), 212. Also see 153 where Hobhouse says that the development of society is "a Common Good." First published in 1913,

Common good is no less an awkward feature of Hobhouse's moral theory than it is an awkward and puzzling feature of Green's. Notwithstanding this awkwardness, self-realization is plainly *a* common good, as it is for Green, in the sense that each person's self-realization (and happiness) comprises a separate component of common good. Common good is the development of each person as a "social personality," making the good of each the good of all.[26] Indeed, each person's self-realization becomes an essential common good where self-realization becomes widespread, sophisticated and robust. Where everyone both enjoys self-realizing opportunities and takes advantage of them, self-realization becomes a dynamic common resource that further serves to enrich and stimulate everyone's self-realizing opportunities. And precisely because self-realization is such a serviceable and formidable resource the more widespread it becomes, it steadily transforms liberal societies into protean forums of mutually stimulating individualities. For Hobhouse, as for Green, self-realization thus promotes common good while simultaneously constituting it. And as with Green, to the extent that Hobhouse emphasizes self-realization's instrumentality primarily, as he occasionally does, he risks being read as just another covert moral egoist after the fashion of Skorupski's reading of Green (which Chapter 4 discusses). Accordingly, each individual's achievements constitute common goods merely in the sense of being instrumentally valuable to the projects of others. Each, then, is merely a precious resource and therefore a means.

Of course, whatever holds for better or worse for self-realization equally holds for moral self-realization. As a *kind* of self-realization, moral self-realization is crucial. Merely self-realizing lives would be self-defeating. Without their also being morally self-realizing in some measure, social life would be insufferable. And as moral self-realization flourishes, so does social life as an arena of satisfying and fulfilling opportunities. That is, common good as a fellowship flourishes as well.[27]

Development and Purpose was extensively rewritten and reissued in 1927. According to Barker, "This [*Development and Purpose*] was, perhaps the work which he [Hobhouse] valued most highly; and . . . the new edition, largely rewritten, may be regarded as his last testament." Barker, "Leonard Trelawny Hobhouse 1864–1929," 545. See too Hobhouse's posthumous, "The Problem," in *L. T. Hobhouse*, ed. J. A. Hobson and Morris Ginsberg (London: George, Allen and Unwin, 1931), 291, where Hobhouse describes common good "as a life effectually shared by all, not repressive of personality, but opening for it a door to fuller and more harmonious development." So, as an arena of "fellowship," Hobhouse's conception of common good follows Green's conception of common good as a community of reciprocal advantage.

[26] L. T. Hobhouse, *Morals in Evolution* (New York: Henry Holt, 1919), 63.

[27] If common good is something richer and more substantive than just individual self-realization, then Hobhouse also risks committing himself to two separate standards of *ultimate* value. Consequently, his consequentialism is open to the criticism that it is tragically dualistic much like Sidgwick's.

Common good is indeed normatively significant for Hobhouse even if its precise significance remains obscure, and his overall moral theory jeopardized, because the concept itself is so poorly conceptualized. Hobhouse's theory of "social mind" helps eliminate some of these ambiguities however. In *Social Development and Purpose*, for instance, Hobhouse argues at length, much like Ritchie as we shall see later on, that the emergence of human consciousness drastically transforms the blind, haphazard struggle of evolution by investing it with direction thus making it "orthogenic." Orthogenic evolution becomes increasingly teleological as rational selection invests natural selection with purpose.[28]

Now, for Hobhouse, mind is no "side product" but rather "the central fact of the history of life upon the earth."[29] Hence, morality is an orthogenic event of unparalleled significance. We have invented, and continue to reinvent, morality in our ongoing efforts to rationalize and therefore tame natural selection's fortuitous flow. Morality is simply one of the ways in which we gain control of the conditions of social life. In becoming self-determining, mind "is guided, that is to say, by values which belong to its own world, and finally it begins to master the very conditions which first engendered it."[30] Beginning from inchoate sentiment, we gradually discover our moral voices as we begin speaking morality's family of languages with increasing skill and sophistication. Localized moral sentiments harden and spread as moral traditions and then as common-sense morality. Ultimately, common-sense morality gives way to systematic rational ethics whose demands are categorical, impartial and universal. In short, in gradually subduing blind evolutionary struggle by inventing vital institutions including morality, mind becomes more socially robust insofar as its institutional creations become more widely venerated. Social mind is simply organic evolution at long last consciously directing itself via *shared* institutions like morality.[31]

---

[28] As Hobhouse remarks in *Development and Purpose*, 473, "The individual mind then becomes aware of the conditions which have made it what it is and of the ultimate meaning of its own efforts and emotions and the harmonious development of life then becomes the object of intelligent purpose." Also see Hobhouse, *The Labour Movement*, 151, n1 where Hobhouse says, much like Ritchie as we will see subsequently, that with the evolutionary emergence of humans, "rational" selection begins replacing "natural" selection. See, too, Hobhouse, *Social Evolution and Political Theory*, 205, where he claims that social progress consists in the "replacement of natural selection by social selection."

[29] Hobhouse, *Development and Purpose*, 14. For a complete, but earlier account of Hobhouse's theory of the evolution of consciousness, see L. T. Hobhouse, *Mind in Evolution* (London: Macmillan and Co., 1915).

[30] Hobhouse, *Development and Purpose*, 13.

[31] See, too, Part II, Ch. VIII, "The Line of Ethical Development," *Morals in Evolution*. See especially 631 where Hobhouse says that as "mind grasps the conditions and possibilities of its own development," human evolution, including moral evolution, becomes a "purposive, self-directed movement" instead of a "blind, unconscious, fitful process." Unreflective moral tradition gradually gives way to rational ethics.

Though hardly less enigmatic than common good, Hobhouse's conception of "social mind" nevertheless ought to dissuade us from saddling Hobhouse with a thick notion of common good qua the independent good of society as a whole. For Hobhouse, social mind is not some "superpersonality" with independent, individual-transcending interests, never becoming anything more than a "social union of personalities."[32] Consequently, it never becomes more than the mass of ideas, traditions and institutions that inform the behavior of its members:

The kind of unity, which attaches to the social mind, is not definable in general terms. It varies from case to case. In more complex societies there are for example many institutions, each with its distinct ethos, and the existence of this ethos means that the institution lays a plastic hand on all who enter it, and with greater or less thoroughness moulds their life and actions. As an individual may and probably does belong to more than one institution, he is subject to influences of this kind from more than one quarter. There is thus in a sense more than one social mind that claims him, and this alone will suffice to warn us against the supposition that the social mind is necessarily something common, for example, to all members of the same political community ... By the social mind, then, we mean not necessarily a unity pervading any given society as a whole, but a tissue of operative psychological forces which in their higher developments crystallize into unity within unity, and into organism operating upon organism.[33]

For Hobhouse, then, societies aren't organisms with discrete common goods in the much thicker sense Hobson often appears to have thought. Hence, Hobhouse does not countenance sacrificing individuals in the name of promoting some fanciful and independent real common good. Nor does he treat societies "as if" they were such fantastic creatures. Only individual self-realization is good and we ought to promote it, or maximize its existence in the world if one prefers, as long as strong moral rights are tenaciously respected. But, of course, whether Hobhouse's consequentialism nevertheless justifies sacrificing some individuals in the name of promoting overall individual self-realization is another matter.[34] But before we turn to Hobhouse's theory of moral rights and the way in

---

[32] Hobhouse, *The Rational Good*, 230.
[33] Hobhouse, *Social Evolution and Political Theory*, 97–8. Mind, including presumably social mind, mysteriously conditions organic evolution from the outset, expressing itself more fully over time. It is "really one and homogeneous everywhere, in the flea and in the dog, in the savage and the poet, and it is only its instrument which is less or more polished." Hobhouse, *Development and Purpose*, 466.
[34] See Hobhouse, *Liberalism*, 202–5, where Hobhouse says that because each person's good is the good of the whole of which he or she is a part, sacrificing individuals for the good of the rest may be justified especially when the only alternative is the much greater evil of social disorder. But sacrifice may be permissible even when success of the "common effort" is at stake.

which they constrain his consequentialism, we need first to attend to his much qualified praise for what he viewed as the undeniable charms of utilitarianism.

THE LONG SHADOW OF UTILITARIANISM

In *The New Liberalism*, Michael Freeden suggests that utilitarianism "paved the way" for the emergence of "advanced liberalism" and that Green's version of the latter, in particular, "absorbed" much from its utilitarian predecessors and rivals.[35] Indeed, the new liberalism never seems to have wholly evaded the conceptual orbit of utilitarianism. Even Hobhouse's version of new liberalism never quite succeeded in emancipating itself from Mill's improved utilitarian legacy. New liberalism and liberal utilitarianism may have been rivals but their rivalry was anything but unfriendly. Not surprisingly, then, Hobhouse was not shy about paying his intellectual debts to Mill as well as Green: "The [his] theory of harmony stands in close relation on the one side to the Utilitarian principle as developed by J. S. Mill, and on the other hand to the form taken by Ethical Idealism in the hands of T. H. Green."[36] But why might most historians of political thought nevertheless find this acknowledgment of debt sufficiently surprising? After all, wasn't the new liberalism heir to philosophical idealism and wasn't the latter unquestionably hostile to classical utilitarianism?

Though kind to Mill, Hobhouse criticized Bentham extensively especially in *Liberalism*.[37] For Hobhouse, Benthamism constituted a "second type" of older liberal theory born in response to natural rights liberalism, which was an earlier first type. Despite the fact that Benthamism was an immense improvement over natural rights liberalism, both forms of older liberalism nevertheless turned laissez-faire into an ideological apology for nineteenth-century status quo.[38]

---

[35] Michael Freeden, *The New Liberalism* (Oxford: Oxford University Press, 1978), 18. According to Peter Clarke, Hobhouse and Graham Wallas were permanently marked by the utilitarianism of Thomas Case while undergraduates at Corpus Christi College, Oxford. Wallas, in particular, "relished the fact that he had been taught by almost the last exponent of the utilitarian system." See Peter Clarke, *Liberals and Social Democrats* (Cambridge: Cambridge University Press, 1978), 11.

[36] Hobhouse, *The Rational Good*, 193.

[37] In *Liberals and Social Democrats*, 73, Clarke claims that Hobhouse rediscovered Bentham between 1902 and 1904, "promptly pressed" him "into service as an opponent of war" and brought him "forward as the father of English Radicalism."

[38] For a similar discussion of the development and interaction of natural rights liberalism with utilitarian liberalism, see Ch. VII, "Modern Ethics" in *Morals in Evolution*.

In criticizing Bentham, Hobhouse repeated many of Green's objections to Benthamism. Like Green, Hobhouse admonished Benthamite utilitarians for devaluing individuality and basic rights by making liberty and democracy merely "means to an end."[39] Thus, Benthamite utilitarianism is inherently illiberal insofar as "it does seem to contemplate the weighing of one man's loss against another's gain, and such a method of balancing does not at bottom commend itself to our sense of justice."[40]

Moreover, Benthamism naively supposes that policy makers, notwithstanding that most citizens are politically unsophisticated, are intelligent enough to calculate how best to promote the general good.[41] Benthamism also wrongly presumes that individuals are essentially selfish and therefore wrongly concludes that they must be either educated or compelled to pursue the general welfare.[42] Lastly, Benthamism, in taking pleasure and not *happiness* as the ultimate good, errs insofar as it reduces good to serial and fleeting moments of pleasure. Being transitory and serial, pleasure can't be experienced in the aggregate and, therefore according to Hobhouse, aggregative pleasure can't be a legitimate object of desire. Hence, in a fashion fully in keeping with Green no less than Bradley, Hobhouse adamantly insists that good must be something stable and abiding if it is to be a coherent object of desire:

But Pleasure, both in ordinary language and in technical philosophic discussion, has generally meant a passing and partial condition, intense or languid as the case may be, but not depending for its intensity on any permanent conditions ... To know what objects will *permanently* satisfy is to possess the secret of happiness, but for the moment the important point is that some *object* is essential, and the most serious criticism of Benthamism is that it seems to ignore the necessity ... We are happy *in* something, and the something must be worth while [my italics].[43]

---

[39] Hobhouse, *Liberalism*, 39.   [40] *Ibid.*, 40–1.

[41] *Ibid.*, 41. Also see Hobhouse, *Morals in Evolution*, 590, where Hobhouse says that whereas the principle of utility may have been a useful standard of reform for combating earlier, brazen political and economic abuses, it was far too blunt a normative instrument for guiding further more complicated reforms. We simply are intellectually incapable of thinking through all the ramifications for future as well as present generations, of subtler, more nuanced applications of the principle of utility.

[42] Hobhouse, *Liberalism*, 41–2. See, in addition, Hobhouse, *The Elements of Social Justice*, 18–20.

[43] Hobhouse, *The Elements of Social Justice*, 17–18. Also see Hobhouse, *Morals in Evolution*, 597, where Hobhouse says that if the "self is more than a series of fleeting states, happiness is more than a succession of pleasurable feelings." And see *The Rational Good*, 194, where Hobhouse says "But we shall not resolve happiness into a series of pleasurable states." And see Chapter 1 for Bradley's and Chapter 2 for Green's nearly identical view that good defined as maximum aggregative pleasures was an experiential fiction.

Nevertheless, Hobhouse seems to have become much less critical of Benthamism in his later writings. For instance, in *The Elements of Social Justice*, Hobhouse praises Benthamism for wisely subordinating "politics to ethics" and for properly attempting to apply an uncomplicated yet inclusive theory of good as the "touchstone" of practical reasoning.[44] Furthermore, by insisting on "actual results in feeling," Benthamites correctly contend for the "control of action by rational values as against mere animal instinct on one side, or a vague and unchecked enthusiasm on the other."[45] In "On Happiness," Hobhouse praises Bentham and his followers for endeavoring to promote the "happiness of *all* men, or as he himself used to say, 'of the greatest happiness of the greatest number' (my italics)."[46] Here, Hobhouse interprets Bentham's notion of good in a non-aggregating way. Whereas this interpretation of Bentham's famous maxim anticipates, as we shall shortly see, Hobhouse's own non-aggregating rendering of good, it contradicts his previously noted fears that Benthamism justifies sacrificing a minority for the sake of the happiness of a majority. Like Green before him, Hobhouse looks to Mill's revised utilitarianism as being a healthy improvement on Bentham. He admired Mill for "spann[ing]" the transition from old to new liberalism by his willingness to theorize resourcefully and iconoclastically. But this also meant that Mill was the "easiest person in the world to convict of inconsistency, incompleteness, and lack of rounded system." Still, Hobhouse supposed, Mill's "work will survive the death of many consistent, complete, and perfectly rounded systems."[47] No doubt, he was anxious about the fate of his own work because he fully appreciated that it was no less eclectic than Mill's.

Now according to Hobhouse, Mill bravely sought to accommodate advanced liberal principles with his unwavering commitment to utility as the final standard of right. By trying to accommodate strong moral rights with the principle of utility, he fashioned and defended with considerable skill what recent scholars refer to as liberal utilitarianism, a project that, in my view, Hobhouse likewise saw himself as advancing further.[48] Moreover, Hobhouse thought that Mill understood better than Bentham the way in which social and individual well-being were compatible and interdependent. He correctly saw that individual well-being depended on individuals

---

[44] Hobhouse, *The Elements of Social Justice*, 14. [45] *Ibid.*, 22.

[46] L. T. Hobhouse, "About Happiness" in *L. T. Hobhouse*, 294. [47] Hobhouse, *Liberalism*, 58.

[48] For the best defense of liberal utilitarianism, and Mill as a liberal utilitarian, see Riley, *Liberal Utilitarianism: Social Choice Theory and J. S. Mill's Philosophy*.

mastering themselves morally so as the better to create an external environment in which the individuality of all could flourish. And insofar as
everyone begins flourishing, insofar as everyone becomes happier, "common life is fuller and richer for the multiplicity of types that it includes, and
that go to enlarge the area of collective experience."[49]

In Hobhouse's view, Mill also judiciously abandoned older utilitarianism's provincial conviction that only pleasure was good. By allowing that
pleasures differed qualitatively and hence evaluatively, Mill thereby raised
the "question what sort of experience it is that will yield pleasure of the
most desirable quality."[50] He recognized, albeit inadequately, that the kind
of life that tended to generate happiness was more important normatively
than the happiness it tended to generate. Hence, Mill, at least in his earlier
writings, implicitly conceded that good had to be something more substantial and complicated than evanescent, serial pleasures which, as far as
Hobhouse was concerned and as we saw earlier, couldn't possibly be
experienced in an aggregative way in any case. Mill more or less understood
that the self was more than a series of fleeting states and that happiness was
therefore more than a succession of pleasurable feelings. That is, Mill
effectively, if not quite overtly, admitted that good was some sort of
abiding or ongoing experience, namely life as an active and satisfying
whole.[51] For Mill, in short, only self-development was good.[52] Only
"realized good" was both contingently possible and authentic.

For Hobhouse, then, Mill nearly succeeded in transforming the older
utilitarianism into something that was acceptable and inspiring, something that was not so crudely and unworkably hedonistic. Unlike other
utilitarians, he correctly avoiding reducing happiness into pleasure.
Hence, what Hobhouse says about the relationship between self-realization
and happiness, discussed at length earlier in this chapter, he might
conceivably have said about the relationship between self-development
and happiness in Mill.

---

[49] Hobhouse, *Liberalism*, 60.   [50] Hobhouse, *The Rational Good*, 196.

[51] But see *ibid.*, 194, where Hobhouse says that he diverges from Mill in not defining happiness as a sum
of pleasures.

[52] We should proceed cautiously when comparing self-development and self-realization. As Michael
Freeden has usefully noted, self-development has historically implied growth, improvement and
human flourishing whereas self-realization has historically been associated with the unfolding of
potentiality. He also warns that though the former has been central to European liberalism, the latter
has not. Unfortunately, according to Freeden, current liberal theorizing tends to ignore this distinction
thereby wrongly endowing the liberal tradition with perfectionist obsessions. See Michael Freeden,
"A Non-Hypothetical Liberalism: The Utilitarian Communitarianism of J.A. Hobson," paper
delivered at the 1993 Annual Meeting of the American Political Science Association, 6.

However, Hobhouse's theory of good is "almost" like Mill's because whereas for Hobhouse happiness and worthwhile living are separate attributes of good, they are arguably identical notions for Mill. As some recent interpreters of Mill have maintained, Mill defined good as happiness, which he, in turn, defined as those activities that exercise our higher capacities, particularly our rational deliberative capacities.[53] For Mill, in other words, good was not a compound of activity and happiness as it seems to have been for Hobhouse. Rather, good, happiness and higher activities were one and the same. Nevertheless and very crucially, for both Mill and Hobhouse, good was ultimately *non-hedonic* and *objective*.[54] In this sense, Mill prepared the way for Hobhouse's new liberal consequentialism.

Moreover, in claiming above that "happiness" and the "kind of life in which it is sought" are but "two elements in the same whole," Hobhouse is suggesting that a worthwhile fulfilling life tends to be a happy life. Self-realizing activity and personal happiness wither and flourish together. In fact, happiness seems to sustain or corroborate the existence of the former. The happier one feels, or the more satisfied one feels with one's life, the more confident one can be that one is truly living a worthy, self-realizing life: "Viewed as feeling, then, the Rational Good is happiness, viewed as the object of this feeling it is the fulfilment of vital capacity as a consistent whole."[55]

The Rational Good is not the only text in which Hobhouse examines the relationship between self-realization and happiness. His *Morals in Evolution*, written about the same time, explores this relationship in a similar but slightly nuanced fashion: "But here again the object is not chosen as a means to happiness, but valued as an end, and the same quality that makes it valued makes of the experiences active and passive which it yields, a life in living which we feel happy."[56] In an endnote to this passage, Hobhouse continues by suggesting that the relationship between self-realization (or "Will" as he refers to it here) and happiness can be clarified by asking, "whether the value of a given object consists in the pleasure derivable from it, so that if we imagine the pleasure removed the value would disappear also." After asserting that an affirmative answer would

---

[53] See David Brink, "Mill's Deliberative Utilitarianism," *Philosophy and Public Affairs*, 21 (1992), 73–7 and 79–82. And see Elizabeth S. Anderson, "John Stuart Mill and Experiments in Living," *Ethics*, 102 (1991), 19–20.

[54] See, as well, Morris Ginsberg, "The Contribution of Professor Hobhouse to Philosophy and Sociology," *Economica* (November, 1929), 262. According to Ginsberg, Hobhouse's moral theory was "essentially eudaemonistic without being hedonistic."

[55] Hobhouse, *The Rational Good*, 156–7.   [56] Hobhouse, *Morals in Evolution*, 599.

render the object (or action) merely a "means to pleasure" and that a negative answer would make pleasure "adventitious and irrelevant," Hobhouse adds:

The true answer rather is that the pleasure we take in a thing is merely *another expression* for the value we attach to it. But the value is attached to the thing. Or if we prefer the phrase, the pleasure is *in* the thing, related to the thing, not a subsequent effect which the thing *happens* to produce and which might as well be produced by anything else [my italics].[57]

Depicting pleasure as but "merely another expression" of value is rather unenlightening. Fortunately, however, Hobhouse discusses the relationship between self-realization and happiness elsewhere. His debt to Green is particularly helpful in this regard. The full extent of this debt has been an issue of some dispute among scholars though not so much in terms of the specific relationship of concern here.[58]

There is little question that Hobhouse drew a great deal from Green. In both *The Metaphysical Theory of the State* and in *The Rational Good*, he acknowledges his indebtedness to Green and discusses his differences with him in some detail.[59] However, his comments on Green in *The Rational Good* are more germane. After comparing his theory of good to that of Mill, Hobhouse explains why his own moral theory is but a "further definition" of Green's theory. He then shows how his and Green's theories diverge. In a very revealing passage, Hobhouse separates himself from Green on the relationship between self-realization and happiness as follows:

In the first place, Green insists on treating the element of pleasure in the good rather as a *secondary consequence* than as an integral and essential element. In this he has as much over-estimated the part of impulse as the empirical school over-stated the part of experienced feeling. If the argument of previous pages is sound, feeling [pain and pleasure] holds the reins, though impulse is often a refractory steed, and the more rational we become, the clearer is the coincidence between the lines of life

---

[57] *Ibid.*, 599.
[58] According to Collini, despite the strong similarities between Mill and Hobhouse, the latter was "much closer" to Green inasmuch as a great deal of Hobhouse's moral and political theory was "little more than a restatement" of Green's *The Principles of Political Obligation*. See Collini, *Liberalism and Sociology*, 126. Likewise, Freeden sees Hobhouse as a "disciple" of Green as much as he was a disciple of anyone. Freeden adds, however, that Hobhouse's theory was not "solely a development of Green's." See Freeden, *The New Liberalism*, 66–7. Peter Weiler, by contrast, claims that Hobhouse tried to synthesize Mill and Green. See Peter Weiler, "The New Liberalism of L. T. Hobhouse," *Victorian Studies*, 16 (1972), 141–61 and 145.
[59] For Hobhouse's assessment of Green in *The Metaphysical Theory of the State* (London: Allen and Unwin, 1918), see especially 118–33. And for a concise summary of Hobhouse's general attitude towards Green, see Clarke, *Liberals and Social Democrats*, 25–6.

which we seek to lay down and those in which, if not actual happiness, at least real peace and inward satisfaction are found.[my italics][60]

For Hobhouse, plainly, self-realization and happiness are somehow more internally interwoven than they are in Green (but not so tightly interwoven that they are identical as with Mill). Like self-realization, happiness is an "integral and essential element" of good for Hobhouse whereas it is merely a "secondary consequence" for Green. In short, Hobhouse felt that happiness (or pleasure at least) was a kind of contingent marker, or token, of self-realization for Green. By contrast, it was constitutive of good itself in his own moral theory. Happiness and self-realization were simply two mutually reinforcing attributes of good. The latter was not just pulled along in the train of the former as pleasure was for Green following Aristotle.[61] For Aristotle, too, pleasure, (though not happiness) was similarly a "sign of virtue superven[ing]" on it. Pleasure "mingle[s]" with virtuous activity by "augment[ing]" it. As the subtitle of Book II of the *Nichomachean Ethics* reads, virtue is "exhibited" by pleasure.[62]

But if happiness is effectively part of the meaning of good, especially in the later *The Rational Good*, shall we conclude that Hobhouse became, in some sense, a *utilitarian* consequentialist? Analysis of his theory of justice may help us as we begin resolving this issue.

JUSTICE AND PRIMA-FACIE RIGHTS

According to Hobhouse in *Liberalism*, the domain of justice was fundamentally the domain of freedom and of strong moral rights much as it was

---

[60] Hobhouse, *The Rational Good*, 200–1.

[61] Note as well Ginsberg's remark in *L. T. Hobhouse*, 184, that "Hobhouse is anxious, as against Green, to retain what he considers to be an element of value in Utilitarianism, namely, the emphasis on happiness as a feeling attendant upon the successful realisation of the capabilities of human nature. Feeling is an integral element in the good, though it must not be severed from the objects with which it is connected in experience."

[62] Curiously, Hobhouse seems to read the relationship between virtue and happiness in Aristotle much as he reads the relationship between self-realization and pleasure in Green. See, for instance, *Morals in Evolution*, 555, where Hobhouse says that, for Aristotle, the "man who resolutely makes the best of his own powers and actively realizes them, is the happiest." But, see Aristotle, *The Nicomachean Ethics*, trans. W. D. Ross (Oxford: Oxford University Press, 1954), Book X, "Pleasure, Happiness" where Aristotle says that virtuous activities are the happiest by nature as well as the "pleasantest." Insofar as contemplation is the most self-sufficient activity, it is the happiest activity of all and the most pleasant *in addition*. Whereas happiness lies "in" virtuous activity, pleasure merely "augments" it by coloring it as a "sort of adventitious charm" (16 and 265–6). Hence, Aristotle's theory of the relationship between pleasure, happiness and virtue actually parallels Hobhouse's view of the relationship between pleasure, happiness and self-realization. Hobhouse, in short, underestimates his similarities with Aristotle on this score.

for Mill. In Hobhouse's judgment, Mill likewise perceptibly grasped how strong moral rights were vital to the task of promoting both individual and public well-being. He correctly perceived that strong moral rights were the "permanent conditions to social health."[63] That is, as Hobhouse saw it, Mill quite rightly recognized that moral rights secured the kind of fecund juridical environment in which everyone's individuality might thrive. To the extent that rational self-mastery constitutes a vital dimension of individuality, the development of the latter entails growing respect for rights yielding richer opportunities for the further flourishing of individuality and, hence, increased general well-being.

So Hobhouse was duly sensitive to the symbiotic relationship between justice (external freedom primarily) and moral individuality (internal freedom) in Mill. Indeed, this dynamic feature of Mill's moral and political theory (which we saw earlier reappears in Green as the interaction between "outward" or "juristic" freedom and "inner" freedom or good will) also reappears as a salient feature in Hobhouse's version of new liberalism. For Hobhouse, social freedom (or "freedom of man in society") is necessary to the development of moral personality (or "moral freedom"), which, in turn, generates greater social freedom thereby encouraging even more opportunities for moral personality to thrive. Moral personality's fecundity is the cornerstone of Hobhouse's perfectionism.

This symbiosis between external and internal freedom in Hobhouse, which surely owes just as much to Green as to Mill, led Hobhouse to deploy a rights theory noticeably similar to their instrumental rights theories. In a passage from *Liberalism* that neither Mill nor Green would eschew, Hobhouse resolutely affirms:

Personality is not built up from without but grows from within, and the function of the *outer order* is not to create it, but to provide for it the most suitable *conditions* of growth. Thus, to the common question whether it is possible to make men good by Act of Parliament, the reply is that it is not possible to compel morality because morality is the act or character of a free agent, but that it is possible to create the *conditions* under which morality can develop, and among these not the least important is freedom from compulsion by others. [my italics][64]

That Hobhouse means basic rights by "conditions" is especially evident where, a few pages later, he discusses why positive economic rights, such as the right to work and the right to a living wage, are just as essential as negative, non-interference rights. Both kinds of rights are "conditions" for

---

[63] Hobhouse, *Liberalism*, 59.   [64] *Ibid.*, 76.

promoting self-realization.[65] Both kinds, hence, empower individuals to make the most of themselves morally and otherwise. Both kinds enable individuals to develop themselves and make themselves as happy as best they can. In *Liberalism*, then, moral rights and freedom are conceptually intertwined. Good justifies them in identical ways. Hence, whatever gives us cause to celebrate freedom gives us just as much cause to celebrate moral rights.

Hobhouse clarifies the relationship between rights and freedom in his later *The Elements of Social Justice*:

> The ultimate foundation of liberty is that it is a condition of spiritual growth. This is the "general" liberty underlying, inspiring, and also transcending all "liberties." But there would be no liberty for us all if any fool, rogue, or fire-eater had liberty for his part to develop his folly, roguery, or violence at our expense ... It is here that physical restraint becomes necessary and that "liberty" must be particularized into "liberties." Liberty – we come back to the initial paradox – itself demands restraints.[66]

Moral rights, then, demarcate liberty as they do with Green. They are so many "definitions" of liberty with the best system of rights comprising an optimal "system of harmonized liberties."[67]

However, Hobhouse's description of the best constellation of rights as a "system of harmonized liberties" is unhelpfully formalistic. Hobhouse acknowledges as much where he critically examines two alternative ways of fleshing out a liberal system of rights. The first alternative was made famous by Herbert Spencer's principle of equal liberty (though Hobhouse does not identify Spencer) according to which "to every man full liberty, provided that he does not interfere with the like liberty of another."[68]

In Hobhouse's view, the equal liberty principle is innocuous at best, and mischievous at worst. Interpreted literally, equal liberty destroys liberty amounting to little more than a cynical equal right to retaliate: "The liberty

---

[65] *Ibid.*, 83–4. For further evidence that Hobhouse means rights by "conditions," see *Social Evolution and Political Theory*, 197–201. And for a recent example of liberal theorizing that sees itself as a "continuation of the 'revisioning' of liberalism undertaken by" the new liberals and that also justifies basic rights as external "conditions" for promoting, but not guaranteeing, the development of internal moral freedom, see Jack Crittenden, *Beyond Individualism* (Oxford: Oxford University Press, 1992). For Crittenden, those who develop the latter become "compound individuals" transcending the confines of atomistic individualism. Their ideal is the "modern liberal ideal" of "self-realization" or "in Hobhouse's phrase, 'full development of personality'" (155). Their ideal is "beyond individualism."

[66] Hobhouse, *The Elements of Social Justice*, 83.   [67] *Ibid.*, 84.

[68] *Ibid.*, 60. This is Hobhouse's paraphrasing of Spencer's equal freedom principle. For Spencer's rendering of equal freedom, see especially *Social Statics* [1851] (New York: Robert Schalkenbach Foundation, 1970), 69 and 79.

of A to knock down B is not sufficiently confined by the corresponding liberty of B to knock down A, if he can."[69]

As a second alternative way of infusing liberal rights with substance, Hobhouse invokes Mill's distinction in his liberty principle between self-regarding and other-regarding acts. For Hobhouse, Mill's liberty principle is more congenial than Spencer's because Mill's principle deftly captures the way in which moral rights secure individuals from serious harm (protecting our "most vital of all interests" as Mill would say).[70] Thus, Hobhouse, inspired by Mill, resolves that "in the body of rights, we have found a system of restraints [against harm] which is the basis of a system of liberties."[71]

Of course, we may wonder what constitutes a legitimate harm (positive or negative, commission or omission) deserving the sanctuary of a basic right. When two rights (liberties) collide, which of the two gives way as a genuine restraint against harm? Here, Hobhouse appeals to his notion of common good as a criterion for prioritizing rights:

If, on the other hand, A's ends and B's cannot be reconciled, a different question arises. We have now to think not only of their respective wills, characters, opinions, etc., but of the *results* in which these issue, and, as these *results* are incompatible, we have to choose between them ... Whichever end is supported by the *common welfare* is a "right," which sets a limit to any liberty that might encroach upon it, while itself carrying the liberty to pursue it. [my italics][72]

So the best "results" in terms of what best promotes the common good is Hobhouse's criterion for systematizing basic moral rights. Moreover, as we become more experienced in promoting common good, our conception of harm not only becomes more nuanced but also widens.[73] Consequently,

---

[69] Hobhouse, *The Elements of Social Justice*, 60. Also see *Liberalism*, 36. There Hobhouse condemns Spencer's equal freedom principle in similar but more colorful language: "My right to keep my neighbor awake by playing the piano all night is not satisfactorily counterbalanced by his right to keep a dog which howls all the time the piano is being played." For a parallel yet more recent misunderstanding of Spencer's liberty principle, see Alan Gewirth, "Political Justice" in *Social Justice*, ed. Richard B. Brandt (Englewood Cliffs: Prentice-Hall, 1962), 149–51. Hobhouse also misconstrues Spencer, as so many have including G. E. Moore most famously, as a simplistic ethical naturalist who conflates fact and value by equating the course human evolution has happened to take with the course it ought to be taking. For instance, see Hobhouse, *Social Evolution and Political Theory*, 21–5. For a discussion of Spencer's principle of equal freedom, see my *Equal Freedom and Utility*, especially ch. 11.

[70] Note, in this regard, Hobhouse's remark, "That, in his [Mill's] phrase, 'individuality is an element of wellbeing' is, I believe, a permanent truth." Hobhouse, *The Labour Movement*, 152.

[71] Hobhouse, *The Elements of Social Justice*, 62.

[72] *Ibid.*, 64. Also, see Hobhouse, *Morals in Evolutions*, 63, where Hobhouse says that every member of society has a right to the conditions of realizing common good in which the good of each is the good for all.

[73] See Hobhouse, *Liberalism*, 50.

our conceptions of freedom and moral rights also become more robust and positive.

If moral rights, then, take their justification from common good, then they cannot be indefeasible. Presumably, this is why Hobhouse calls them "prima facie" rights.[74] Moral rights are not absolute but merely stringent. They are neither stubbornly inflexible nor slaves to incidental expediency.[75] The realization of common good rests upon the near universal sanctity of certain conditions, namely security of person broadly conceived and security of meaningful opportunities. Without strong moral rights standing hard by both kinds of security in all but exceptional circumstances, fruitful cooperation would be impossible and common good severely diminished at the very least.

In *The Elements of Social Justice*, Hobhouse also claims that a "true moral right is one which is demonstrably justifiable by relations to the common good, whether it is actually recognized or not." By contrast, a "legal right" is a claim recognized by law as a right and a "recognized moral right" is merely the "actual moral judgement" which the community happens to uphold as a moral right.[76] Hence, while the range of "recognized moral rights" and "legal rights" is limited only by the powers of social recognition and legal codification, "true moral rights" comprise a very limited subset of this range. "True moral rights" are simply those rights from the large set of possible rights that are actually essential to common flourishing.[77] They are contingently necessary conditions for realizing common good although they are certainly not natural rights in the sense of predating society.[78]

---

[74] *Ibid.*, 44.

[75] See in particular *ibid.*, 42, where Hobhouse says that rights should neither be "absolute principles" nor overly "subservient" to the demands of common welfare.

[76] *Ibid.*, 39–40.

[77] In a lengthy footnote, *ibid.*, 35, criticizing Green's interpretation of Locke's theory of rights, Hobhouse distinguishes four, instead of three, kinds of rights. While "rights" always exist wherever social relations exist, "recognized rights" emerge wherever society becomes "durable." "Crystallized and enforced rights" arise wherever "political society with a developed judiciary and police" appears. A "moral right," whether embodied in the above kinds of rights or not, is a "claim which is a true element in the common good."

[78] See *ibid.*, 37, where Hobhouse says that rights are not "conditions precedent to society." And see *Social Evolution and Political Theory*, 197, where he also says: "The older thinkers spoke of them [moral rights] as 'natural rights,' but to this phrase, if uncritically used, there is the grave objection that it suggests that such rights are independent of society, whereas, if our arguments hold, there is no moral order independent of society and therefore no rights which, apart from the social consciousness, would be recognized at all." But on the next page, Hobhouse appears to concede the existence of natural rights where he says that, "the rights of man are those expectations which the common good justify in him [an 'impartial' person] in entertaining, and we may even admit that there are natural rights of man if we conceive the common good as resting upon certain elementary

Regrettably, justifying moral rights according to common good is less than satisfying given the latter's ambiguous nature discussed earlier. Nevertheless, insofar as common good is the harmonious cultivation of everyone's personality, moral rights ultimately derive their justification from their success in *indirectly* promoting everyone's self-realization: "In general terms, a true right is an element in or condition of the real welfare of its possessor, which on the principle of harmony is an integral part of the common welfare."[79] So moral rights guarantee, or empower, each individual with the equal opportunity to develop him- or herself in harmony with others. Hobhouse's debt to Mill is, indeed, profound, and especially so if Wendy Donner's egalitarian Mill is the real Mill.[80]

Thus, for Hobhouse (no less than for Donner's Mill), common good requires juridically institutionalizing external freedom as extensive equality of opportunity. Freedom devoid of the latter is merely "apparent" freedom, *particularly* with respect to contractual exchanges where the contracting parties possess unequal wealth. Unless the state intervenes on behalf of the weaker parties, most bargains, according to Hobhouse, become "forced bargain[s]" with the weaker participants consenting as "one slipping over a precipice might consent to give all his fortune to one

---

conditions affecting the life of society, which hold good whether people recognize them or not." But we shouldn't be misled by what Hobhouse is actually conceding here. Rights are natural only in the sense that they sanctify those basic necessary conditions of human flourishing. As with Ritchie, as we shall see in Chapter 5, rights constitute juridical strategies that we gradually discover best promote happiness overall. But such discovery is the discovery of invention rather than of some metaphysical normative intuition. This is what Hobhouse and Ritchie, following Green, mean by *recognizing* rights. *The Elements of Social Justice* and *Social Evolution and Political Theory* are the only works in which Hobhouse systematically distinguishes "moral" from other kinds of rights. Nonetheless, I take him to mean "moral" rights by rights in his other writings unless he stipulates otherwise.

79 Hobhouse, *The Elements of Social Justice*, 40–1.

80 For Wendy Donner, Mill regards the "liberty of self-development as a vital human interest that must be protected as a right." And for Donner, this basic right is the source of Mill's enthusiasm for positive welfare rights as well as negative rights. So Donner effectively tries to close the gap between Mill and new liberalism but from the side of Mill. Her Mill would warmly embrace Hobhouse's comment in *Liberalism*, 21, that the "struggle for liberty is also, when pushed through, a struggle for equality." And her Mill would readily concur with Hobhouse that state interference is not so much a question of increasing or decreasing constraints but simply reorganizing them (81). See her *The Liberal Self* (Ithaca: Cornell University Press, 1992), especially ch. 8. Mill, however, was unwilling to prohibit drunkenness, as Green and Hobhouse were, in the name of self-development or harm to others. At least in this regard, self-development was less a right for Mill compared to Green and Hobhouse. For Green's defense of legislating temperance, see Peter Nicholson, "T. H. Green and State Action: Liquor Legislation," *History of Political Thought*, 6 (1985). For Hobhouse's parallel views, see *Liberalism*, 80–1. For Mill's characterization of drunkenness as purely self-regarding and therefore not a liberty-violating harm (excluding cases where intoxicated individuals had a history of violence), see J. S. Mill [1859], *On Liberty* in *Collected Works of John Stuart Mill*, ed. John M. Robson (Toronto: University of Toronto Press, 1977), Vol. XVIII, 295.

who will throw him a rope on no other terms."[81] "Apparent" freedom, in short, is a cruel chimera for those bargaining in desperation and from significant economic weakness.

So, in Hobhouse's view, the "apparent" freedom of the unfettered market needs to be made "real" if liberalism is to fulfill its promise. Accordingly, private property must be regulated. Hence, Hobhouse sought to equalize property relations so that, to borrow from Mill, each person could "lead his own life, developing his faculties in his own way, and make the most of himself by his own efforts." And hence, like Mill before him, he saw himself as simply extending the underlying principles of older versions of liberalism and utilitarianism by making "apparent" freedom sufficiently "real."[82]

In "The Historical Evolution of Property, in Fact and in Idea," published about the same time as *Liberalism*, Hobhouse discusses the vital role which property plays as an "instrument of personality." For Hobhouse, property is an "integral element in an ordered life of purposeful activity" and is, thus, an "integral element in a free life."[83] However, each person's property should not exceed that which he or she can effectively use. Property "for use" therefore must be distinguished from property "for power." Whereas property "for use" is essential if everyone is to have opportunities to develop as personalities, the "accumulation of vast masses of property *for power* in the hands of a relatively narrow class" handicaps most people's pursuit of individuality and happiness.[84] Whereas the former provides "freedom and security," the latter entails the "control of persons through things."[85]

Property "for use" is, therefore, both an instrumental and redistributive principle. Indeed, its moral instrumentality is the source of its redistributive urgency. *All* citizens must have access to property if *all* were to realize themselves morally, civically and otherwise. Property empowers self-development and, consequently, common good recommends its common availability. Even Locke's theory of property, in Hobhouse's view, justifies property for use only:

---

[81] Hobhouse, *Liberalism*, 50. Also see *Development and Purpose*, 183, where Hobhouse says that rights and duties are "conditions" for the development of harmony as "many-sided development."

[82] Hobhouse, *Democracy and Reaction*, 224. Hobhouse continues on 225 that it is unsurprising that Mill openly "gravitated in later life" towards socialism. And see Hobhouse, *The Labour Movement*, 91, where Hobhouse describes industrial cooperation as "extend[ing]" the principle of private property.

[83] L. T. Hobhouse, "The Historical Evolution of Property, in Fact and in Idea" in *Property, Its Duties and Rights*, ed. Charles Gore (London: Macmillan and Co., 1913), 9.

[84] *Ibid.*, 22.   [85] *Ibid.*, 10.

Be this as it may, we find in Locke the basis of a view which is at once a justification of property, and a criticism of industrial organization. Man has a right, it would seem, first to the opportunity of labour; secondly, to the fruits of his labour; thirdly, to what he can *use* of these fruits, and nothing more. Property so conceived is what we have here called property for *use*. [my italics][86]

As far as Hobhouse understood (or wanted to understand) Locke's theory of property, one person's use of property can negate its use by another allowing the former to control the latter by denying him or her the possibility of living meaningfully.[87] In short, the former *injures* the latter.

In Hobhouse's judgment, then, Locke was sensitive to the enervating effects of unequal property even in the seventeenth century. Therefore, as far as Hobhouse was concerned, Locke would have quickly condemned these same yet far more debilitating effects in the nineteenth century and, consequently, he would have embraced new liberalism's spirited endeavor to widen our notion of serious harm.[88]

Hobhouse's reasoning for enlarging the meaning of harmful action went beyond his recognition of the importance of equalizing opportunities for the sake of fostering individuality. Part of earlier liberalism's failure, as Hobhouse makes clear elsewhere, also stemmed from its inability to understand that community itself was the source of much wealth. Society creates value by creating a stable, secure environment in which private property can be enjoyed and by providing cooperative opportunities for production and exchange.[89] Hence, justice requires that this social value or "surplus" return to the community with only the remainder going to individuals as deserved "residue." Accordingly, we must distinguish the "social from the individual factors in wealth, by bringing the elements of social wealth into the public coffers, and by holding it at the disposal of society to administer to the prime needs of its members."[90]

Hobhouse's strategy for insuring that socially created wealth would remain public property was basically two-fold. First, he recommended that private ownership of land be converted to a system of "State tenantry" of small tenants paying rent to the state equivalent to the socially created

---

[86] *Ibid.*, 27. Hobhouse admits, however, that Locke imprudently allows that individuals may rightfully acquire extensive monetary wealth beyond whatever resources and goods they are capable of consuming. This issue has, of course, been the source of considerable controversy among modern interpreters of Locke.

[87] See, as well, Hobhouse, *The Elements of Social Justice*, 155.

[88] For Ritchie's different assessment of Locke on this score, see his "Locke's Theory of Property," in D. G. Ritchie [1893], *Darwin and Hegel, Collected Works of D. G. Ritchie*, ed. Peter Nicholson (Bristol: Thoemmes Press, 1998), Vol. II.

[89] *Ibid.*, 162.   [90] Hobhouse, *Liberalism*, 98.

value of the land under their cultivation.[91] Second, he proposed that everyone else be assured continuous employment at a "living wage" or public assistance if necessary.[92] Basic income was a fundamental right. Both strategies would guarantee all citizens either access to the means of production or an adequate share in the common stock. Both strategies would equalize the "race to run against fate" so that everyone would enjoy genuine equal opportunities to flourish as distinct personalities.

Hobhouse, it would seem, is suggesting that individuals can be harmed *indirectly* as well as *directly*. One can be *directly* harmed by being physically assaulted or one can be *indirectly* harmed by being denied equal opportunities or by being robbed of one's share in socially created value. Either way, one is harmed insofar as one is severely disempowered from cultivating one's unique attributes. Hence, as a strategy of empowerment, the new liberalism linked arms with socialism thus becoming nothing less than what Hobhouse sometimes referred to as "Liberal Socialism."[93]

Liberal socialism was not egalitarian socialism plainly enough. Inequalities of wealth, power and position were permitted as long as each person's wealth was the "residue" of value he or she alone created *and* as long as these inequalities also worked out to the common good. (Common good, lest we forget, was Hobhouse's ultimate criterion of value.) Now the latter proviso might seem less confining on the face of it than Rawls's difference principle especially given common good's deep ambiguity. After all, even Hobhouse concedes rather remarkably that the "existence of millionaires on the one hand and of paupers on the other" is just as long as such "contrasts are the result of an economic system which upon the whole works out for the common good, the good of the pauper being included therein as well as the good of the millionaire."[94] But we must not forget as well that common good for the pauper meant creating for him or her new, meaningful opportunities for self-realization that he or she previously lacked.

Notwithstanding the cogency of Hobhouse's efforts to extend the meaning of serious harm, his commitment to private property was plainly contingent. By distinguishing property "for use" from property "for power," and by regarding the latter as indirectly harmful, Hobhouse again revealed just how obviously goal-based his juridical commitments

---

[91] For instance, see *ibid.*, 92.   [92] *Ibid.*, 92.

[93] See especially *ibid.*, 87 and 88–91. Also see Clarke, *Liberals and Social Democrats*, for an excellent analysis of the relationship between new liberals and socialism in England before and after WWI.

[94] Hobhouse, *Liberalism*, 70.

were. Property-ownership had a point. Indeed, like freedom and other basic rights, it had a consequentialist moral point. Property-ownership was legitimate only to the extent that it promoted the good of individual flourishing, particularly moral flourishing. Hence, property-ownership was legitimate *only* insofar as it did not unfairly empower some at the expense of others by undermining equal opportunities for all and by wrongly distributing socially created value. In short, Hobhouse's theory of property was as deeply instrumental as were those theories of his utilitarian predecessors. Following them, he denied that private property was an axiomatic natural right.[95] And following Green explicitly, he held that basic property rights, like all moral rights, were created by social recognition. Here especially, Hobhouse helps us appreciate just how effortlessly the new liberalism moved between utilitarianism and idealism.

MORAL RIGHTS AND GLOBAL PURPOSES

For Hobhouse, as we have now come to see, moral rights were instrumental in much the same way that they were instrumental for some of his liberal predecessors. In other words, good is prior to right in Hobhouse just as it is in Mill, and arguably, Green. But by prioritizing good, Hobhouse was not necessarily committing himself to consequentialism as it is *typically* understood today. As much as Hobhouse's theory of good and right resembled that of his liberal utilitarian forebears in many essentials, it was not conventionally consequentialist. As much as moral personality was an axiological value for Hobhouse, he did not hold that we were obligated to maximize it in an aggregating or pooled way. Still, as we have seen, Hobhouse looked to the *results* of actions in order to evaluate them. For him, right actions, particularly those sheltered by moral rights, were those that promoted "the development of personality in *each* [and every] member of the community" (my italics).[96] As Hobhouse also says:

What, for example, is my right? On the face of it, it is something that I claim. But a mere claim is nothing. I might claim anything and everything. If my claim is of right it is because it is sound, well grounded, in the judgment of an impartial observer ... Further, if his decision is in any sense a rational one, it must rest on a *principle* of some kind, and again, as a rational man, any principle which he asserts

---

[95] *Ibid.*, 54. Michael Freeden has indicated to me that Hobhouse's views on property are, in all likelihood, deeply indebted to those of J. A. Hobson. Also see Clarke, *Liberals and Social Democrats*, 126–7, for Hobhouse's debt, regarding socially created value, to Hobson's theory of unproductive surplus as unearned income belonging to the community.

[96] Hobhouse, *Liberalism*, 70.

he must found on some good *result* which it serves or embodies, and as an impartial man he must take the *good of every one* affected into account [my italics].[97]

Hobhouse was what *we* would term a consequentialist though it is far from clear just what kind he was. Clearly, he was not a consequentialist of the traditional, hedonic utilitarian variety. And just as clearly, he was not a good-aggregating consequentialist inasmuch as he never explicitly and systematically argued that maximizing good entailed promoting the greatest good among the greatest number. Nevertheless, Hobhouse defined good as self-realizing happiness and urged that it be vigorously promoted. Hence, he was some sort of consequentialist.

But this is a less-than-venturesome claim. Here Wayne Sumner's "three stage" construction of the elements of consequentialism may serve us profitably.[98] For Sumner, a basic theory of good constitutes the first stage in constructing a consequentialist moral framework. Moreover, this theory of good must be both good-based and goal-based. That is, good must be prior to right and it must be a "synoptic" or global goal. A global goal is a state of affairs valuable from the point of view of anyone. Hence, a global state of affairs is one that is agent-neutral (non-subjective) and categorical (non-relative). It is objectively valuable, period. Now Hobhouse's moral theory includes this first stage. For Hobhouse, self-realizing happiness is an agent-neutral and categorically valuable state of affairs. It is valuable, period.

The second stage in constructing a consequentialist moral framework, according to Sumner, consists of specifying some method for operationalizing one's global value. Sumner notes that aggregation is the most familiar method but he also mentions the "equal distribution of goods across individuals, or a pattern which attends solely to the minimum individual share" as options.[99] Though Hobhouse's moral theory is non-aggregative, it nevertheless stipulates that self-realization be generously distributed across society. The best society would be one in which *all* were self-realizing in morally acceptable ways.[100]

---

[97] *Ibid.*, 68.
[98] Wayne Sumner, *The Moral Foundations of Rights* (Oxford: Oxford University Press, 1987), 167–75.
[99] *Ibid.*, 171.
[100] R. M. Hare, much like Cummiskey, argues that Kant's categorical imperative can be interpreted in a liberal utilitarian way, which, we can surmise, Mill and the new liberals might well have found agreeable. Like the categorical imperative, according to Hare, "utilitarianism is simply, the morality which seeks the ends of *all* in so far as *all* can seek them consistently in accordance with universal maxims" (my italics). R. M. Hare, "Could Kant Have Been a Utilitarian?", *Utilitas*, 5, 1 (1993), 10.

Cummiskey, as we saw earlier, has argued that operationalizing good distributively can constitute a legitimate form of consequentialism. Likewise, Freeden has defended what he refers to as "modified constrained consequentialism" which he says incorporates a "communitarian view-point" rather than an "aggregative one." "Modified constrained consequentialism" includes "as a central goal the protection of those attributes that right-based theories deem precious."[101] David Brink, too, interprets Mill's consequentialism in much the same way in claiming that Mill's theory of value is "distribution-sensitive" inasmuch as it includes, besides rational deliberation, "forbearing" and "cooperative social relations" as "part of each person's good."[102]

Sumner's third stage in constructing a consequentialist framework specifies what we are to do with our global value. Most consequentialist moral frameworks favor maximization. More, rather than less, of a partic-ular axiological value is always preferable. Once again, Hobhouse's theory meets Sumner's test insofar as it requires us always to maximize qua promote (albeit distributively) self-realization. Indeed, all new liberals with whom this study is concerned meet Sumner's test.

Thus, according to Sumner's criteria, Hobhouse's moral theory would appear legitimately consequentialist by *our* standards. Yet in arriving at this conclusion, we should not be surprised if Hobhouse's theory, despite all its formal attractiveness, proves practically cumbersome. As Green recog-nized, developing crisp maximizing strategies for something so amorphous as self-realization is surely problematic.

I have suggested that Hobhouse was a consequentialist though not a conventional utilitarian consequentialist. Still, we must not forget that though, as we saw earlier, he displayed limited enthusiasm for Benthamite utilitarianism, he thought highly of Mill's juridical, liberal utilitarianism in many respects. Indeed, like Green before him, he regarded improved utilitarianism as sharing much with, if not *mimicking*, his own version of liberal consequentialism:

Indeed, if happiness be rightly defined as consisting in harmony of life, the divergence from the Utilitarian teaching is *less* marked than appears at first sight ... Harmony tends to fullness of life, to complete development of person-ality, though it also limits this development in any individual by the condition that his activity must be such as to promote the development of others. Thus a harmonious development of man in society forms the one aspect of the ethical

---

[101] Michael Freeden, *Rights* (Minneapolis: University of Minnesota Press, 1991), 89 and 98.
[102] Brink, "Mill's Deliberative Utilitarianism," 98.

ideal as the universal happiness forms the other, the two being related as the *content* of feeling to *feeling* itself. [my italics][103]

In sum, Hobhouse developed the same kind of amicable attitude towards Millian liberal utilitarianism that Green did. For both, improved Millian utilitarianism was a splendid and heartening exercise even if improved utilitarians never quite got practical reasoning right. The "new" liberalism was as thoroughly retrospective as it was new.

CONCLUSION

Conceptual rivalries and preoccupations of the moment invariably and indelibly warp our assessment of those of the past. This holds as much for liberalism and its tradition as for any philosophical tradition and, hence, it holds for how we interpret Hobhouse's new liberalism.

Hobhouse, I have argued, privileged good over right. Moreover, not unlike Green, he basically defined good non-hedonically in terms of self-realization with moral self-realization enjoying pride of normative place. But though it would be imprudent to suggest, further, that Hobhouse was a good-aggregating consequentialist, he nevertheless insisted that self-realization ought to be maximized as equitably as possible and that a spirited theory of moral rights (including qualified property rights) was most conducive to this end. Hence, Hobhouse's mature maximizing strategy was robustly juridical as well as redistributive and was, therefore, solidly liberal.

Like Mill and Green before him, Hobhouse struggled, if not always successfully, to forge a liberal consequentialist theory of good that was capable, at a minimum, of accommodating the separateness of persons. Yet mere *accommodation* is an uninspiring clarion call. A liberal theory of good must celebrate separateness in the sense of celebrating *flourishing* individuality if it is to inspire our allegiance. Now Hobhouse's liberal consequentialism may exhibit its share of faults but timidity in celebrating this kind of individuality surely isn't one of them. Like his enthusiasm for juridical constraints on the pursuit of good, his enthusiasm for the cultivation of individuality should warm the doubting hearts of even the hardiest neo-Kantian critics of consequentialism. *If* liberal consequentialism is at all plausible and compelling, *if* it liberates us from the dictatorship of one of our most tyrannical of tyrannizing conceptual dichotomies, then L. T. Hobhouse, as much as any new liberal, deserves better from current liberal theorizing.

[103] Hobhouse, *Development and Purpose*, 182–3.

CHAPTER 4

Excursus: Green, Hobhouse and contemporary moral philosophy

INTRODUCTION

Hobhouse once said approvingly that in Green "we get most of the cream of Idealism and least of its sour milk."[1] What follows next examines additional aspects of this philosophical, new liberal cream as Green reconstituted it and as Hobhouse further modified it. As we have already begun to see, Green and Hobhouse married communitarianism, consequentialism and liberalism. I shall now endeavor to assess more carefully whether this marriage of what we have come to consider philosophic rivals succeeded or was just a misconceived exercise in overly enthusiastic eclecticism. And I hope to do this by helping myself generously to components of their respective moral psychologies.

Regardless of how successfully Green and Hobhouse marry competing philosophies, their efforts nevertheless look ahead to more recent attempts to rescue philosophical liberalism from the rivalry between liberalism and communitarianism that has artificially straitjacketed much contemporary political theorizing. Some will therefore recognize Joseph Raz's anti-individualist liberalism of human flourishing in Green and Hobhouse's new liberalism. Some may also recognize mirrored in their moral and political theories Jack Crittenden's liberal "self beyond individualism, a self constituted by autonomy and relationships."[2] But few, I doubt, will also recognize as they should Harry Frankfurt's perfectionist liberalism as well.

But more importantly, and perhaps more controversially, I would like to insist that Thomas Hurka's consequentialist perfectionism restates and reinvents salient aspects of Green and Hobhouse's new liberalism, albeit with greater sophistication and nuance. Hurka's much understated debts to the new liberals aside, his perfectionism nevertheless helps us appreciate just how thoroughly consequentialist the new liberals were. But this upshot

---

[1] Hobhouse, *The Elements of Social Justice*, 43.　　[2] Crittenden, *Beyond Individualism*, 8.

should be unsurprising, for after all, as I have been emphasizing, the new liberalism emerged against the backdrop of nineteenth-century utilitarianism. The new liberalism absorbed as much as it rejected from its utilitarian predecessors. In particular, as we have begun seeing, new liberals absorbed much from J. S. Mill's liberal utilitarianism.

Some of this chapter's plan, then, consists in showing how Green and Hobhouse's moral psychology of desiring and willing grounds their efforts to accommodate liberalism and communitarianism, an accommodation that contemporary liberals and communitarians are reinventing though few recognize the spurious novelty of their efforts.[3] Following Kymlicka, I want to "examine the resources available to liberalism" to meet some of the objections leveled against it by communitarians. But unlike Kymlicka, my chief concern is not what contemporary analytic liberals "can say," or can be made to say, but what "particular [new] liberals have actually said."[4] Most of my immediate plan, however, entails reinforcing my claim that new liberals like Green and Hobhouse liberalized consequentialism as much as they liberalized communitarianism as a way of showing, as I have been suggesting, that the new liberalism was fundamentally consequentialist.

This chapter, in particular, exhibits my predilection for using intellectual history to provoke our normative thinking about philosophical problems that continue to vex us. It aims, in Conal Condren's words, "to enrich the theoretical world we now inhabit."[5] That is, it seeks to remind us of the great bearing that intellectual history has for the practice of contemporary moral and political theory by helping us appreciate just how elusively complex normative theories like consequentialism have been and, therefore, just how dynamic, flexible and potentially rich in undervalued possibilities they continue to be.

---

[3] See Simhony and Weinstein, "Introduction" in *The New Liberalism: Reconciling Liberty and Community*, ed. Simhony and Weinstein, for an in-depth discussion of how contemporary liberals and communitarians, in their efforts to accommodate liberalism with communitarianism, are rediscovering much of what new liberals already discovered.

[4] Will Kymlicka, "Liberalism and Communitarianism," *Canadian Journal of Philosophy*, 18, 2 (June, 1988), 181. Kymlicka adds that modern liberals from Mill through Rawls and Dworkin provide resources from which to draw in answering communitarians. Ironically, he labels these liberals "new liberals," as opposed to classical liberals like Locke, ignoring earlier, self-described new liberals who provide more compelling resources. In *Liberals and Communitarians*, ix, Mulhall and Swift likewise raise the possibility that modern liberalism can be sufficiently modified so that it "does not conflict with, and perhaps can even take on board, the arguments which communitarians have to offer." With Simhony, I would contend that the new liberalism already achieved this modification.

[5] Conal Condren, "Political Theory and the Problem of Anachronism" in *Political Theory*, ed. Andrew Vincent (Cambridge: Cambridge University Press, 1997), 56.

DESIRE AND WILL

According to Green in *Prolegomena to Ethics*, will is refined desiring. Desire, in turn, is for specific, enduring *experiences* rather than transitory sensations. In desiring a "bottle of fine wine" or in desiring to "hear a certain piece of music," we desire the "experience of tasting the wine or hearing the music."[6] Moreover, desire is the "consciousness of opposition between a man's self and the real world, and an effort to overcome it by giving a reality in the world . . . to the object [experience] which, as desired, exists merely in his consciousness."[7] Overcoming this opposition between self and the world, realizing the experience desired, satisfies by "extinguish[ing]" the desire.[8] In "overcoming" the gap between itself and the world, the self realizes and satisfies itself by "carry[ing] itself out into the world."[9]

Will, insofar as it is partially constituted by desire, is therefore an effort to overcome the gap between oneself and the world, to carry oneself out into the world. However, will is more than desire, more than just an attempt to appropriate the world. While desires ebb and flow often as passing fancies and often conflicting with each other, will is resolute desire. Will is a "new principle that supervenes upon" desires "through the self-conscious subject's *identification* of itself with one of them." The desired experience is an individual's "final pursuit" in which "he desires in the sense that for the time he *identifies* himself with it" (my italics). In living for himself, he "lives for it." The "single self of which he is conscious, the unit in which all the influences of his life centre, but which distinguishes itself from them all, is for the time directed to making it [the desired experience] real."[10]

Will, therefore, is not just an individual's strongest desire that momentarily happens to defeat weaker competing desires. Such an erroneous conception of will implies that our desires are no more than brute forces mechanically determining our inner lives. In willing, our actions are not

---

[6] Green, *Prolegomena to Ethics*, Sect. 131.   [7] *Ibid.*, Sect. 131.   [8] *Ibid.*, Sect. 131.
[9] *Ibid.*, Sect. 136. In Sect. 136, Green also claims that thought features in all desiring [but not for infants presumably]: "Thus thought and desire are not to be regarded as separate powers, of which one can be exercised by us without, or in conflict with, the other. They are rather different ways in which the consciousness of self, which is also necessarily consciousness of a manifold world other than self, expresses itself. One is the effort of such consciousness to take the world into itself, the other its effort to carry itself out into the world; . . . " In short, all desiring is purposive and therefore "freedom evaluable" as Richard Flathman would say. Desires do not deterministically drive behavior willy-nilly. Also see Sect. 145 where Green says that willing is analogous to perception, which is "not a sensation or congeries of sensations, but supervenes upon certain sensations through a man's attending to them" by "taking them into self-consciousness . . ." Also see Note 45 below.
[10] *Ibid.*, Sect. 138.

simply the results of victorious, more powerful impulses. Willing is not the involuntary triumph of overpowering "solicitations" over weaker ones. Rather, in willing, each of us "takes it [a particular desire] into himself ... in a way which wholly alters it from what it was as a mere influence affecting him."[11] In willing, we enact ourselves by acting on our desires instead of allowing our desires to act on us uncontrollably. We consume desires selectively as opposed to being consumed by them. We consciously determine ourselves and thus begin acting morally:

A man, we will suppose, is acted on at once by an impulse to avenge an affront, by a bodily want, by a call of duty, and by fear of certain results incidental to his avenging the affront or obeying the call of duty ... So long as he is undecided how to act, all are, in a way, external to him. He presents them to himself as influences by which he is consciously affected but which are not he, and with none of which he yet identifies himself; or, to vary the expression, as tendencies to different objects, none of which is yet *his* object. So long as this state of things continues, no moral effect ensues. It ensues when the man's relation to these influences is altered by his identifying himself with one of them, by his taking the object of one of the tendencies as for the time his good. This is to *will*, and is in itself moral action, though the circumstances may prevent its issuing in that sensible effect which we call an overt act ... The object is one which for the time the man identifies with himself, so that in being determined by it he is consciously determined by himself.[12]

Will, in sum, is an act of conscious self-determination by which an individual decisively commits him- or herself to a particular desire. Willing therefore constitutes a higher-order desiring that moralizes desiring. Moreover, when an individual patterns his or her will over time in a special way by repeatedly "identifying" with certain kinds of desires, he or she develops character. The "formation of character" is the "growth

---

[11] *Ibid.*, Sect. 144. Also see Sect. 145 where Green continues, "Just as each of us is constantly having sensations which do not amount to perceptions, make no lodgment in the cosmos of our experience, add nothing to our knowledge, because not gathered into the focus of self-consciousness and through it referred to objects or determined by relation to each other; so there are impulses constantly at work in a man – the result of his organisation, of habits (his own or his ancestors), of external excitement, &c. – of which he is more or less aware according to the degree to which their antagonism to each other calls attention to them but which yet do not amount to principles of imputable action, or to desires of which it is sought to realise the objects, because the self-seeking, self-determining person has not identified himself with any of them." In other words, in contrast with desires, impulses are biological forces impelling us. Impulsive behavior is therefore not "freedom evaluable" in Flathman's sense. See, too, Sect. 120 where Green says that self-consciousness as the "faculty or possibility of desire," transforms what would otherwise be mere impulses into desires.

[12] *Ibid.*, Sect. 146. Note that in this passage, Green suggests that will is not simply a matter of identifying with immediate desires but also a matter of identifying with their objects.

of some habit of will."[13] By its formation, we begin transforming ourselves into virtuous personalities.

In Sect. 6 of "Lectures on the Principles of Political Obligation," Green claims that the "condition of a moral life is the possession of will and reason." As in *Prolegomena to Ethics*, he contends that will is an individual's capacity of being "determined to action by the idea of a possible satisfaction of himself." A "state of will is the capacity as determined by the particular objects in which the man seeks self-satisfaction; which becomes a character in so far as the self-satisfaction is habitually sought in objects of a particular kind." Will, more simply, is being determined by objects one desires and simultaneously being committed decisively to them. Green then adds, "Practical reason is the capacity in a man of conceiving the perfection of his nature as an object to be attained by action."[14]

Practical reasoning is thus a higher, "autonomous" kind of willing in which individuals make their own perfection the object of desires they resolutely "identify" with.[15] In reasoning practically, one takes one's own perfection "into himself" and "lives for it." One realizes oneself by "carry[ing]" one's desire for perfection "out into the world." One systematizes one's desires by "forming them into a totality."[16]

Hobhouse likewise conceives will as a complex if not necessarily higher-order desiring in the strong sense. In *The Rational Good*, Hobhouse holds that desire is a cognitive impulse directed at a simple end and that volition is a cognitive impulse directed at an overarching end involving several interrelated desires. Will is an even more sophisticated, cognitively enriched impulse, namely for a comprehensive end "*dominating* all life" (my italics).[17] Just as desire unifies our lower impulses and volition "introduces unity of direction" into our desires, will implies "some supreme unifying principle, rule, or end of action, setting out the real meaning of our life as a whole."[18] Will "is a gathering of much, ideally of the whole, conational energy of our nature canalized into a deep and steady stream

---

[13] *Ibid.*, Sect. 101. Robert Audi has suggested to me that Green's conception of willing can better be understood in terms of intention. When one identifies with a particular desire and commits to it, one forms an intention. Developing character, then, is a matter of making specific intentions habitual.

[14] Green, *Lectures on the Principles of Political Obligation*, Sect. 6.

[15] For the connection between willing one's own perfection, practical reasoning and autonomy of the will, see especially Green, "On the Different Senses of 'Freedom' as Applied to Will and the Moral Progress of Man," Sects. 5 and 21.

[16] T. H. Green, "Notes on Moral Philosophy," *Collected Works of T. H. Green*, ed. P. Nicholson, Vol. v (Bristol: Thoemmes), 191.

[17] Hobhouse, *The Rational Good*, v.   [18] *Ibid.*, 46.

flowing within determinate limits in ordered activity to foreseen ends."[19] It brings continuity to our experiences enabling us to "conceive ourselves as a persistent identity . . . as personalities."[20] Will, in short, forges each of us into distinctive personalities much as it does for Green.

In *Social Development*, Hobhouse again suggests that will is the synchronizing of our impulses, volitions and desires which infuses our lives with meaning by giving our lives "consistency of direction" according to "certain governing principles." Will unifies our lives into a coherent "system of ends."[21] Will, moreover, becomes "rational will" when it *consciously* unifies our lives around our deepest "permanent" or "root-interests" by either privileging one over the rest or by balancing each against the other. The rational will is "thus our [root] nature in the shape in which it can act as an organised whole."[22] And since its "true principle" is "harmony," rational will is identical with practical reasoning, which Hobhouse defines in *The Rational Good* as the "mass of impulse-feeling harmonized, or in process of finding harmony" and as "the impulse to develop harmony."[23]

Of the several root-interests, Hobhouse claims that our "interest in others, or the social interest" is among the most fundamental with sympathy and our concern for society as a whole being its most conspicuous manifestations. This root-interest is generated by our need for "reciprocity," by our need to respond to others and for their response in turn.[24] "What we imperiously need, like our daily bread, is to be in relation with others."[25] Even many of our other root-interests in Hobhouse's view, such as pride and self-respect, imply a need for others.[26] We can achieve neither without being acknowledged by others and acknowledging them simultaneously. For this reason, rational willing not only entails

---

[19] *Ibid.*, 52. Hobhouse regards willing and moral obligation as interconnected. Willing gives rise to feelings of moral obligation to the extent that desires resist will's unifying mastery. Given life's "tragic complexities," which pit duty against our ties of affection, willing and desire will forever conflict. Willing will never fully succeed in harmonizing our desires, condemning us perpetually to feelings of moral obligation of some kind. We will never perfect our wills and therefore we will never be fully self-realizing (53).

[20] *Ibid.*, 49.

[21] Hobhouse, *Social Development*, 142. Also see *Mind in Evolution*, 341, where Hobhouse says that enlightened self-interest means subordinating one's actions to the "whole system of purposes that make up the self."

[22] Hobhouse, *Social Development*, 173.

[23] *Ibid.*, 173 and Hobhouse, *The Rational Good*, 115 and 124.

[24] Other "root-interests" include our "egoistic" interest in bodily survival and reproduction, our "cognitive" interest in understanding our world and our "constructive" interest in remaking it. See Hobhouse, *Social Development*, 167 and 174.

[25] Hobhouse, *Social Development*, 155–7 and 174.   [26] *Ibid.*, 169.

harmonizing root-interests within ourselves individually but equally between ourselves.[27]

Now Hobhouse also insists, as was shown in Chapter 2, that the harmonious development of our lives as the balanced cultivation of our individual capacities and skills is what makes us truly self-realizing personalities. Whereas lives lived from momentary impulse to momentary impulse, from fleeting desire to fleeting desire, are chaotic and irrational, lives rich in personality exhibit dynamic focus. They possess direction, consistency and thus rationality. They are "strongly marked" with individuality: "By Personality is meant that constitution of the self which our account has postulated, that operative unity which, by the continual interrelation of action and experience, gives to each man's active life whatever cohesion and whatever individuality it manifests."[28] Thus, insofar as becoming a self-realizing personality in this sense is also equivalent to consciously unifying our lives around our "root-interests," then becoming a self-realizing personality is a matter of *willing* rationally. Willing rationally, as we just saw, consists in harmonizing our lives in accordance with our "root-interests."

And as we should also recall from Chapter 3, self-realizing actions are additionally harmonious inasmuch as results match our intentions in performing them and insofar as they generate feelings of pleasure. Rational, "strongly marked" self-realizing lives are intricately harmonious. They are orchestrated performances whose authors find them gratifying as much as others find them inspiring.

For both Green and Hobhouse, rational will plays a crucial and similar role in their respective conceptions of character and personality. The capacity to will rationally is the source of developed character for Green and of personality for Hobhouse. We elaborate and refine ourselves as ongoing projects through each act of rational will. For both, rational will is the fount of each person's singularity, of each person's identity.

Green's conception of rational will nevertheless differs from Hobhouse's in one fundamental respect. For Green, as we have seen, in willing we *identify* with particular desires by resolutely committing ourselves to them. We *choose* them doggedly. We create an identity by identifying with them so tenaciously. We carry ourselves out into the world, making a real mark in it, by aggressively desiring some desires over others. And when we do so habitually and rationally according to an ongoing deliberate pattern, we develop character.

---

[27] See, for instance, *Ibid.*, 168–9.   [28] Hobhouse, *The Rational Good*, 141.

By contrast for Hobhouse, in willing rationally we *unify* our underlying desires giving our lives direction, coherence and continuity. We make ourselves whole personalities not so much by decisively committing our-selves to a particular subset of desires (Green) but by bringing our desires into focused harmony. Harmony, not commitment, makes us selves with character and individuality.[29] While every person is a self, not every self succeeds in becoming a personality. Or at least not every self succeeds in becoming a *self-realizing* personality.

Green's theory of will surely rings familiar to modern, analytical philo-sophical ears. In his celebrated "Freedom of the Will and the Concept of a Person," Harry Frankfurt distinguishes between "first-order desires," "second-order desires" and "second-order volitions." "First-order desires" are simple unreflective desires for this or that X. "Second-order desires," by contrast, are desires to have certain desires. In "second-order" desiring, we want to want X and thus engage in "reflective self-evaluation." "Second-order volitions" are more peremptory "second-order" desires in which we desire to have certain desires be those which "effectively" move us "to act." To have a second-order volition is to want a certain desire to be one's will, to be one's effective desire. Second-order volitions, in Frankfurt's words, are therefore a matter of "decisively" committing to, and "identif[ying]" with, one of our lower-order desires.[30] Hence, willing freely for Frankfurt is in part what it is for Green, namely a question of *choosing* and energetically *identifying* with some of our primary desires by gathering them into ourselves.[31]

More recently, Frankfurt has modified his psychology of free will in response to critics, like Gary Watson, who charge that the "structural

---

[29] Harmony is not an irrelevant feature of Green's conception of willing for, as we saw above, willing systematizes our desires. However, harmony is not the defining feature of willing for Green the way that it is for Hobhouse.

[30] Harry Frankfurt, "Freedom of the Will and the Concept of a Person," *The Journal of Philosophy*, 47, 68 (1971).

[31] Note that Green and Frankfurt do not mean quite the same thing by will. By will, Green means what Frankfurt means by second-order volition whereas Frankfurt means "effective desire" or desire that actually moves one to act. Freedom of the will as decisive commitment is also what Raz, *The Morality of Freedom*, 382, partially seems to have in mind by autonomy: "To be autonomous one must identify with one's choices and one must be loyal to them." It is also what Charles Taylor seems to be thinking of by "self-articulation" though probably not what Richard Rorty is thinking of by aesthetic "self-enlargement" which he says is incompatible with an ascetic "desire to purify" oneself, "to will one thing, to intensify, to become a simpler and more transparent being." See Richard Rorty, "Freud and Moral Reflection" in *Essays on Heidegger and Others, Philosophical Papers*, Vol. II (Cambridge: Cambridge University Press, 1991), 154. And it is what Bradley seemed to have had in mind by self-realization as a process in which the self "fixes and closes itself; in short, gets hardened" as character. *Ethical Studies*, 50–5.

feature to which Frankfurt appeals is not the fundamental feature of either
free agency or personhood; it is simply insufficient to the task he wants it to
perform."[32] According to Watson, Frankfurt's hierarchical structure of
desiring fails to explain why anyone would identify decisively with some
first-order desires and not others. And why, asks Watson, privilege second-
order volitions? What gives *them* special authority? One's only recourse
would seem to entail ascending to third-order volitions but then why stop
there or anywhere? Thus, for Watson, decisive commitment looks like an
arbitrary refusal to ascend to higher orders of volition, calling the entire
psychology of ordered desiring into question. Moreover, while Watson
concedes that there may be something to identification and decisive
commitment, he wonders why, in any case, such psychological acts cannot
be themselves regarded as first-order desires to courses of action.[33]

Responding to such criticisms, Frankfurt has suggested that decisively
committing oneself to certain desires does not simply consist in arbitrarily
refusing to ascend to higher orders of desiring. Identifying with one's
desires is more substantive than that. Decisively endorsing some desires
over others exhibits "wholeheartedness." In wholeheartedly identifying
with certain desires, an agent no longer "holds himself apart" from them
but, in Greenian fashion, internalizes them and takes responsibility for
them. He or she "constitutes" him- or herself by them.[34] As such, wholeheartedness offers little that is new to Frankfurt's original theory of decisive
commitment. But Frankfurt adds that wholehearted commitment also
entails establishing coherence, and eliminating inconsistency, within
one's volitional complex: "In the absence of wholeheartedness, the person

---

[32] Gary Watson, "Free Agency" in *Free Will*, ed. Gary Watson (Oxford: Oxford University Press, 1982), 107.

[33] *Ibid.*, 108–9.

[34] Harry Frankfurt, "Identification and Wholeheartedness" in *The Importance of What We Care About* (Cambridge: Cambridge University Press, 1988), 170. Also see D. G. Ritchie, "Free-Will and Responsibility," *International Journal of Ethics*, 5 (1895), 414, where Ritchie observes: "We are only said to act quite freely, quite voluntarily, when the act is one that we do 'with our whole heart,' one that we choose not only in the sense that it is our act, for which we are in some degree responsible, but in the sense that we put ourselves into it, so to speak. For such acts, acts which are the outcome of our inclinations, we are obviously responsible in the fullest sense." In an endnote (436), Ritchie adds that on "the difference between the negative and positive meanings of 'freedom' in ethics and politics, I cannot do better than simply refer those who are not already acquainted with it to the discussion of the subject" in Green's "On the Different Senses of 'Freedom' as Applied to Will and to the Moral Progress of Man." Ritchie, one of Green's foremost students at Balliol College, was Professor of Logic and Metaphysics at St. Andrews University from 1894 until his death in 1903. Chapter 5 will discuss Ritchie's new liberalism in detail. According to Peter Nicholson, Ritchie was "one of the best exponents and defenders of Green's ideas." See Peter Nicholson, "Introduction," *The Collected Works of D. G. Ritchie*, 6 vol. (Bristol: Thoemmes Press, 1998), xvii.

is not merely in conflict with forces 'outside' him [external desires like a rejected but overpowering desire to smoke]; rather, he himself is divided."[35]

Frankfurt, then, seems now to be shadowing unknowingly Hobhouse more than Green. Hobhouse's theory of will, with its emphasis on harmony and coherence, anticipates rather nicely what Frankfurt intends by whole-heartedness in his improved theory of will. Hobhouse's theory of will has an equally familiar modern echo in Thomas Hurka and Joseph Raz's perfectionist liberalisms. For Hurka, a well-rounded life is a unified life in which our desires are hierarchically structured around dominant organizing ends entailing varied, challenging activities. Such lives are ongoing, orchestrated harmonies characterized by rich "unity-in-diversity." They are deeply rational because they require such skilled coordination. And they exhibit strength of will because they also require dedication and self-discipline.

By contrast, weakness of will characterizes lives permeated by whimsical, disjointed and often conflicting desires. Weak-willed persons never develop character, never become personalities. Their lives are irrational lacking resolve, coherence and complex structure. They remain impoverished, disunified, devoid of poignant harmony: "By succumbing to weakness [of will], the person abandons unified activity for a particular momentary goal and so severs the ties between her acts. If weakness of will is intrinsically bad, this disunity is surely the main reason."[36] For Raz, autonomy is the "ideal of free and conscious self-creation" in which one "progressively gives shape to one's life."[37] However, becoming autonomous is "not to be identified with the ideal of giving one's life a unity."[38] Raz thus concurs with Hobhouse who warns that mere unity of desires too often starves personality: "It is perhaps superfluous to point out the obverse truth [of harmony], that the cheapest way of approaching unity is to starve the self by suppressing all sides of it save one, as, e.g., by consistent asceticism, or sensualism, or even professionalism."[39] Such self-denial effectively

[35] Frankfurt, "Identification and Wholeheartedness" in *The Importance of What We Care About*, 165. Also see 173 where Frankfurt says that wholeheartedly deciding is reflexive as when one firmly makes up one's mind about something. It is something that one does to oneself. "It seems to me," Frankfurt adds, "that in this light the closest analogue to a situation in which someone makes up his mind is, rather surprisingly perhaps, a situation in which two people make up their differences. People who do that after a quarrel pass from a condition of conflict and hostility to a more harmonious and well-ordered relationship." I would like to thank Lee Overton for bringing to my attention Frankfurt's more recent retheorizing of decisive commitment as wholeheartedness.

[36] Hurka, *Perfectionism*, 123.   [37] Raz, *The Morality of Freedom*, 387 and 390.   [38] *Ibid.*, 370.

[39] Hobhouse, *Mind in Evolution*, 34. Hobhouse similarly condemns Plato's ideal city because it fetishizes cramping, ascetic political unity at the expense of "true organic" political unity. See Hobhouse, *Social Development*, 308.

constitutes what Berlin has condemned as freedom-subverting "retreat to the inner citadel."[40]

Now John Skorupski has very recently proposed ways of improving Green's moral psychology that parallel Frankfurt's efforts to rescue his own theory from its critics but without appealing to the mysteries of Frankfurtian wholeheartedness. Skorupski characterizes Green's theory of desire "in the full sense," as making particular "solicitations" one's own by identifying with them rather than with others. Skorupski then invokes Sidgwick's criticism that Green thereby conflates desire and volition because desiring something is not equivalent to resolving to satisfy a desire. Notwithstanding whether Green conflates desire and volition (which I have shown that he does not), Skorupski also suggests that we can improve Green's moral psychology by reconceptualizing full-bodied desire as endorsing the objects of solicitations for *reasons*. Such solicitations earn their legitimacy from the authority of *reasons* we are able to invoke on their behalf. Left unimproved, Green's "model makes it [reason] a *servant* whose only discretion lies in *picking* which passion to serve" which is "not enough to give the will autonomy. Autonomy, however, "lies in being able to recognize that there is reason to bring about an outcome irrespective of whether I desire that outcome – even if I do not desire it – and in being able to act on that recognition."[41]

Authorizing specific desires by invoking reasons, then, equips us with a strategy for bringing the danger of infinite regress, so troubling to Frankfurt's critics, to a halt. Otherwise, all we can do is "pick" our passions without reason, i.e. willy-nilly. And picking passions willy-nilly means picking them arbitrarily. Reason can no more afford to be a "servant" of the passions than their "slave" in order to salvage autonomy from the slippery slope of infinite regress.

Skorupski's solution to the dangers of infinite regress in Green follow Raz's recommendation for arresting infinite regress in Frankfurt. For Raz, our lives are our own insofar as our emotions, moods, desires and beliefs are responsive to reasons. That is, we act autonomously insofar as we conduct ourselves with a "semblance" of rationality. Conducting ourselves accordingly "sometimes means no more than forming beliefs and emotions where they are reasonable, where their formation and persistence is under the

[40] See Isaiah Berlin, "Two Concepts of Liberty," in Isaiah Berlin, *Liberty*, ed. Henry Hardy (Oxford: Oxford University Press, 2002), 181–7.
[41] John Skorupski, "Green and the Idealist Conception of a Person's Good," *T. H. Green: Ethics, Metaphysics, and Political Philosophy*, ed. Maria Dimova-Cookson and William J. Mander (Oxford: Oxford University Press, 2006), 58.

control of our rationality, even though there is *no self-awareness or decision*"
(my italics).[42] Hence, for Raz, it is enough for our actions to be intelligible
to us, even if only after the fact, for our lives to be sufficiently our own.
Potential intelligibility gives our lives ample "semblance of rationality" and
somehow obstructs infinite regress. Compared to Skorupski, then, Raz's
solution to the challenge of infinite regress appeals to a thinner notion of
acting for a reason.

Raz aside, Green's model of desire and willing, as I have been suggesting,
is richer than Skorupski allows. For Green, as we have seen, willing is not
merely an act of resolution but an act of *self-conscious* resolution. In willing,
we determine ourselves by an "idea" of ourselves. Hence, willing is acting
autonomously in Skorupski's sense, providing Green's moral psychology
with the resources to meet the kinds of criticisms that Watson and others
have brought against Frankfurt.[43]

In his study of Green's *Prolegomena*, David Brink echoes Skorupski's
appreciation of Green's rejection of Humean moral psychology. For Brink
as well, Green's conception of willing makes reason more than the slave of
our passions.[44] But Brink's Green theorizes reason in robustly Scanlonian
terms. Reason does not merely *serve* our passions by just *picking* between
them. Willing is a "process of deliberative endorsement" in which some
desires are transformed into motives. In willing, we reflect on our desires,
endorsing some over others because of how they fit into our idea of the
kind of person each of us wants to become. In short, in willing, we act for a
formidable reason. And, as Brink points out, our capacity to will is the
source of our moral responsibility. Moral responsibility requires that
reason be more than a "servant" as well as more than a "slave."[45] And it

---

[42] Joseph Raz, "When We Are Ourselves: The Active and the Passive" in *Engaging Reason* (Oxford: Oxford University Press, 1999), 20.

[43] In this regard, see as well Green's claim in "On the Different Senses of 'Freedom' as Applied to Will and the Moral Progress of Man," Sect. 10, that we must not "regard the will as independent of motives, as a power of deciding between motives without any motive to determine the decision, which must mean without reference to any object willed." In short, we conceptualize willing erroneously if we think of it as simply picking between desires for no reason.

[44] To deny reason's enslavement is to reject psychological egoism as Brink also points out.

[45] See Brink, "Introduction," xxxix. Brink also explores how Green's moral theory rests on his argument linking knowledge to self-consciousness. According to Brink, Green holds that "epistemic responsibility" makes transforming true belief into knowledge possible. And because "epistemic responsibility," in turn, requires self-consciousness, knowledge therefore requires self-consciousness. Epistemic responsibility requires a "cognizer to be able to distinguish and distance an appearance from herself, to frame the question whether she should *assent* to the appearance, and to assess reasons for assent by relating this appearance to other elements of consciousness" (xxix). Likewise, moral responsibility requires a cognizer who is able to distance herself from her passions and desires so that she can frame the question whether she should assent to them for good reasons.

must be more than either if willing is to avoid degenerating into infinite regress.

Brink's account of Green helps us see that other neo-Kantians, like Korsgaard and Gewirth, repeat Green unawares and therefore with an inflated sense of novelty. For Korsgaard, the reflective structure of human consciousness distances us from our brute desires and impulses and consequently compels us to act for reasons. We have no choice but to endorse our impulses before acting on them. We are condemned to "reflective endorsement" and thus to acting for reasons. To be human is to endorse impulses for reasons. Moreover, the reflective structure of our consciousness also forces us to develop a conception of our identities, which purportedly informs or grounds our reasons. Or rather, we necessarily act *for* reasons and therefore *from* a sense of identity. We ask ourselves whether beings with our identities could will as a law the maxim of acting on the particular impulses or desires animating us. And to the extent that we respond negatively, we have an obligation. Impulses and desires that fail the test of universalization fail to provide reasons for acting. Lacking reasons, we are therefore obligated not to act on them. Hence, Korsgaard concludes that obligating ourselves is "simply a fact about human nature," which is why she identifies herself as a "procedural realist."[46]

Notwithstanding the overall cogency of Korsgaard's account of obligation, her conception of reflective endorsement plainly parallels Frankfurt's account of willing and therefore Green's notion of willing as well. Taking Korsgaard seriously points back to Green as much as laterally to Frankfurt though Green is largely ignored and forgotten by defenders and critics of both Korsgaard and Frankfurt. For Korsgaard, paralleling Green, morality begins with reflection on our impulses and desires. For her as well as for him, willing consists in endorsing those impulses with which we identify. Willing for both is therefore ineluctably moral as well. In willing, we actualize our identities by committing to a subset of first-order desires.

---

[46] Christine Korsgaard, *The Sources of Normativity* (Cambridge: Cambridge University Press, 1996), 112–13. Also see Korsgaard, 103–4, where she explains: "The reflective structure of human consciousness *requires* that you identify yourself with some law or principle which will govern your choices. It requires you to be a law to yourself. And that is the source of normativity." Moreover, she continues: "But when we do reflect we *cannot but think* that we ought to do what on reflection we conclude we have reason to do. And when we don't do that we punish ourselves, by guilt and regret and repentance and remorse" (my italics). In other words, being reflective creatures by nature, we cannot help but act for reasons insofar as we cannot help but endorse some impulses and desires over others. We cannot help but act from principle for to act for a reason is to act from principle. And to act from principle is to act from a powerful sense of identity. When we fail to act from the principles, we feel guilty and ashamed.

We act for higher-order reasons and thus begin realizing ourselves morally. Moreover, to the extent that we fail to act for reasons and thus fail to reflect upon our desires endorsing some at the expense of others, we act wantonly and immorally. And, "if you live at random, without integrity or principle, then you will lose your grip on yourself and one who has any reason to live and to act at all."[47]

We should not overexaggerate how far Korsgaard's neo-Kantianism replays Green's no less than we should precipitously conflate Frankfurt's neo-Kantianism with Green's. For instance, though Korsgaard regards herself as improving and correcting Kant by trading on Aristotle as did Green, she nevertheless sees herself as more traditionally neo-Kantian than Green saw himself. Moreover, Korsgaard sees reflective endorsement of lower impulses and desires as simultaneously making laws for ourselves, as simultaneously universalizing and endorsing maxims as moral laws. While Green is sympathetic to such thinking, it is not as central to his practical reasoning as it is for Korsgaard. Furthermore, she readily concedes that her account of morality is "naturalistic" inasmuch as it grounds normativity in psychological and biological facts about us, namely our reflective consciousness.[48]

Alan Gewirth's neo-Kantianism reveals nearly as much about Green's conception of willing as Korsgaard's. While reading Green backwards through Gewirth is as risky methodologically as reading him backwards through Korsgaard, Gewirth at least briefly appeals explicitly to Green on several occasions in defending his account of morality as self-fulfillment. Gewirth thus sensitizes us to facets of Green's theory of willing (and

---

[47] *Ibid.*, 121. Also see Korsgaard's criticism, shared by Green, that Kant's categorical imperative is formalistically empty insofar as it merely prescribes that our motives be self-consistent. Like Green, she wants to make the categorical imperative substantive, which reconceptualizing it as the "moral law" qua Kingdom of Ends purportedly does. See especially 97–100 and 134.

[48] *Ibid.*, 160. But Korsgaard also says rather obscurely that her account is "not quite" fully naturalistic. She insists that she has not claimed that the "bare *fact* of reflective endorsement – is enough to make an action right" (160–1). But see Cohen and Nagel's respective criticisms that her neo-Kantianism risks collapsing into normativity as brute endorsement. Cohen, drawing on earlier criticisms that Frankfurt's original theory of willing is arbitrarily subjective and prone to infinite regress, likewise faults Korsgaard's conception of reflective endorsement for being no less ungrounded. As Cohen argues, there "is no restriction either in Frankfurt's presentation or in fact on what the content of second-order volition can be, or, better, for this claim will suffice here [Korsgaard], no restriction sufficiently restrictive to yield moral obligation." See G. A. Cohen, "Reason, Humanity and the Moral Law" in *ibid.*, 188. For Nagel's criticisms, see Thomas Nagel, "Universality and the Reflective Self" in *ibid.*, 206, where he complains that Korsgaard's theory of moral obligation "cheapen[s]" moral motives because it makes morality turn on who one happens to think one is. Nagel doesn't have in mind what Cohen and Frankfurt's critics have in mind, namely that reflective endorsement is criterionless and therefore prone to infinite regress. The later phenomenon nevertheless clearly cheapens morality too.

Hobhouse's too) that we might otherwise devalue. Just as contextualized history of political thought can provoke our thinking afresh regarding conceptual philosophical problems vexing us, so analytical moral and political theory can stimulate us to read historical texts more critically.

On Gewirth's recent account, self-fulfillment differs from both self-realization and self-actualization. Whereas self-realization suggests that selves are not fully "real" unless realized, self-actualization suggests the opposite, holding that unactualized selves contain real though latent potentialities. By contrast, according to Gewirth, self-fulfillment comes in two varieties, namely aspiration-fulfillment and capacity-fulfillment. Now Gewirth seems mostly inclined to read Green as defending an implausible version of aspiration-fulfillment. For Gewirth, Green represents the ill-formulated, "occurrent" version of aspiration-fulfillment, which makes every successful action self-fulfilling. Agents fulfill themselves when they simply get what they want most. Gewirth rightly insists that such an account of self-fulfillment as brute aspiration-fulfillment "overlooks the aspect of aspiration as one's deepest higher-order desires that involve a person's general conception of himself as embodying certain wished-for values." As Gewirth reminds us, not "every particular action has such a general involvement; many are trivial and transitory in relation to the depth and intimacy of desires that characterize aspirations."[49] On the other hand, Gewirth *also* classifies Green as exemplifying capacity-fulfillment perfectionism.[50]

So which Green is the "real Green" on Gewirth's understanding and classification? Gewirth is clearly confused about how to characterize Green. Perhaps, his confusion about Green reflects a deeper confusion in his own theory.

According to Gewirth, aspiration-fulfillment properly formulated (not the ill-conceived "occurrent" version) views self-fulfillment as fulfilling one's "deepest" as opposed to our momentary desires. Our "deepest" desires "reflect most directly the values and indeed the very definition of the self as an enduring conative entity." Our aspirations are "higher-order desires" that are "desires to have not only the objects of one's desires but also to be a person who is characterized both as having those desires and as

---

[49] Gewirth, *Self-Fulfillment*, 26–7. Gewirth, by the way, admits that his account of Green is derived from J. B. Schneewind, *Sidgwick's Ethics and Victorian Moral Philosophy* (Oxford: Oxford University Press, 1977).
[50] Gewirth, *Self-Fulfillment*, 15. But also see 7, n5, where Gewirth confuses his characterization of Green even more by claiming that Green, Bradley and Bosanquet make self-realization, and not self-fulfillment, fundamental.

being successful in attaining them." They are "supreme desires, in that their objects are what one most wants to have."[51] More succinctly: "In aspirations, the self tends to identify itself in part with the other two aspects [its deepest desires and the objects of its desires]; far from taking a detached view of its desires and their objects, its attitude towards them is evaluative, conative, and proactive. But at the same time the self turns its desires on itself, in that, by a higher-order desire, it aspires to be a certain kind of person."[52]

No doubt with criticisms of Frankfurt's initial account of willing in mind, Gewirth recognizes that aspiration-fulfillment raises the problem of infinite regress or, as he nicely puts it, "a bottomless pit of reflection." However, because aspiration-fulfillment concerns one's very deepest desires, reflection will not go on endlessly. Our deepest desires "anchor," by providing "centrality and perspective," to our other, less fundamental desires. They provide powerful reasons endorsing some desires over others thus thwarting infinite regress.

By contrast, capacity-fulfillment concerns bringing out what is "best in oneself," namely one's best capacities. What is best in oneself is not "preexisting or ready-made" like a "pearl that already exists in an oyster and needs only to be extricated." Rather, the best in ourselves is something we develop out of the "preexisting materials" that constitute our various capacities.[53] Capacity-fulfillment has to do with bringing our natural abilities, talents and potentialities to fruition.[54]

In sum, while aspiration-fulfillment pertains to actual desires, capacity-fulfillment concerns desires one ought to have depending upon the potential capabilities and skills one happens to have. For the former, the question is: "What will satisfy my deepest desires?" For the latter, it is: "How can I make the best of myself?"[55] Capacity-fulfillment is therefore, according

---

[51] *Ibid.*, 23–4.
[52] *Ibid.*, 25. Also see 38 where Gewirth explains the importance of autonomy for aspiration-fulfillment: "The second-order desires of desire-autonomy that one has on the basis of reflective evaluation – what one desires to desire as a result of such evaluation – can be considered to be one's desires in a more stable and authentic sense than the desires one has and pursues without subjecting them to critical scrutiny. In this way, too, the depth of desire that characterizes aspirations is brought more fully into line with the person's autonomy because he is more fully in control of his desires."
[53] *Ibid.*, 60 and 65.
[54] "It is a creative process: in fulfilling the self one creates oneself, but along lines that are implicit in such of one's prior capacities as one chooses to fulfill because they are what is best in oneself. So to fulfill oneself requires not that one already be fulfilled but rather that one moves from relatively indeterminate powers to exercise them as one chooses so as to make them more determinate." *Ibid.*, 65.
[55] *Ibid.*, 14.

to Gewirth, more normative than aspiration-fulfillment.[56] In addition, on Gewirth's account, for aspiration-fulfillment, happiness is desire satisfaction whereas, for capacity-fulfillment, happiness consists in actually developing one's best capacities whatever they are.

Gewirth's notion of capacity-fulfillment would appear, then, to thwart infinite regress even more precipitously than aspiration-fulfillment insofar as it is inherently normative. By grounding self-fulfillment in our underlying abilities, and not in our passing desires as aspiration-fulfillment does, it provides criteria for how we ought to go about fulfilling ourselves. Even more than aspiration-fulfillment, it offers powerful reasons for committing to some desires over others, for escaping the abyss of perpetual reflection. It offers powerful reasons, assuming that equating *unique* capacities with *morally best* capacities does not beg any questions. But if Gewirth is question-begging after all, then capacity-fulfillment provides no safe harbor from the tumult of infinite regress. Or to put it otherwise, what is so special about the capacities I happen to have? Why ought I to develop them all unless I can establish on independent grounds that they are worthwhile? And, for that matter, why privilege my "deepest" desires as aspiration-fulfillment alternatively suggests? Notwithstanding Gewirth's claim that capacity-fulfillment in particular saves perfectionism from boundless regress, his ethics of self-fulfillment qua capacity-fulfillment palpably replays Green's. Like Green, in willing, we begin fulfilling ourselves morally by making the best of ourselves, by developing our talents and capacities to the full. To paraphrase Green, we become all that we have in us to become. Aspiration-fulfillment is likewise redolent of Green for in fulfilling our aspirations, we begin acting morally by decisively committing ourselves to some desires over others, namely to those that are somehow more fundamental or "deeper" (as Gewirth would say). In other words, Green's (and Hobhouse's to a lesser degree) perfectionist account of willing combines features of Gewirth's aspiration-fulfillment and capacity-fulfillment.[57] Now either Green's account conflates conceptual

---

[56] Capacity-fulfillment's purported normative richness is borne out by the rights claims that Gewirth insists that it entails: "My argument in this section has rested on the premise that since reason is the epistemically best of human capacities, whatever is justified by reason must also be among the best of human capacities and thus must be a part of capacity-fulfillment. It was on the basis of this premise that I held that practical acceptance of the universalist morality of human rights is itself a part of capacity-fulfillment. In this way the bestness of the process – the justificatory use of reason – gets transferred to the bestness of the product – the universalist morality of human rights." *Ibid.*, 92.

[57] For examples of where Gewirth, like Frankfurt and Hurka too, seems to shadow Hobhouse as much as, or more than, Green, see *ibid.*, 24–5 where he describes aspiration-fulfillment as hierarchically ranking

distinctions that Gewirth skillfully formulates that should not be conflated or Gewirth's efforts to secure these distinctions are analytically clumsy if not arbitrary. Green would not see much difference between appeals to our "deepest" desires (aspiration-fulfillment) and appeals to our natural talents and potentialities (capacity-fulfillment) that uniquely individuate each of us. And nor should we.

Brink's account of Green's theory of willing leads easily to Korsgaard and Gewirth. And viewing Green retrospectively through the lens of Korsgaard and Gewirth highlights the limitations of Skorupski's interpretation of him. Green's theory of willing is less misleading than Skorupski thinks because Green, anticipating Korsgaard and Gewirth, provides what he supposes are compelling reasons for willing, or committing to, some desires over others. Skorupski's improved Green is a very modest improvement because Green was nearly already what Skorupski would prefer him to be.

New liberal conceptions of willing continue resonating unexpectedly. Those laboring in the trenches of the history of political thought can take heart that their efforts have more than antiquarian value. Moreover, as we shall now see, Green's (and Hobhouse's) conception of *good* willing foreshadows contemporary theorizing in other suggestively instructive ways.

---

and harmonizing our desires. In fulfilling her aspirations, she "is not buffeted about by each desire in turn in an unending cycle of frenetic activities; instead, she can sort out and coordinate her desires so that some are seen to be means to others, and she can maintain some sense of an organizing principle that enables her to pursue her main goals while putting her subordinate ones into their proper place." Also note the palpable similarities between aspiration-fulfillment as satisfying our "deepest" desires and Hobhouse's conception of willing as unifying our lives around our "root" interests. See, too, Gewirth's description of capacity-fulfillment (186–7), which sounds more like Hobhouse's account of willing than Green's. George Sher has recently defended a form of perfectionist liberalism similar to Hobhouse and Gewirth's in significant respects. According to Sher, certain human capacities or goals are "fundamental," being "rooted" in our mental constitution. These "near-universal and near-inescapable" goals belong to agents "so deeply" that they underlie all our more specific desires much the way root-interests underlie everyday desires for Hobhouse. You ought to "develop whichever of your abilities would contribute the most to the achievement of your fundamental goals." Sher therefore insists that his version of self-realization ethics compared to other versions therefore neither lacks content nor begs the question of which of our innumerable capacities we should develop. See George Sher, *Beyond Neutrality* (Cambridge: Cambridge University Press, 1997), 208. And also much like Hobhouse, Sher maintains: "the elements of a [self-realizing] good life include knowledge, rational action, close relationships, and various other forms of contact with the world. This means that whether someone lives a good life cannot depend exclusively on the quality of his experience. But neither is the quality of his experience irrelevant. We can hardly deny that happiness, pleasure, enjoyment are among life's goods, so any satisfactory unifying theory must appeal to a property or relation that is capable of belonging to experiential as well as nonexperiential states" (229). Hence, like Hobhouse but unlike Green, happiness does not piggyback on self-realization contingently but partially constitutes it.

GOOD WILL

Michael Sandel has argued that liberalism "undoes" itself because liberals typically and wrongly assume a flawed individualistic psychology.[58] As we are beginning to see, this portrayal conveniently ignores new liberals like Green and Hobhouse. Their respective conceptions of good willing make Sandel's claim more plainly specious still.

David Johnston has suggested that modern perfectionist liberalisms typically distinguish "personal autonomy" from "moral autonomy." According to Johnston, a personally autonomous agent "chooses his own projects and values." He is a "self-defining subject, a self-fashioning individual, or a subject of free and conscious self-creation."[59] A morally autonomous agent is not only self-defining but also possesses an "effective sense of justice" and consequently acts with restraint.[60] Personally autonomous agents, we might say, possess effective wills while morally autonomous agents possess effective good wills. Moral autonomy, then, is a species of personal autonomy in much the same way that good will is a species of will. Fanatics may be personally autonomous (possess strong wills) but not morally autonomous (possess good wills). Moral saints possess both.

For new liberals like Green and Hobhouse, effective good will is a species of effective will, a species of personal autonomy. For both, good will is also the most exalted species of will. Goodness is, for both, the desire most worth *identifying* with, most worth *unifying* one's life around.

In *Prolegomena to Ethics*, Green says that good will is the "unconditional good" and constitutes, in part, "perfect character."[61] It is the "morally good" which is a category of good in the "wider sense."[62] Thus, good will as the "unconditional good," as character perfection, is a narrower species of good.

Now if good will is a narrower kind of good, then will is good in the "wider" sense. Hence, in willing, in resolutely *identifying* with some of my lower-order desires, I begin acting morally but only in the "wider," generic sense. I act morally in the narrower sense when I resolutely *identify* with my desire to be a moral person. All willing is good but only willing on behalf of good will itself is unconditionally good. Green's conception of good willing is therefore deeply Kantian to the extent that for him, as for Kant, will is

---

[58] See, for instance, Michael Sandel, "The Procedural Republic and the Unencumbered Self," *Political Theory*, 12, 1 (February, 1984), 83.

[59] David Johnston, *The Idea of a Liberal Theory* (Princeton: Princeton University Press, 1994), 75.

[60] *Ibid.*, 71–7.   [61] Green, *Prolegomena to Ethics*, Sects. 194–5.   [62] *Ibid.*, Sect. 171.

the ability to choose (or "identify" with as Green would say) what reason commends, namely moral goodness.[63]

Furthermore, will and good will reinforce each other symbiotically. On the one hand, society is a necessary condition for any kind of willing. As Green says in a well-known turn of phrase, "social life is to personality what language is to thought."[64] Only by living in a particular kind of society with particular social roles, values and possibilities can one actualize oneself as a particular personality. Only in particular societies can one develop any first-order desires whatsoever from which to choose and identify with:

Only through society is any one enabled to give that effect to the idea of himself as the object of his actions, to the idea of a possible better state of himself, without which the idea would remain like that of space to a man who had not the senses either of sight or touch. Some practical recognition of personality by another, of an 'I' by a 'Thou' and a 'Thou' by an 'I,' is necessary to any practical consciousness of it [personality], to any such consciousness of it as can express itself in act.[65]

Naturally, how successfully we will ourselves as personalities depends upon *what* kind of society we live in. How each 'I' and each 'Thou' practically recognizes each other determines how well each 'I' and 'Thou' develop themselves as personalities. Only societies whose members recognize each other as ends possessing rights enable their members to become authentic personalities: "So human society presupposes persons in capacity – subjects capable each of conceiving himself and the bettering of his life as an end to himself – *but* it is only in the intercourse of men, each recognized by each as an end, not merely a means, and thus as having reciprocal claims, that the capacity is actualised and we really live as persons" (my italics).[66] Effective willing, in sum, depends upon good will.

On the other hand, good will depends upon will. As we saw earlier, the "possession of will" is a necessary but not sufficient "condition of a moral life." In order to become a moral personality, one must at least be able to

---

[63] See Kant, *Fundamental Principles of the Metaphysics of Morals*, 40.
[64] Green, *Prolegomena to Ethics*, Sect. 183.   [65] *Ibid.*, Sect. 190.
[66] *Ibid.*, Sect. 183. Also see Sect. 370 where Green observes: "In thinking of ultimate good he ['the educated citizen of Christendom'] thinks of it indeed necessarily as perfection for himself; as a life in which he shall be fully satisfied through having become all that the spirit within him enables him to become. But he cannot think of himself as satisfied in any life other than a social life, exhibiting the exercise of self-denying will, and in which 'the multitude of the redeemed,' which is all men, shall participate. He has other faculties indeed than those which are directly exhibited in the specifically moral virtues – faculties which find their expression not in his dealings with other men, but in the arts and sciences – and the development of these must be a necessary constituent in any life which he presents to himself as one in which he can find satisfaction."

become *a* personality. And the latter, as we have just seen, depends, in turn, upon the cultivation of good will itself.

The symbiotic relationship between will and good will recalls and reformulates the symbiotic relationship between Green's conceptions of "outward" and "inner" freedom discussed in Chapter 2. To the extent that an individual wills by merely identifying with some desires and not others, he or she begins becoming a personality, enjoying a measure of "inward" freedom. To the extent that an individual wills rationally by making "himself an object to himself," by identifying with his desire to be a particular kind of person, he begins becoming an "autonomous" personality and therefore becomes more inwardly or positively free. And to the extent that he wills the good by making "himself a [moral] object to himself," he begins becoming morally "autonomous," achieving full "inward" freedom.[67]

By contrast, "outward" or "juristic" freedom is merely the opportunity to act on one's preferences, of being negatively uncoerced and positively empowered to follow one's first-order desires. An "outward[ly]" free agent is "free to act" though not necessarily "free to will."[68] Such an agent enjoys opportunities to actualize his or her desires whatever they happen to be. The "reflecting man," however, is not satisfied with just being "free to act" on his desires. He wants more, namely to will and to will well. He "distinguishes himself from his preference[s], and asks how he is related to [them] – whether he determines [them] or how [they] are determined."[69] But he also gradually comes to appreciate that this "more" that he wants, this fuller "inward" freedom that he now prizes, depends upon securing "outward" freedom uncompromisingly. To come to prize "inward" freedom is to prize "outward" freedom even more fervently. And prizing the latter ever more zealously insures that the former, and the latter in turn, will flourish still more.

What is more, for Green, good will is a special kind of willing insofar as it is the only kind that is "really" a common good in the sense of being a wholly non-competitive good. Only by willing to be good, only by steadfastly *identifying* with one's desire to be good, do individuals realize a good over which competition is supposedly impossible. The confirmed "disposition" to be good is the sole species of good that is perfectly compossible.

---

[67] Green, "On the Different Senses of 'Freedom' as Applied to Will and the Moral Progress of Man," Sects. 6–8.

[68] *Ibid.*, Sect. 8. Also see Frankfurt, "Freedom of the Will and the Concept of a Person," 15 and 17, for a similar distinction between freedom of action and freedom of the will.

[69] Green, "On the Different Senses of 'Freedom' as Applied to Will and the Moral Progress of Man," Sect. 8.

Willing to be good is an invaluable common resource, which is also wondrously unlimited. Decisively committing to one's desire to be good helps everyone and harms no one. As Green says in remarks cited previously in Chapter 2, the "only good in the pursuit of which there can be no competition of interests, the only good which is really common to all who may pursue it, is that which consists in the universal will to be good – in the settled disposition on each man's part to make the most and best of humanity in his own person and in the persons of others."[70] Green's liberalism thus seems powerfully non-individualistic in Raz's sense because it privileges such a fecund common good like the will to be good. For Raz, a distinguishing trait of non-individualist liberalisms, such as his own, consists in their commitment to non-competitive public goods.[71]

Green's conception of common good nevertheless remains notoriously hard to decipher (as we began to see in Chapter 2), and may not make much sense as Skorupski claims even though mutual respect, including respect for each other's rights, would seem a genuine, non-competitive common good if anything would.[72] But Skorupski's assessment is compelling if Green's ethics indeed exemplifies what Skorupski labels "moralistic egoism." According to Skorupski, moralistic egoists, like Green, hold that pursuing one's own good is the "only *ultimate* practical-reason-giving

---

[70] Green, *Prolegomena to Ethics*, Sect. 244. Note that A. C. Bradley, who wrote the Analytical Table of Contents for *Prolegomena to Ethics*, subtitles Sects. 240–5 "Virtue as the Common Good." See, too, Sect. 283 where Green explains that the development of personality as such even in its more mundane forms, not just moral personality, is equally a common good: "It ['social authority'] can have its origin only in an interest of which the object is a common good; a good in the effort after which there can be no competition between man and man; of which the pursuit by any individual is an equal service to others and to himself. Such a good may be pursued in many different forms by persons quite unconscious of any community in their pursuits; by the craftsman or writer, set upon making his work as good as he can without reference to his own glorification; by the father devoted to the education of his family, or the citizen devoted to the service of his state." See, as well, Sect. 234. Green means much the same thing when he says, following Bradley, that each citizen "has primarily to fulfil the duties of his station" (Sect. 183). Compare this to Raz, *The Morality of Freedom*, 319, who remarks: "All I argue for is that individuals inevitably derive the goals by which they constitute their lives from the stock of social forms available to them, and the feasible variations on it. If those social forms are morally valid, if they enshrine sound moral conceptions, then it is easy for people generally to find themselves with, and to choose for themselves, goals which lead to a rough coincidence in their own lives of moral and personal concerns . . . By being teachers, production workers, drivers, public servants, loyal friends and family people, loyal to their communities, nature loving, and so on, they will be pursuing their own goals, enhancing their own well-being, and also serving their communities, and generally living in a morally worthy way."

[71] Raz, *The Morality of Freedom*, 198–9.

[72] But see Green, *Prolegomena to Ethics*, Sect. 245, where Green holds that common good remains unrealized where citizens merely enjoy "negative" rights to "be let alone." And by merely leaving each other alone, their lives remain competitively uncoordinated rather than mutually re-enforcing. Negative rights-respecting societies are therefore incompletely morally self-realizing.

consideration."[73] Hence, moral egoism has "nothing moral in it" as Mill would say because it is not grounded in impartiality. And common good indeed makes little sense if impartiality is morally irrelevant. If common good is to serve as a principle of practical reasoning, then impartiality must be taken seriously.

Now Green indeed sometimes appears to advocate moralistic egoism in discussing common good. In having discovered how one's pleasures and pains depend on the pleasures and pains of others, morally disposed persons "must be able in the contemplation of a possible satisfaction" of themselves to "include the satisfaction of those others, and that a satisfaction of them as ends to themselves." Such persons invariably seek a "permanent well-being in which the permanent well-being of others is included."[74] In other words, one's own good remains the prevailing reason for acting. But fortunately for others, acting accordingly just happens to constitute their good as well.

In struggling to make sense of Green's notion of common good, Brink likewise seems initially inclined to read him as an egoist. Because, according to Green, others are my "alter egos," I have reason to promote their self-realization as contributing to my own.[75] Their self-realization is not only their good but mine as well and vice versa, making self-realization a common good. But if this is all common good comes to, then Skorupski is right and Green is fundamentally a moral egoist. Each is a common good to the rest instrumentally. And this commonality holds for the common goodness of each person's good will as well. Good willing may be indeed some kind of unlimited resource, but instrumentality is what makes any resource a resource.

Notwithstanding good willing's limitlessness and instrumentality, it is nevertheless hard to see how its exercise does not entail competition. What if, despite the purity of my will to be good, I must choose between aiding my best of friends or assisting some "distant Mysian" (to borrow from Brink)? Or worse yet, what if I simply cannot respect my friend's rights without simultaneously violating the rights of someone distant and unknown to me? Such dilemmas typify casuistry because they typify everyday life whether we are fully conscious of them or not. Brink, then, is entirely correct in suggesting that moral self-realization does not guarantee "extreme harmony" although it might well foster considerable, and nearly

---

[73] Skorupski, "Green and the Idealist Conception of a Person's Good," 49.
[74] Green, *Prolegomena to Ethics*, Sect. 201.
[75] Brink, "Introduction," *Prolegomena to Ethics*, xl–xli.

as precious, "moderate harmony." That is, a world in which people decisively committed themselves to becoming moral persons, would surely go far in achieving wide-ranging harmony, but distant, faceless Mysians would invariably suffer, however little, from our good will towards our loved ones, friends and associates. And sometimes they would suffer a lot insofar as protecting those close to us can only be done by mistreating those far from us, with just war being the most compelling example. Even though morality is universal in scope for Green, it is nevertheless not universal in degree. Because, in his view, our moral obligations expand outward con-centrically, we are fated to at least a moderate disharmony of interests. Moral self-realization, though a limitless mutual resource, cannot make obligations compossible. Still, as sympathetic critics like Brink and Skorupski insist, we have good reason to commend Green for reminding us how much the good of others constitutes our very own.[76]

Good will, for Hobhouse, is likewise a narrower kind of willing and is thus a purer kind of good as well. It is a "rational" form of willing which, as we earlier saw for Hobhouse, means *consciously* unifying our lives around our permanent, "root" interests primarily. To will rationally is to will one's life as a harmonious project according to "conceptions, ideals, or principles which appeal to personality as a whole."[77] Good will, however, is more than just rational will for, by the former, we also make the "permanent

---

[76] Skorupski, "Green and the Idealist's Conception of a Person's Good," 49–50, and Brink, "Introduction," *Prolegomena to Ethics*, cviii–cix. Brink, however, contends that Green, following Aristotle, possesses the resources for at least avoiding moral egoism. According to Brink, both Aristotle and Green viewed friendship as non-instrumental self-love wherein friends are concerned with each other's well-being for the other's own sake and for the "constitutive" contribution the well-being of each makes to the well-being of the other (xlvii–xlviii). By implication, each person's moral self-realization, as Green conceives it, is intrinsically valuable as well as constitutively valuable in the same way. Moral self-realization, in short, is utterly non-conflictual. For Brink's application of the problem of the remotest Mysian to Green's ethics, see li–lv. Note especially his remark that Green encourages us to "think of the degrees of connectedness and continuity in terms of a set of concentric circles with myself occupying the inner circle and the remotest Mysian occupying the outer circle" (liii). Brink also suggests that Green's moral theory is impartial insofar as its scope is universal, extending all the way out to distant Mysians. Yet, it endorses partiality insofar as the good of distant Mysians counts less than my own and as those close to me (liii). And this partiality is simply another way of conceding that self-realization is not, after all, a non-competitive common good. Or, once more following Brink, while Green's conception of common good can accommo-date "moderate" harmony of interests, it cannot accommodate conflict-free, "extreme" harmony (liii–liv). Brink's account of Green's conception of common good is otherwise obscure. For instance, Brink says ambiguously that Green "links" self-realization and common good by making the latter an "ingredient" of the former (xl–xlii and liii–liv). For a fuller discussion of the ethical import of the remotest Mysian, see Julia Annas, *The Morality of Happiness* (Oxford: Oxford University Press, 1993), ch. 12. Annas borrows this notion of the remotest Mysian from Plato's *Theaetetus*.

[77] Hobhouse, *Mind in Evolution*, 350.

welfare of others," and not just our "own permanent welfare," our over-riding conscious end.[78] We privilege our root-interest in their welfare as a paramount interest.

For Hobhouse, too, good will is a necessary condition of will. Like Green, as noted in the previous chapter, Hobhouse insists that each of us is a "transpersonal reference."[79] The self-realization of each depends upon the self-realization of all.[80] Hence, others must have opportunities to cultivate themselves, to will themselves as harmonious personalities. In short, each of us must become a moral personality by exhibiting good will. To recall Hobhouse once more from Chapter 3, social "development 'as a moral being' will mean a development which harmonizes with social life, and so *fits in with* and *contributes* to the development of others" (again my italics). And becoming a moral personality by "fit[ting] in with" and "contribut[ing]" to the development of others means "remodel[ing]" one's will. Full self-realization is not "any sort of realization of any sort of self."[81] It entails both respecting others' rights (both their negative rights to be left alone and their positive rights to be empowered with opportunities) and acting beneficently.[82]

Will, in sum for Hobhouse, is a kind of internal freedom as it is with Green. And as with Green, Hobhouse's theory of willing resonates with the same symbiotic interaction between different kinds of freedom that we saw in Chapter 3 characterized his theory of freedom. For Hobhouse, as a kind of internal freedom, will is the "self in its active [internal] unity," while good will (also a kind of internal freedom) is "moral freedom" or the "harmony of the whole self in the multitudinous relations which constitute the web of its interest."[83] "Moral freedom," as a "willing partnership of the citizen in the common life," makes, in turn, external "freedom of man in society" possible, optimizing everyone's chances of becoming both as

---

[78] *Ibid.*, 352.   [79] Hobhouse, *The Rational Good*, 145.

[80] "The perfection of the human soul," Hobhouse insists, "is a function of the perfection of others." Hobhouse, *Mind in Evolution*, 388.

[81] Hobhouse, *The Rational Good*, 200. Hobhouse adds, "Self-realization must mean (a) not any kind of experience in which some psychical capacity is fulfilled, but an orderly development of an organic whole, and (b) this development, if it is to form part of a 'common' good, must be conditioned by the equally desirable development of other human beings."

[82] In *Social Development*, 259, Hobhouse says that both rights and duties are "conditions of or elements in [the] common good" of personality. See as well Hobhouse, *The Rational Good*, 161–2, where Hobhouse observes that the "self must have some other person to care for" otherwise it is "stifled." Every individual "should look beyond himself." Even if "he is bringing up his child or serving the State, or stubbing Thornaby waste, he is doing his part in a harmonious movement."

[83] Hobhouse, *The Elements of Social Justice*, 51 and 56.

internally and morally free as possible.[84] And becoming internally free gives each the psychological dexterity to become more morally free. In the language of will and willing, the flourishing of good will stimulates the flourishing of will, which, in turn, further enlivens good will.

This symbiotic dynamic between will and good will (and external and moral freedom) reinforces the thoroughly communitarian disposition of Hobhouse's social ontology. Hobhouse's self is no abstract, sallow specter. Our interests, especially our root-interests, are not related to will and good will voluntaristically thereby reducing the self to an antecedently individuated, metaphysical phantom. Our interests are never arbitrary expressions of preference that we, as unencumbered selves, simply select from a capacious menu of possibilities. Each of us, as "transpersonal reference," is thoroughly embedded in a particular community where our interests are mostly provided, or contoured, in advance.[85]

Even Green, despite his neo-Kantian enthusiasms, consumed too much Hegel to think that we could have most any will simply by decisively committing ourselves arbitrarily to some subset from the panoply of possible human desires. For Green, lest we forget, humans can only develop their capacities in society and they only develop particular capacities in particular societies. "Social life is to personality what language is to thought" only because social life and language are always of a particular kind. New liberal self-realization is thickly situated.[86]

PLEASURE AND HAPPINESS

In *Perfectionism*, Hurka contends that "natural tendency doctrines" comprise one of the many varieties of perfectionism. "Natural tendency doctrines" hold "optimistically, that humans tend naturally to develop their nature to a high degree, and perhaps to the highest degree possible."[87] The "extensional" version of such doctrines holds, furthermore, that humans often desire states "co-extensive" with the development of their natures simply because such states are contingently co-extensive. For Hurka, Plato,

---

[84] Hobhouse, *Social Development*, 35.

[85] We are, to borrow from Stephen Mulhall and Adam Swift in *Liberals and Communitarians* (15), "parasitic on society" for the very way we understand and realize ourselves. Our identities, in short, are not prior to our ends. Nor are they entirely constituted by society either. Though, for Hobhouse, we are confined to particular evaluative horizons, we should nevertheless aspire, as Talyor or Walzer might say, to transcend them critically.

[86] And precisely because we are so thoroughly situated and constituted by our interactions with each other, we are each a common good to each other.

[87] Hurka, *Perfectionism*, 24.

Marx and Green are "extensional" perfectionists who have been wrongly interpreted as utilitarians because they insist that realizing human capacities also tends to be co-extensively pleasant.[88]

Now Hurka is correct to classify Green as an "extensional" perfectionist for whom pleasure was contingently co-extensive with self-realization (effective willing). As Green says, "it is not pleasure as such, or by itself, that he [the morally good individual] is seeking to produce, but pleasure as an *incident* of a life of which the value or desirability does not consist in its pleasantness" (my italics).[89] Such persons fully appreciate that good is never "a succession of pleasures but a fulfillment of itself, a bettering of itself, a realisation of its capabilities, on the part of the human soul."[90] Insofar as one's interests are the latter, "he must indeed anticipate pleasure in their realisation, but the objects, not the pleasure, form the actuating content of his idea of true well-being."[91] Or as Green puts it somewhat differently in a passage previously cited, whereas good is pleasure for utilitarians, "in this treatise the common characteristic of good is that it satisfies some desire." In "all satisfaction of desire there is pleasure, and thus pleasantness in an object is a necessary incident of its being good."[92]

This last passage differs somewhat from the preceding two in the way that Green casts his conception of good. Whereas in the first two passages, good consists in *realizing* capacities, in the last it consists in *satisfying* desires. (And as we have seen insofar as willing one's own moral perfection is the highest form of desiring, the second passage further implies that morally good consists in satisfied good willing.) Of course, one might insist that one cannot realize capacities without simultaneously satisfying desires but realizing and satisfying are nevertheless dissimilar. Notwithstanding these subtle and perplexing differences, pleasure is nonetheless a contingent by-product in both cases.

In any case as we saw in Chapter 2, pleasure is psychologically unavailable as a source of well-being for Green since the desire for well-being is necessarily a desire for an "abiding satisfaction of an abiding self." That is, in desiring well-being, we desire something enduring possessing depth. We desire an "ordering of life" that creates a personality.[93] Since pleasures

---

[88] *Ibid.*, 25–6. Hurka also notes that Rawls's Aristotelian Principle exemplifies non-perfectionist extensionality.

[89] Green, *Prolegomena to Ethics*, Sect. 238.   [90] *Ibid.*, Sect. 239.

[91] *Ibid.*, Sect. 234.   [92] *Ibid.*, Sect. 171.

[93] See especially *ibid.*, Sect. 234. Green explains, "The demand for an abiding self-satisfaction has led to an ordering of life in which some permanent provision is made, better or worse, for the satisfaction of those interests which are not interests in the procuring of pleasure, but which may be described most generally as interests in the development of our faculties, and in the like development of those for whom we care."

follow each other serially, each vanishing as soon as the next appears, nobody can possibly experience aggregated pleasure. Hence, as we saw, aggregate pleasure cannot be a coherent object of desire and, thus, cannot be a source of abiding well-being.[94]

We can better appreciate Green's aversion to utilitarianism by returning once more to his theory of will and good will. As we saw, Green held that, in willing, we identify with some of our desires by taking them into ourselves and resolutely living for them. And in good willing, we steadfastly identify with our desire to be a particular kind of person. We decisively commit ourselves to our desire to become a *moral* person. We will our own moral perfection as an ongoing endeavor. But if we try to will unadorned pleasure, we doom ourselves to frustration for such pleasures are so ephemeral. How can we, Green might say, identify with something so precarious? How can we perfect ourselves by decisively committing ourselves to something so evanescent? Hence, pleasures can never be the basis for identity and, consequently, for genuine personality including genuine moral personality. One might just as futilely try to will the experience of infinite space or time as try to will aggregate pleasure as good.[95] Because the quality of the will depends on the kinds of objects willed, willing incoherent objects, like pleasure, is self-defeating bad will.

Though Hurka says little about Hobhouse, we might classify him as an "extensional" perfectionist too. Following Bradley and Green, Hobhouse faulted Benthamism for reducing good to no more than serial and fleeting moments of pleasure. Like Green, as we saw previously, he urged that good had to be stable and abiding if it was to be a coherent object of will.

In other words, for Hobhouse, attempting to will pleasure amounts to attempting to will our lives, not around "root" interests, but around passing sensations of pleasure. Attempting to unify our lives around pleasure therefore leaves our personalities unfocused and chaotically structured. As a consequence, we never develop "strongly marked" identities.

---

[94] For a more complete analysis of Green's objections to pleasure as a credible object of desire and criticisms of Green's position, see Chapter 2. For Kant's similar objections, see Kant, *Fundamental Principles of the Metaphysics of Morals*, 24.

[95] For a valuable analysis of Hegel's dissatisfaction with utilitarianism for being psychologically incoherent on grounds that anticipate Green, see A. S. Walton, "Hegel, Utilitarianism and the Common Good," *Ethics*, 93 (July, 1983). No doubt, Green (and Bradley) owed much to Hegel's criticisms of utilitarianism. And see Brink, "Introduction," *Green's Prolegomena to Ethics*, xxxviii–xxxix and lxxvii, which overstates Green's rejection of classical, though not Millian, utilitarianism. Brink insists that Green rejects "evaluative hedonism" because he rejects "psychological hedonism" since a "sum of pleasures is not itself a pleasure." In the next section, I argue that Green's anti-utilitarianism was ambivalent despite his criticisms of psychological hedonism.

Of course, insofar as we fail to develop internal harmony of will, we can never develop external harmony of will or good will.

Hobhouse's simultaneous debts to Mill and Green, noted in Chapter 3, are worth revisiting here. Recall how in *The Rational Good*, Hobhouse acknowledges his indebtedness to both Mill and Green though with some reservations.[96] Regarding Mill specifically, he says:

To the first [personality] belong[s] the mode of action that we have called will, and the mode of feeling that we call happiness. To the second [impulses and experiences], the mode of conation that we call Desire and the modes of feeling that we call pleasure and pain. We should, therefore, diverge from Mill in his definition of happiness as a sum of pleasures. Happiness and pleasure are states of mind possessing the same feeling-tone. We may, if we like, take the term pleasure as generic and say that happiness is a mode of consciousness dependent on the relatively stable character and position of the personality as a whole, and endowed with pleasurable feeling-tone. But we shall not resolve happiness into a series of pleasurable states.[97]

Willing, therefore, is not just the quest for stable personality rather than for maximum pleasure. Once again, we see that when successful, it also engenders happiness, which is a *lasting*, rather than fleeting, "mode of consciousness." A fulfilling life rich in personality is equally a happy life. Both flourish or wane concurrently so that either inscribes the other's existence. The kind of concord between happiness and personality nevertheless varies somewhat. It varies "not only according to individual temperament and circumstances, but also according to the current ideas of life and society" reminding us of how self-realization was nevertheless socially contextualized for Hobhouse.[98]

Regarding his indebtedness to Green, we should recall especially Hobhouse's concession of how his moral theory diverged from Green's only modestly. But whereas Green treated happiness as a "secondary" by-product of good, Hobhouse viewed happiness as "integral and essential" to good. For Hobhouse, good was partially constituted by happiness. So it seems, then, that while Green is a straightforward "extensional" perfectionist, Hobhouse is not. Hobhouse is clearly a perfectionist and a eudaemonist but not in the sense that his eudaemonism piggybacked contingently on his perfectionism. His eudaemonism was integral, and

---

[96] "The theory of harmony stands in close relation on the one side to the Utilitarian principle as developed by J. S. Mill, and on the other hand to the form taken by Ethical Idealism in the hands of T. H. Green." Hobhouse, *The Rational Good*, 193.
[97] *Ibid.*, 194.   [98] Hobhouse, *Mind in Evolution*, 431.

not external, to his perfectionism.[99] The history of moral philosophy going back to Aristotle is, of course, replete with skirmishes over how closely moral goodness and happiness are linked. And if, as a matter of fact they are not inexorably linked, as contemporary moral psychologists such as Owen Flanagan claim, then Green, ironically, turns out being the "better" psychologist than the more scientific Hobhouse.[100]

CONSEQUENTIALIST PERFECTIONISM

Plainly, a great deal of idealism invests Green's conceptions of will and self and his criticisms of utilitarianism. A great deal of idealism also lingers on in Hobhouse's version of perfectionism despite the latter's efforts to distance himself from idealism's sour milk. And as we have seen, Bradley's idealism, in particular, reverberates in the respective perfectionisms of Green and Hobhouse. Like Green and Hobhouse, Bradley faults utilitarians for foolishly believing that good resides in fruitlessly attempting to experience a sum of evanescent pleasures. Like Green and Hobhouse, he holds that utilitarians consequently misunderstand the nature of the self reducing the self to a series of pleasurable experiences. And like them, he also rejects Kantianism as an alternative to utilitarianism because Kantianism impoverishes goodness of will reducing it to an empty formalism. The categorical imperative demands merely that one be self-consistent.[101]

---

[99] Ritchie, as we shall see in greater detail in the next chapter, was also a straightforward extensional perfectionist like Green. For Ritchie, pleasure was likewise a contingent offshoot of good qua self-realization. See, for instance, D. G. Ritchie [1905], "Moral Philosophy: On the Methods and Scope of Ethics," *Philosophical Studies* in *Collected Works of D. G. Ritchie*, Vol. v, ed. P. Nicholson (Bristol: Thoemmes), 299.

[100] "My own view is that the tensions among various ideals – happiness, personal maturity, psychological health, moral goodness – are real. These tensions partially explain why the ethical life is almost never found unproblematically appealing and is almost never seen as easily integratable with all our other legitimate aspirations." Owen Flanagan, *Varieties of Moral Personality* (Cambridge, MA: Harvard University Press, 1991), 318. But he also says: "Happiness, goodness, and psychological health are not inexorably linked. There do exist, however, some relations among the three concepts, some patterns of co-occurrence, which we can seek to amplify by paying attention to creating social and political arrangements which raise self-esteem, project reasonable ethical standards, and widely distribute the resources necessary for happy, good, and healthy lives" (332).

[101] According to Don MacNiven, the "job of the will is to subjugate desire" for Kant whereas for Bradley its "job is to bring together the disparate elements of the psyche into a coherent harmony." Hobhouse's debts to Bradley seem palpable. (See Don MacNiven, "Bradley's Critiques of Utilitarian and Kantian Ethics," *Idealistic Studies*, 14, 1 [1984], 81). Compare Sandel's view that utilitarianism's faulty (Parfitian) conception of the self as a series of desires paved the way for the equally faulty and opposite neo-Kantian conception of the architectural self which supposedly exists behind its desires selecting some and discarding others while authoring a life plan. (See Michael Sandel, "Morality and the Liberal Ideal," *The New Republic*, 190, 18 [May 7, 1984], 17.) Again, for a

Nevertheless, for all their idealist criticisms of utilitarianism, for all the idealist "cream" that they imbibed, Green and Hobhouse were consequentialists. More precisely, they were consequentialist perfectionists.

In *Perfectionism*, Hurka contends that the "best perfectionism is a maximizing consequentialism that is time- and agent-neutral, telling us to care equally about the perfection of all humans at all times." Its "ultimate goal" is the "greatest development of human nature by all humans everywhere."[102] Though agent-neutral, in practice it tells each of us to attend to our own lives disproportionately. Because each of us is better able to promote his or her own perfection over that of others, each can do more for overall perfection by focusing on cultivating his or her own perfection.[103] Hence, Hurka concludes, the best practical strategy is an *indirect* strategy grounded in strong moral rights guaranteeing equal freedom. Strong rights promote overall perfection by providing citizens with the equal freedom, a necessary though insufficient condition, to cultivate their own separate conceptions of perfection in their own way. (And because our separate quests for perfection are purportedly compossible, they reinforce each other thereby amplifying general perfection further.) Hence, the best perfectionism is as solidly liberal as it is consequentialist.[104]

Green's perfectionism was a maximizing, liberal consequentialism in Hurka's best perfectionist sense. In the first place, recall from Chapter 2 that for Green, promoting the "exercise by the greatest number of a [good] will" was the criterion of moral rightness. But given good will's ambiguous nature, we are fully entitled to "take refuge" in the greatest happiness of the greatest number as a substitute criterion of moral rightness as long as we interpret happiness "except as including and dependent upon [this] unimpeded" exercise of the greatest good will among the greatest number. But

---

thoughtful analysis of Bradley's criticisms of utilitarianism and Kantianism, see Nicholson's invaluable *The Political Philosophy of the British Idealists*, especially 17–23. Nicholson also maintains that, despite the many similarities between Bradley and Green, "it is unlikely that Green influenced the main positions or most of the detailed argument of *Ethical Studies*, and that it is going too far to describe Bradley as Green's 'disciple.'" (50).

[102] Hurka, *Perfectionism*, 55.
[103] "The acts best for others are also best for oneself, and each can choose rightly by agent-neutral standards, given only agent-relative aims." *Ibid.*, 68.
[104] "This connects perfectionism with liberalism and also gives liberalism a new rationale. The liberal commitment to liberty need not rest on agnosticism about the good or on the view that only free choice is good. It can be grounded in a deep fact about human perfection: that each person's achievement of it must be largely her own." *Ibid.*, 153. Consequentialist perfectionism, according to Hurka, also favors a moderately egalitarian distribution of basic resources because all citizens must enjoy empowering equal opportunities if they are to cultivate their personalities successfully. Hurka's consequentialist perfectionism, like Raz's, is thus a form of what Hobhouse labeled "liberal socialism" when referring to his own perfectionist liberalism.

we can now better appreciate why greatest happiness of the greatest number can substitute so effectively as a backup moral standard. Because successful good willing was generally "co-extensive" with pleasure for Green, promoting the latter, a far easier practical target, fortunately promoted the former by-and-large. Indeed, Green's insistence that happiness be interpreted as being "dependent" on the exercise of good will implies such extensionality.[105]

Issues of utilitarian substitution aside, we should recall what I regard as an extremely significant passage from *Prolegomena to Ethics* cited previously in Chapter 2:

When from the nature of the case, however, a consideration of effects can alone enter into the moral valuation of an act, the effects to be considered, according to our view, will be different from those of which the Utilitarian, according to his principles, would take account. They will be effects, not in the way of producing pleasure, but in the way of contributing to that perfection of mankind, of which the essence is a good will on the part of all persons. These are the effects which, in our view, an action must in fact tend to produce, if it is one that *ought to be done*, according to the most limited sense of that phrase; just as these are the effects *for the sake of which* it must be done, if it is done *as* it ought to be done.[106]

The expression "consideration of effects alone" is revealing for it suggests that there is another perspective (that of promoting good will qua unconditional good) from which to consider the "moral valuation of an act." Green continues, "There is no real reason to doubt that the good or evil in the motive of an action is *exactly* measured by the good or evil in its consequences, as rightly estimated – estimated, that is, in their bearing on the production of a good will or the perfecting of mankind."[107] In other words

---

[105] Also see Green, "Lecture E. T. 78," where Green says that "there is a tendency to greater general happiness" in pursuing self-realization. Also recall Green's remark, cited in Chapter IV, in *Prolegomena to Ethics*, Sect. 356 that if the Millian utilitarian "is committed to no more than a certain doctrine of the criterion of morality – the doctrine that the value of actions and institutions is to be measured in the last resort by their effect on the nett sum of pleasures enjoyable by all human, or perhaps all sentient beings, the difference between him and one who would substitute for this 'nett sum, etc.' 'the fulfilment of human capacities' may be *practically* small" (my emphasis). Here, Green suggests that maximizing the development of personality among *all* individuals can "substitute" for maximizing greatest happiness among them rather than the other way around as in the passage from Sect. 286. So, these two criteria can stand in for each other in terms of their "practical" implications for right action.

[106] Green, *Prolegomena to Ethics*, Sect. 294. Other British idealists did not fail to notice the consequentialist nature of Green's moral philosophy. For instance, in *Six Radical Thinkers* (London: Edward Arnold, 1907), 241, John MacCunn observes that, like the utilitarians, Green's "eye is on results." Moreover, "Barring its [utilitarianism's] hedonism against which he [Green] waged a lifelong war, he does generous justice to the practical value of utilitarianism as a political creed."

[107] Green, *Prolegomena to Ethics*, Sect. 295. In the same section, Green continues: "With the whole spiritual history of the action before us on the one side, with the whole sum and series of its effects before us on the other, we should presumably see that just so far as a good will, i.e. a will determined

and *quite remarkably*, one's success in promoting the good will of others exactly reflects the purity of one's motives. Purity of motive, like happiness, is "co-extensive" with consequences qua good will but unlike happiness, it is unequivocally "co-extensive."

Green, therefore, was an "extensional" perfectionist in a double sense. On the one hand, he held (as did Bradley more or less as we saw in Chapter 1) that promoting self-realization, particularly moral self-realization, was *usually* co-extensive with maximizing happiness. Thus, greatest happiness for all could serve as a second-best (handier) substitute criterion for moral rightness *most of the time*. Indeed, the practical convergence between utilitarianism and his own theory was rooted in such co-extensional efficacy. Hence, Green could be mistaken for a utilitarian though he clearly was not one.

On the other hand, he also held that promoting moral self-realization, *particularly* moral self-realization qua effective good will, for all was *always* co-extensive with acting virtuously.[108] Hence, greatest moral self-realization for all can serve as the infallibly best criterion for moral rightness *all of the time* because acting virtuously was constitutive of promoting moral self-realization non-aggregatively and vice versa. That is why Green concludes that actions are not deemed good (or bad) solely in terms of motives exclusively nor results exclusively. They are deemed good in terms of both, making both mutually co-extensive. They are not, to repeat remarks cited previously, "good in virtue of any results except results in way of production of good character, nor good in virtue of these results unless proceeding from a character *interested* in production of such results" (my italics).[109] Results matter morally when they are about moral motives; that

---

by interest in objects contributory to human perfection, has had more or less to do with bringing the action about, there is more or less good, i.e. more or less contribution to human perfection, in its effects."

[108] I emphasize "particularly" because moral self-realization, besides exhibiting good will as we have seen, also includes acting justly towards others by respecting their rights.

[109] Green, "Note D on Pleasure and Kant's Moral Philosophy." In addition, *Prolegomena to Ethics*, Sect. 377, Green says, "the statement that the act of self-sacrifice has value in itself is not to be understood as denying that it has its value in its consequences, but as implying that those consequences, to be of intrinsic value, must be *of a kind* with the act itself, as an exercise of a character having its dominant interest in some form of human perfection." Promoting human perfection as the "bettering of men would mean their advance in a goodness the same in principle as that which appears in the sacrifice enjoined, and this sacrifice itself would be regarded as already an *instalment* of the good to be more largely attained in its consequences" (my italics). And see Sect. 293 where Green says that "actions which *ought* to be done, in the fullest sense of the word, are actions expressive of a good will, in the sense that they represent a character of which the dominant interest is in conduct contributory to the perfection of mankind, in doing that which so contributes for the sake of doing it." In other words, right actions simultaneously *promote* by *expressing* good will. By

is, when motives are not simply a means to some different, external value such as is the case with conventional utilitarianism.

Avital Simhony has argued, as I noted previously, that I confuse consequences with consequentialism in interpreting Green. In her view, "Consequences do not play a consequentialist role in Green's moral philosophy."[110] According to her, Green sought to transcend the dichotomizing rivalry between deontology and consequentialism by steering a "middle path" between the Scylla of Kantian formalism and the Charybdis of utilitarian disrespect for persons as ends.[111] Hence, Green was no consequentialist and he certainly was no utilitarian. But, of course, intending to steer a middle course does not guarantee success in doing so.

Contrary to Simhony, certain kinds of consequences do matter morally for Green, namely those that coincide with certain kinds of motives. For Green, acting from consequentialist perfectionist motives by decisively committing to being a moral person invariably produces the desired consequentialist perfectionist results. Promoting moral self-realization and acting virtuously are thus perfectly co-extensive allowing the former to substitute perfectly in place of the latter as a criterion of right.[112]

---

suggestive and controversial comparison, see W. D. Ross [1930], *The Good and the Right* (Indianapolis: Hackett, 1988), 46–7: "An act is not right because it, being one thing, produces good results different from it; it is right because it is itself the production of a certain state of affairs."

[110] Avital Simhony, "Was T. H. Green a Utilitarian?," *Utilitas*, 7, 1 (May, 1995), 122.

[111] Ibid., 135. Simhony adds on the same page that I confuse consequences with consequentialism in Green because I fail to appreciate that the "[c]onsequentialist consideration of consequences relates to the evaluation of action by reference *only* to the maximization of a specified [presumably external] good" (my italics). But, as we are beginning to see, there are different ways of theorizing maximization.

[112] Green is not always consistent in insisting that maximizing moral self-realization perfectly matches, and therefore perfectly reveals, morally good motives. Hence, Simhony's criticism of my account is not without textual evidence. For instance, in *Prolegomena to Ethics*, Sect. 294, Green says, "if two actions could be alike in their moral effects (as they very well may be in production of pleasure) which represent, the one a more virtuous, the other a less virtuous character, they would still be quite different in moral value. The one would be more, the other less, of a good, according to the kind of character which they severally represent." However, if Green means "production of pleasure" only by "moral effects" as the phrase in parentheses suggests, then Green is not arguing inconsistently. He is merely reiterating that the production of pleasure does not always mark the existence of good will. Yet in his discussion in Sect. 111 of *Lectures on the Principles of Political Obligation* of the difficulties in determining whether political rebellion is morally justifiable, Green notes: "But where the probable effects of a certain line of action are at the time of taking it very obscure, we cannot be sure that relatively the best character will lead a man to take the line which turns out best in the result, or that because a line of action has turned out well in result, the character of the man who adopted it was good." However, precisely because of this ignorance, we have no alternative but to judge his action "retrospectively" in terms of its results. As Green adds in Sect. 112, we have little option but to "fall back on the generalization, that the best man – the man most disinterested in perfecting humanity . . . is most likely to act in a way that is good as measured by its results."

One might stubbornly resist admitting that Green was a consequentialist by insisting that, for Green, motives and consequences are the "inner" and "outer" sides of action. As the "outer" side, consequences merely disclose motives which are foundational. Were we omniscient, we would not need consequences to decipher motives.[113] But we are not omniscient and we therefore have little choice but to fall back on consequences. Given the doubly co-extensive nature of Green's moral theory, maximizing happiness *often* unveils motives for us whereas promoting self-realization, particularly its moral variety, *always* does.[114] Both kinds of consequences were first-rate ciphers of good motives though the former was less effective,

---

[113] Simhony seems to imply as much: "Being internal, motives cannot be assessed but by the acting agent himself or herself or by the perfect knowledge of God. Green's point, therefore, is that external observers cannot evaluate motives but only the effects of actions which, he claims, mirror their motives." See Simhony, "Was T. H. Green a Utilitarian?," 136. In "On the Meaning of the Term 'Motive,' and on the Ethical Significance of Motives," *International Journal of Ethics*, 4 (1893–94), 93–4, Ritchie similarly observes: "Motives being identical with the spirit in which an act is done are, it seems to me, ideally, the true subject of moral judgment; but, in practice, it is well to confess that motives could be known in their fulness only to an omniscient judge, and for human beings it is wiser on the whole to pronounce judgment on acts in their general aspect. The individual cannot know even his own motives adequately. In the long run, but only in the long run and on the whole good motives cannot bring forth bad (i.e., socially mischievous) acts; and when we judge the character and the motives, we are inferring the nature of the tree from its habitual fruits. But we may err in very many cases; and it is certainly better to *discuss* the right and wrong acts, where we can directly apply a measure and a standard, – viz., their effects on social well-being ... In the case of legislation it is absolutely necessary to deal with acts (the connection between English utilitarianism and the theories of legislation will suggest itself)." For Green's admission that, were we omniscient, we would not need to fall back on consequences, see *Prolegomena to Ethics*, Sect. 295: "For an omniscient being, indeed, the distinction – unavoidable for us – between the judgment that an action ought to be done and the judgment that an action is done as it ought to be done, would not exist. It is occasioned by a separation in the moral judgment of act from motive, only possible for an imperfect intelligence." In short, not being omniscient, we are compelled to evaluate actions "as" they ought to be done, i.e. in terms of their consequences. See, too, Green, *Prolegomena to Ethics*, Sect. 354, where Green insists that because assessing the motives of others is considerably more difficult compared with assessing our own, consequentialist practical reasoning is especially unavoidable when making normative judgments about them. In other words, being more opaque than our own motives, we have little choice to be consequentialists most of the time. But we could perhaps do without such a crutch when evaluating ourselves.

[114] For Kant's likely influence on Green in this regard, see Kant, *Fundamental Principles of the Metaphysics of Morals*, 19 where Kant says: "Its [good will's] usefulness or fruitfulness can neither add to nor take away anything from this value. It would be, as it were, only the setting to enable us to handle it the more conveniently in common commerce [to handle it practically as Green would say], or to attract to it the attention of those who are not yet connoisseurs, but not to recommend it to true connoisseurs, or to determine its value." And see Kant, *The Metaphysics of Morals*, 250–1, where Kant allows that because sympathy likewise naturally tends to accompany duty, it can substitute for duty whenever the latter's motivating power is too weak. Also see Green's robust qualification, in *Prolegomena to Ethics*, Sect. 361, of pleasure's special connection with self-realization where he says that "although pleasure must be incidental to such realization, it is no way distinctive of it" being frequently no less incidental to "animal functions." Hence, being often coterminous with satisfying non-self-realizing desires, pleasure could not serve as a particularly

being more contingent. The latter was an impeccable cipher since the kind of consequences promoted were the very moral dispositions embodied in well-motivated moral behavior.

To underscore this section's argument thus far, for Green, good willing simultaneously instantiated the end it served to promote, namely universal good willing. Acting virtuously was equivalent to promoting virtue, making consequences identical in kind to the actions bringing them about. Acting morally entailed being disposed to promote everyone's moral disposition to do likewise. It meant being in the "right state of mind" as Green would say, which amounts to being in a good will-promoting state of mind. Now Kantian consequentialists like Cummiskey would surely concur that acting according to duty prescribes nothing less. Being disposed to promoting good will in others clearly satisfies what Cummiskey calls a "determining ground" for action untainted by contingent, heteronymous desires. Moreover, because for Green, good willing instantiates the very end it promotes, we can, if necessary, restrict moral appraisal to how effectively such ends are promoted because this extensionality is so hermetically tight. Since any agent's success in promoting good willing overall mirrored the normative status of his or her own will, results mattered morally. Or, at least, they were morally serviceable with uncanny precision. If we were omniscient, we could presumably do without assessing tertiary results, saving us the trouble of having to pose as extensionalist consequentialists when unadulterated deontology will do just fine. We could penetrate the results of actions to the purity of the motives animating them. Normative assessment would be like x-raying external contours for their hidden structural content.

So we have little choice but to rely on good will-promoting results as the best strategy for creatures like ourselves. And insofar as measuring results in terms of promoting good will oftentimes proves cumbersome, then measuring results in terms of promoting pleasure will substitute capably enough much of the time because pleasure-promoting actions usually mark the presence of good will. Bentham and J. S. Mill were not entirely misplaced in looking to pleasure and pain because both phenomena were so visceral, tangible and therefore evaluatively accessible.[115]

effective marker for self-realization. Also see Sect. 333 for Green's reservations about the practical efficacy of utilitarianism where he says that hedonistic utilitarianism, despite contributing to rationalizing social and political life for the better, nevertheless risks producing "practical evils."

[115] In *Pleasure and The Good Life* (Oxford: Oxford University Press, 2004), Fred Feldman defends a form of hedonism that resembles the kind of hedonism I am imputing to Green. Feldman readily acknowledges that his favored version of intrinsic attitudinal hedonism is "extensionally equivalent" to Darwall's Aristotelian theory of flourishing. That is, even though his and Darwall's theories are

Of all of Green's recent interpreters, Brink comes the closest to capturing the consequentialist nature of Green's perfectionism. As noted earlier, Brink properly concludes that Green's ethics could be viewed as some kind of perfectionist utilitarianism.[116] Moreover, Brink fittingly observes that Green holds that motives and effects are both germane to morality. Motives concern *how* acts ought to be done while effects concern *what* ought to be done. Brink does not develop this distinction very far other than to suggest obscurely that the latter asks a broader question that "includes" the former.[117] Nonetheless, he clearly appreciates that Green is a consequentialist for whom motives and results are acutely intertwined.

However, though Brink captures pivotal features of Green's consequentialist perfectionism, unlike my interpretation, he confuses the relationship between Green's perfectionism and assessment of utilitarianism. While Brink agrees that Green was ambivalent about the practical guidance that his perfectionist moral theory afforded, Brink does not appreciate the extent to which Green conceded that utilitarianism could effectively substitute for his moral theory. Brink says only that Green admits that the "precepts of conventional morality and one's own conscience are adequate guides to conduct and that the goal of moral philosophy should be not so much to reform or to resolve perplexity but provide understanding of familiar moral precepts." Rather than appeal to utilitarianism for substitute guidance, Brink's Green falls back on common sense in Sidgwickian fashion.[118]

Green, then, was a consequentialist whatever his intentions. As Hurka observes, perfectionist acts, including those aimed at maximizing perfection, can "sometimes embody perfection, and contribute to the good by

---

distinct, they nevertheless "yield nearly equivalent evaluations of lives." Moreover: "Perhaps it will be easy to see why the theories yield similar outcomes if we take note of the fact that one can be engaged in valuing activity of the right sort if and only if one is taking intrinsic attitudinal pleasure in some worthy or meritorious object. Even if pleasure is no more than a mere sign of virtuous activity (like the bloom of health on the cheek of one in the flower of his age), if the pleasure occurs when and only when the virtuous activity occurs, we can take either as our guide to the value of the life. Given that these items occur in equal amounts within any life, it seems to make little difference whether we select the activity or the pleasure as the foundation of value. The ranking of lives will be the same" (166).

[116] Brink, "Introduction," *Prolegomena to Ethics*, lxv. Brink adds, rather ambiguously, that Green "could perhaps defend a form of perfectionist utilitarianism, but only as a subordinate, if necessary, aspect of self-realization." Again, see Chapter 2, Note 42. For criticism of Brink's willingness to read Green as perfectionist utilitarian, see Avital Simhony, "A Liberalism of the Common Good: Some Recent Studies of T. H. Green's Moral and Political Theory," *The British Journal of Politics and International Relations*, 7 (2005), 140.

[117] *Ibid.*, lx.

[118] But again recall where Brink also notes that "somewhat surprisingly," Green acknowledges that there "isn't likely to be much difference in the real-world application" between perfectionism and utilitarianism (lxiii–lxiv).

instantiating it now rather than by allowing its occurrence later." They can "sometimes be 'constitutive,' not 'productive,' means to excellence, or components of, not preconditions for, the good." (And, I would add, they can sometimes be both simultaneously.) But this does not mean that theories that commend such acts can't be consequentialist. It merely means that their consequentialism is "harder to see."[119]

Hobhouse was also a consequentialist perfectionist but a consequentialist perfectionist whose consequentialism, compared to Green's, was easier to see. Like Green, he admired Mill but even more reverently. Like Green as well, though less ambiguously, he evaluated the moral rightness of actions in terms of their results. For Hobhouse, moral rightness turned upon particular kinds of "good result." Morally right acts promoted the "development of personality in each member of the community."[120]

Hobhouse was unmistakably a consequentialist and a perfectionist. What made his consequentialism so unmistakable, so easy to see, was the tighter, more deeply interwoven "co-extensional" relationship between the development of personality and happiness. Indeed and as we saw in Chapter 3, insofar as "happiness" and the "kind of life in which it is sought" were "two elements of the same whole," one's degree of happiness necessarily mirrored or expressed the degree to which one was self-realizing. Whereas with Green, purity of motive and consequences in terms of promoting moral personality moved in tandem and perfect harmony (with happiness usually moving in tandem contingently), in Hobhouse, happiness and such consequences moved perfectly together. Thus, Hobhouse's consequentialist perfectionism was just as much a Millian perfectionism.[121]

---

[119] Hurka, *Perfectionism*, 60. Also see Amartya Sen, "Rights and Agency," *Philosophy and Public Affairs*, 11, 1 (Winter, 1982), 29, where Sen says: "Whether consequentialism can accommodate agent relative values will depend on the way outcome morality is characterized. In especially narrow formulations, consequences are defined *excluding* the actions that bring them about, and in this case agent relativity of the 'doer relative' kind would be impossible to accommodate. But this is an arbitrary exclusion, and it is not imposed by the broader characteristics of consequentialism." And see J. L. Mackie, *Ethics: Inventing Right and Wrong* (London: Penguin, 1977), 150, where Mackie says that his brand of utilitarianism takes certain activities as constituting good and as well as serving as a means to it. Or as Green says in *Prolegomena to Ethics*, Sect. 195, about his own "broader" consequentialism, illustrating much the same point, "For the end is that full self-conscious realization of capabilities to which the means lies in the self-conscious exercise of the *same* capabilities – an exercise of them in imperfect realization, but under the governing idea of the desirability of their fuller realization" (my italics).

[120] Hobhouse, *Liberalism*, 68.

[121] Insofar as Hobhouse's consequentialist perfectionism was equally a form of utilitarianism, utilitarian practical reasoning was a serviceable substitute variety of practical reasoning. But Green's claim that utilitarian practical reasoning could also stand in as a serviceable substitute, albeit not perfectly given that happiness was an imperfect token of self-realization, is compromised if not contradicted by his claim that trying to will pleasure as end was bootless and self-defeating. This problem is less acute with

CONCLUSION

We have now seen that the new liberalism was a form of consequentialist perfectionism in Hurka's best sense. For both Green and Hobhouse, to become a moral personality by exhibiting good will, to be morally self-realizing, was simultaneously a matter of promoting self-realization. As with subsequent neo-Kantians like Korsgaard and Gewirth, good willing entails deliberative endorsement. But unlike with them, it is a decisive commitment to, a conscious unifying of our lives around, our fundamental interest in promoting everyone's self-realization. In Green's case, decisively committing to promoting everyone's self-realization characterizes good willing because, much like Cummiskey afterwards, Green fully appreciated that Kantianism entails consequentialism. Or we should at least concede that Kantianism is not incompatible with consequentialism.

For Green, in other words, good willing as decisively committing to the dictates of reason meant respecting each as an end which, in turn, surely required promoting everyone's flourishing as best we can. And we do this best by securing the conditions necessary to universal flourishing. Kantianism, in short, implies consequentialism. And Kantian consequentialism contingently requires liberalism because promoting self-realization directly is self-defeating. Each flourishes best wherever freedom and equal opportunity are guaranteed. The best perfectionist-maximizing strategy was one that constrained the pursuit of perfection within the confines of strong negative and positive moral rights. Since, for Green and Hobhouse, no one can give another personality, each must construct it for him or herself. But each requires enabling positive freedom as well as negative freedom. Thus, as a form of indirect consequentialism, the new liberalism was as modestly egalitarian as it was authentically liberal. And this modest egalitarianism further reinforced the new liberalism's perfectionism.[122]

---

respect to substituting Millian practical reasoning because the latter is not narrowly hedonic but aims, rather, at maximizing happiness qua self-development. Similarly problematic is Green's observation in *Prolegomena to Ethics*, Sect. 161 that obsessive pleasure-seeking is counterproductive, making not seeking pleasure directly the best way to get it. It might seem as if Green is merely reaffirming his view that pleasure is contingently tied to acting for other motives such as for the sake of virtue. However, if utilitarianism is self-defeating, then how can it stand in effectively as a substitute strategy for Green's perfectionist practical reasoning. Perhaps it still can if Green intends merely to condemn egoistic pleasure-seeking (egoistic hedonism) rather than universalistic pleasure-seeking (universal hedonism). For a more complete discussion of this substitution problem in Green, see my "The New Liberalism and the Rejection of Utilitarianism" in *The New Liberalism: Reconciling Liberty and Community*.

[122] I am indebted to Hurka's "Indirect Perfectionism: Kymlicka on Liberal Neutrality," *The Journal of Political Philosophy*, 3, 1 (March, 1995) for me helping appreciate just how indirectly perfectionist the

Furthermore, we have seen how the new liberalism was modestly egalitarian insofar as it was a distribution-sensitive consequentialism. Neither Green nor Hobhouse were good-aggregating consequentialists inasmuch as neither argued that self-realization ought to be *aggregatively* maximized. Both, in effect, operationalized perfection by advocating that it be equally distributed across individuals. Neither theorist, that is, was a crude, good-pooling consequentialist. *All* citizens were to cultivate personality. As Hobhouse never tired of stressing, common good "includes every individual."[123] The new liberalism's liberal authenticity is incontrovertible though not incontrovertibly narrowly individualist.[124]

Finally, we have also seen how the new liberalism was "co-extensively" utilitarian though with Hobhouse this "extensionality" was more hermetic. Whereas for Green, happiness was no more than a contingent and somewhat imperfect hallmark of effective will and good will, it was constitutive of both for Hobhouse. Hobhouse's consequentialism of self-realization was more substantively eudaemonic than Green's. Green's new liberalism was nevertheless "co-extensively" and hermetically consequentialist in a way Hobhouse's was not. Notwithstanding occasional lapses of inconsistency, Green generally insisted that good willing unvaryingly promoted good willing because willing as one ought meant willing everyone else's good will, which meant promoting their good will. Promoting good willing simultaneously instantiated its own content. Green thus brings together Hurka and Cummiskey. What a shame only Hurka seems to have read Green just a little while Cummiskey seems not to have read him at all.

---

new liberalism was. Though Hurka's essay focuses on the shortcomings of Kymlicka's attempt to marry perfectionism and liberal neutrality and makes no reference to the new liberals, it is nevertheless analytically useful for understanding them.

[123] Hobhouse, *Liberalism*, 70 and Hobhouse, *The Labour Movement*, 153, where Hobhouse says: "The best social life consists precisely in the harmonious working out to their fullest possible development of the best capacities of all members of the community. And true liberty, to quote Professor Green again, is found when each man has the greatest possible opportunity for making the best of himself." Hobhouse, interestingly, seems to have interpreted Bentham as distribution-sensitive utilitarian. In *The Elements of Social Justice*, 26, n1, Hobhouse says: "In this respect the Benthamite appeal to number is unsatisfactory. The happiness of many purchased at the expense of the few is better than that of the few purchased at the expense of the many. But it is not harmony. Harmony is not an algebraic sum with a positive result, but a pervading relation. It should, however, be noted that Bentham speaks of 'the greatest happiness of *all*, or in the case of competition, the greatest happiness of the greatest number'" (my italics). Such distribution sensitivity arguably introduces a complicating, second criterion of normative evaluation in addition to maximizing utility.

[124] For more detailed discussion of the non-individualist nature of the new liberalism, see Simhony and Weinstein, "Introduction" in *The New Liberalism: Reconciling Liberty and Community*.

PART II

"New utilitarianism"

CHAPTER 5

Vindicating utilitarianism: D. G. Ritchie

INTRODUCTION

In *Darwin and Hegel*, D. G. Ritchie proclaimed that "in Ethics the theory of natural selection has vindicated all that has proved most permanently valuable in Utilitarianism."[1] For Ritchie, utilitarianism, especially Millian utilitarianism, had much to recommend it. Principally, it rescued moral reasoning from the factious and emotive jumble of intuitionism. Whereas intuitionism leaves morality chaotic, utilitarianism systematizes it. Utilitarianism, however, was not without deficiencies of its own in Ritchie's view, particularly its narrowly hedonic conception of good. Even its Millian variety, though not hedonically cramped, underappreciated the thickly textured nature of good. Good was happiness for Ritchie but it was happiness understood more expansively as self-realization. As far as Ritchie was concerned, Millian liberal utilitarianism was not so much wrongheaded as it was incomplete. Mill's conception of good was inchoate and, even more importantly, his meta-ethical reasoning insufficiently exploited the powerful resources being made available by evolutionary theorizing. In typical new liberal fashion, then, Ritchie enriched Millian utilitarianism with a more complex notion of good. And like L. T. Hobhouse after him, but unlike T. H. Green before him, Ritchie wholeheartedly embraced evolutionary theory in his bid to fashion a more compelling, thoroughly (new) liberal version of utilitarianism.

This chapter begins by examining the kind of utilitarianism Ritchie claims natural selection vindicates. With respect to the kind of utilitarianism vindicated, we shall see how he tries to fortify Millian liberal utilitarianism with new liberal concepts such as self-realization and common good. For Ritchie, like his fellow new liberals, promoting self-realization was the criterion of the morally right. Moreover, promoting self-realization just

---

[1] Ritchie, *Darwin and Hegel, Collected Works of D. G. Ritchie*, 62.

happened to maximize happiness because self-realization and happiness were so deeply and psychologically intertwined. And self-realization was a common good as well insofar as each person's self-realization redounded to everyone else's self-realization.

Next, we will explore how evolutionary theory vindicates utilitarianism, concentrating on Ritchie's contention that natural selection among humans gradually gives way to "rational" selection with the emergence of utilitarian practical reasoning. Of course, vindicating utilitarian reasoning via evolutionary theory raises the specter of ethical naturalism, a peril that Ritchie recognized but did not always negotiate with success.

Herbert Spencer was a specter of a related kind for Ritchie, one that haunted him as recommending a seductive but degraded evolutionary utilitarianism. Spencer was a liberal utilitarian too, who likewise viewed utilitarian practical reasoning as a turning point in human evolution. Spencer, however, was a Lamarckian and Ritchie was not.

Nowhere do the similarities between Ritchie and Spencer converge more revealingly than in their critical assessments of natural rights theory. However, nowhere do Ritchie and Spencer *seem* to diverge more sharply than over this issue. This is due largely to Ritchie's misunderstanding of Spencer on natural rights. Analysis of Ritchie's theory of fundamental rights will also return us to familiar new liberal philosophical themes. Together with Green and Hobhouse, Ritchie was a formative figure in the development of the new liberalism.[2] And the fact that Ritchie, as much as Green and Hobhouse, was considerably indebted to Mill reinforces my claim that the new liberalism and nineteenth-century liberal utilitarianism were more like amicable theoretical cousins than estranged rivals.

Finally, examination of Hume's theory of justice, which anticipates Ritchie's evolutionary utilitarianism so closely in certain important respects, should further help us appreciate the potent family resemblances between the new liberalism and its utilitarian predecessors. Mackie's debts to Hume will assist us still more. All new liberals were at least liberal consequentialists even if they were not unambiguously liberal utilitarians.

---

[2] Whether Green should be considered a new liberal is a matter of some debate. I am tempted to classify him as one because of his powerful influence on later new liberals, especially Ritchie. I concur with Peter Nicholson's judgment that Ritchie is "one of the best exponents and defenders of Green's ideas." Though Nicholson sees more continuity between Green and Ritchie than Michael Freeden, John Morrow and Peter Clarke do, Nicholson is nevertheless less tempted than I am to view Green as a new liberal. For Nicholson's assessment of Ritchie's debts to, and differences from, Green, see Peter Nicholson, "Introduction," *Collected Works of D. G. Ritchie*, Vol. 1, xvii and xxii–iii.

SELF-REALIZATION AND HAPPINESS

In an early essay on Mill's *On Liberty* republished as "Individual Liberty and State Interference" in *The Principles of State Interference*, Ritchie observes: "The State has, as its end, the realisation of the best life by the individual. This best life can only be realised in an organized society – i.e., in the State; so that the State is not a mere means to individual welfare as an end; in a way, the State is an end to itself."[3]

Social life therefore has an ethical aim, namely, promoting individual self-realization for all citizens. Living a certain kind of social life is also partially constitutive of self-realization insofar as realizing the best individual life is, in part, realizing the best social life. Self-realization is communally thick.

The best social life, moreover, does not proscribe certain political policies as out of bounds *a priori*. The "spheres" of the state and the individual are not irrevocably fixed. Rather:

It is much better to ask the Utilitarian question: "Is this particular measure expedient in this case?" Bentham would ask, "Will it tend to the greatest happiness of the greatest number?" – a question profitless in its apparent precision. We must alter it into the vague but less misleading one: . . . "Will it make society healthier?" – a formula Mr. Spencer would probably accept. For Mr. Spencer has admirably used the Aristotelian analogy of health in explaining morality. Healthy [moral] activities are (on the whole, and in the long run) pleasant activities, and so the mistake has arisen of treating the accompanying pleasure, which is *merely a conspicuous external trait*, as if it were the end to be sought. [my italics][4]

Politics, then, should be consequentialist in large part; it should be a species of utilitarian-like practical reasoning. Morally right politics strives to promote everyone's self-realization though it *seems* utilitarian because self-realizing activities are generally pleasant, causing us to misidentify good as pleasure. Pleasure is merely a contingent effect of authentic good, namely, self-realization.

In "Moral Philosophy: On the Methods and Scope of Ethics," Ritchie claims that good is self-realization, though we may say that good is happiness provided that by happiness we mean self-realization.[5] Properly understood, happiness is a contingent by-product of self-realization,

---

[3] Ritchie, *Principles of State Interference*, 102.   [4] *Ibid.*, 107–8.
[5] D.G. Ritchie [1905], "Moral Philosophy: On the Methods and Scope of Ethics," *Philosophical Studies, Collected Works of D. G. Ritchie*, Vol. V, 299.

including moral self-realization, which consists of aiming at everyone's well-being:

> He who attains his end is happy and pleased in the attainment of it; but the end is not therefore happiness. If we say the ultimate end is the wellbeing of all mankind, . . . we mean the same thing as the utilitarian when he speaks of the greatest happiness of the greatest number, but it is put in a less misleading way. We can claim all the advantages of utilitarianism.[6]

Green and Hobhouse, as we have seen, also maintained that pleasure invariably accompanied good qua self-realization. However, like Green but unlike Hobhouse, Ritchie held that self-realization generated pleasure merely as an *external* symptom. For Ritchie, like Green, pleasure was not internal to self-realization as one of its components as it was for Hobhouse.

In "Confessio Fidei," Ritchie buttresses his view that good is self-realization by showing why erroneously pursuing happiness as good is so "hopeless." For our pursuit of good to be possible, our ethical end must be "*something* that we have always to hold before us" (my italics). According to Ritchie, following Green, Mill sometimes understood that good had to be *something* other than happiness insofar as he recognized that "happiness can only be attained by not being directly pursued."[7] Mill intimated that good was self-realization rather than pleasure, by highlighting the importance of the development of individuality and the higher pleasures. Unfortunately, according to Ritchie, Mill sometimes continued mistaking pleasure for good, not fully appreciating that pleasure was simply an offshoot of good.[8]

Now the reason why, for Ritchie as for Green and Hobhouse, pleasure is such a "hopeless" pursuit and therefore cannot possibly be good is that pleasures are serial and fleeting. Being serial and fleeting, they cannot be experienced aggregatively and, consequently, aggregate pleasure cannot plausibly be a legitimate object of desire. Aggregate pleasure cannot be "something" that we can "hold before us." There is no such experience as an aggregate pleasure, including an aggregate of maximum of pleasure. Both are fictions. Only fools would waste their time futilely trying to pursue either. But self-realization is another matter because the self is something enduring and its realization is therefore something possible to aim for. Thus, it is not irrational to desire it. And whatever is a rational

---

[6] *Ibid.*, 299.
[7] D. G. Ritchie [1905], "Confessio Fidei," *Philosophical Studies, Collected Works of D. G. Ritchie*, 237.
[8] Recall that both Green and Hobhouse admired Millian utilitarianism generally while faulting it for reasons similar to Ritchie's. See Chapters 2 and 3.

object of desire is a potential candidate for being desirable. According to Ritchie, as Green correctly observes, the "self in a human being is something other than a mere series of feelings, and so in its true nature other than a mere subject for pleasurable sensations." The self "is what renders possible the consciousness of a series of feelings: the self-consciousness, which is manifested in them, must yet be other than they; for, as J. S. Mill himself had seen, it was a 'paradox' that what is only a series of feelings should be aware of itself as a series." Hence, Ritchie, inspired by Green, concludes that in self-consciousness lies the "metaphysical basis of Ethics."[9]

Despite utilitarianism's ill-conceived hedonic conception of good, utilitarianism ironically possesses considerable practical value for Ritchie. The "greatest happiness of the greatest number, may be valid in politics and yet not in morality."[10] Hedonistic utilitarianism converges with new liberalism's practical recommendations. Both are consequentialist and both generate parallel theories of right. The fundamental difference between them lies in their respective theories of good. For utilitarians, good is hedonic whereas for new liberals, like Ritchie and Green, it is non-hedonic and therefore objectively more plausible. Ritchie says: "There is no reason why the Idealist, after making clear his objections to Hedonism, should not join hands with the Utilitarian. In fact, an ethical system like Green's is really, on its practical side, J. S. Mill's Utilitarianism with a securer basis and a criterion provided, which Mill cannot logically provide, for distinguishing the different *qualities* of pleasures."[11]

Even Green conceded, according to Ritchie, that traditional utilitarianism coincided practically with his own moral theory. Even Green appreciated the former's practical, reforming value:

> Thus, the practical tests which Green applies to determine the rightness of any proposed course of conduct, either for the individual or for the State, seem to coincide with those which would be proposed by the Utilitarian. Of this he is quite aware, but he considers that he has a logical justification for applying the test of social well-being to which the Utilitarian, with his Hedonist starting-point, has no claim, and that, having defined the end as the realisation of a permanent self-satisfaction, he escapes the difficulties attending the balancing of pleasures and pains.[12]

---

[9] Ritchie, *Principles of State Interference*, 142. But this conception of the self is not unproblematic in turn. On the one hand, it is "other than a mere subject for pleasurable sensations." On the other hand, it is "what renders possible the consciousness of a series of feelings" making it, in effect, a "mere subject" for sensations of pleasure.

[10] Ritchie, "Moral Philosophy: On the Methods and Scope of Ethics," 342.

[11] Ritchie, *Principles of State Interference*, 145.   [12] *Ibid.*, 142–3.

Ritchie does not just close the gap between Green and utilitarianism by affirming their practical convergence only. He also suggests that there was more hedonism to Green's consequentialism than meets the undiscerning eye: "Even Green, it may be necessary to remind the more vehement of anti-hedonists, defined positive freedom as 'a power or capacity of doing or *enjoying* something worth doing or enjoying, and that, too, something that we do or enjoy in common with others.'"[13] Hence, as far as Ritchie was concerned, Green was a consequentialist for whom morally right actions were those that promoted everyone's self-realization. Insofar as self-realization consisted of "doing or enjoying something worth doing or enjoying," morally right actions were those that availed and encouraged everyone in living a worthwhile and simultaneously happy life. Moreover, morally right actions coincided with those recommended by traditional utilitarianism.

Ritchie's new liberalism was plainly consequentialist much like Green (or at least Green as Ritchie understood him) and Hobhouse's. Like them, he privileged good over right, equating good with self-realization. Right actions promoted everyone's self-realization. Unlike Green and Hobhouse, however, he did not hesitate to declare himself a utilitarian thereby stretching the meaning of utilitarianism and obfuscating its distinctiveness as a species of consequentialism.

Recall from Chapter 4 that both Green and Hobhouse were, to borrow from Hurka, "extensional perfectionists." As we saw there, extensional perfectionism holds that we often desire experiences "co-extensive" with self-development simply because such experiences happen to be co-extensive. Green is therefore an extensional perfectionist insofar as he argues that pleasure is contingently co-extensive with self-realization.[14]

We also saw how Hobhouse is an extensional perfectionist. For him, a self-realizing life is equally a happy life. However, in contrast to Green, as noted in Chapter 3, Hobhouse refuses to "separate happiness from the kind of life in which it is sought." Where Green, according to Hobhouse, treats pleasure as an external "secondary consequence" of good, Hobhouse insists that happiness is an "integral and essential element." Whereas happiness is merely a contingent symptom of self-realization for Green, for Hobhouse

---

[13] D. G. Ritchie, "Review of T. H. Huxley, *Collected Essays*, Vol. I," *The International Journal of Ethics*, 4 (1893–4), 534.

[14] Again, see Green, *Prolegomena to Ethics*, Sect. 238. The co-extensional nature of Green's perfectionism probably accounts for Ritchie's assessment, noted previously, that there is more hedonism in Green's moral theory than seems at first sight.

happiness is constitutive of self-realization. Hobhouse was therefore closer to being a genuine utilitarian consequentialist.

If Green and Hobhouse can be categorized as extensional perfectionists, then Ritchie can safely be categorized as one as well. More like Green than Hobhouse, though all the while ironically calling himself a utilitarian, Ritchie deemed pleasure a contingent by-product of self-realization conveniently marking its existence. We need only eat the cake of happiness and we will likewise get our self-realization. Maximize happiness and you will promote self-realization too.

RATIONAL SELECTION

In "What are Economic Laws?", Ritchie summarizes his account of how "rational selection" replaces "natural selection" with the emergence of utilitarian practical reasoning:

> The ideas of "natural selection" will apply perfectly to human evolution, if we remember that the variations on which natural selection works in human phenomena arise, not merely (1) "spontaneously" or "accidentally" ... but (2) by imitation – which is at least a half-conscious process – and (3) by deliberate effort, as the result of reflection, with a view to obtain certain ends. Where such reflection has really anticipated what is advantageous, natural selection seems to be superseded in successful artificial or rational selection.[15]

During early human evolution, moral codes arise fortuitously persisting in those societies that manage to succeed and endure in the struggle for existence with rival societies.[16] These codes become part of the cultural identities of societies that prevail. In part, successful societies prevail over rivals precisely because of the kinds of moral codes that partially constitute their identities. Other things being equal, success goes to societies that are more internally harmonious thanks to the quality and force of their moral beliefs. Success stimulates rivals to begin mimicking their moral regimens. Moral mimicry is of necessity a primitive type of utilitarian practical reasoning. To imitate a moral convention is to recognize, if even "half-conscious[ly]," its utility as a recipe for success.[17] Through mimicry, the

---

[15] Ritchie, *Darwin and Hegel*, 170.
[16] See, in addition, D. G. Ritchie [1901], "Natural Selection and the Spiritual World," *Darwinism and Politics, Collected Works of D. G. Ritchie*, Vol. 1, 98.
[17] Also see D. G. Ritchie [1901], "Natural Selection and the History of Institutions," *Darwinism and Politics, Collected Works of D. G. Ritchie*, Vol. 1, 130, where Ritchie says, "Conscious imitation because of some expected advantage already implies reflection, which is a further cause of variation among human beings." At the risk of exaggerating similarities between Ritchie and recent

most useful moral conventions spread gradually and, over time, metamor-
phose into our deepest moral intuitions. Moral intuitions, just because they
are intuitions, come to appear innate, seemingly unconnected with considerations of utility. Until the emergence of evolutionary theory, it was
"easy enough to point out that men's moral judgments are not as a rule
based on calculations of consequences." However, the "theory of natural
selection makes it a necessity that those societies should survive in which
the promptings of the tribal self have been most felt; and the mysterious
'feelings' on which the Intuitionist falls back are thus accounted for."[18]

In time, happily enough, intuitionism gives way to critical, utilitarian
practical reasoning that accelerates social harmony and well-being.
Harmony and well-being now become deliberately pursued in their own
right and not only because of the comparative advantages they bestow to
their possessors in inter-societal competition. Utilitarianism rises phoenix-
like from the smoldering ashes of intuitionism as "rational selection"
supersedes the lumbering inefficiency and cruelty of "natural selection"
in normative human affairs. By forecasting policies that promote general
well-being and social stability, utilitarianism speeds up their achievement
minimizing great suffering that would otherwise follow from purely intuitionist ethics and politics.[19] The theory of natural selection, therefore,
breathes new life into utilitarianism:

When reflection appears, however, a higher form of morality becomes possible;
the useful – i.e. what conduces to the welfare of the social organism, is not
recognised merely by the failure of those societies in which it is not pursued, but
by deliberate reflection on the part of the more thoughtful members of the society.
The utilitarian reformer reflects for his society, and anticipates and obviates the
cruel process of natural selection by the more peaceful methods of legislative
change. The theory of natural selection thus gives a new meaning to
Utilitarianism.[20]

naturalistic accounts of the social contract and the problem of the evolution of social cooperation,
see, for instance, Brian Skyrms, *The Stag Hunt and the Evolution of Social Structure* (Cambridge:
Cambridge University Press, 2004).

[18] Ritchie, "Natural Selection and the Spiritual World," 104–5. Ritchie's distaste for intuitionism was
almost visceral and was the source of his preoccupation with debunking it. But note that his account
of intuitionism explains our moral intuitions in terms of their utilitarian, survival value.

[19] D. G. Ritchie, "Evolution and Democracy," *Ethical Democracy: Essays in Dynamics*, ed. S. Coit
(London: G. Richards, 1900), 16. Also see Hobhouse, *Social Evolution and Political Theory*, 205
where Hobhouse says that moral progress consists in the "replacement of natural by social selection."

[20] Ritchie, "Natural Selection and the Spiritual World," 105. Also see Ritchie, *Darwinism and Politics*,
82–3, where Ritchie asks whether, by substituting "rational" for "natural" selection in our lives, we
may not hope to make "mutual help conscious, rational, systematic, and so to eliminate more and
more the suffering going on around us?"

To summarize, rational selection "marks the rise of civilization out of barbarism." While itself a product of natural selection, rational selection imposes a "check" on it.[21] Though the "rise of ethical ideals may be explained *historically* in terms of natural selection," once these ideals have arisen, "they make social progress something different from mere organic evolution ..."[22] There is "no absolute gap between Nature and man," though the bridge between them keeps getting longer. What is "dumb and blind in the struggle of plant and animal gains a consciousness of its meaning and a voice to express its needs in human society."[23] Utilitarianism is this consciousness and this voice.

But until the advent of evolutionary theory, our utilitarian consciousness remained confused and its voice weak. Fortunately, the theory of natural selection has "vindicated" all that is worthy in utilitarianism, eliminating confusion from our utilitarian consciousness and giving utilitarianism a stronger, clearer voice. Prior to the theory of natural selection, hedonistic utilitarianism was suffused with several shortcomings. For instance, as intuitionists were fond of complaining, earlier utilitarians never adequately distinguished between pleasure and happiness. They never explained how the "calculus of pleasures" was supposed to work with respect to measuring intensity of pleasure against its duration and with respect to interpersonally comparing pleasures. And they never justified how we can "jump from 'Every sentient being naturally pursues his own pleasure' (supposing it were true) to 'Every one ought to seek the happiness of other.'"[24]

However, evolutionary theory puts utilitarianism on a "scientific basis" ostensibly rescuing it from intuitionist objections and thereby also rescuing moral theorizing from intuitionism's perilous arbitrariness. In other words:

Natural selection ... is a perfectly adequate cause to account for the rise of morality ... Morality, to begin with, means those feelings and acts and habits which are advantageous to the welfare of the community. Morality comes to mean the *conscious and deliberate* adoption of those feelings and acts and habits which are advantageous to the welfare of the community; and reflection makes it possible to alter the conception of what the community is, whose welfare is to be considered. [my italics][25]

---

[21] Ritchie, "Natural Selection and the Spiritual World," 99–100.
[22] D. G. Ritchie, "Review of Benjamin Kidd, Social Evolution," *The International Journal of Ethics*, 5 (1894–5), 110–11.
[23] D. G. Ritchie [1895], *Natural Rights, Collected Works of D. G. Ritchie*, Vol. III, 70.
[24] Ritchie, "Evolution and Democracy," 15. See as well D. G. Ritchie, "Note C, Utilitarianism," *Principles of State Interference*, 168.
[25] Ritchie, *Darwin and Hegel*, 62–3.

And, for its part, utilitarianism corrects the fatalism that is liable to infect social evolutionary theory. Utilitarianism, by making the greatest happiness of the greatest number our criterion of right, instills in us optimism about social reform. It also encourages us to begin appreciating that our true standard of action is the "good of the whole community."[26] By stressing the "deliberate adoption of the common good as the end of action," utilitarianism points us in the correct normative direction.[27] The "practical value" of utilitarianism "remains if we interpret the common good as the well-being of the social organism of which the individual is a member."[28]

Ritchie is never clear how we get from utilitarian common good to common good as everyone's self-realization (which is what he means above by "common good as the well-being of the social organism"). The answer may lie in the relationship between self-realization and happiness discussed earlier. Earlier utilitarians "failed to notice that, *while apparently* their ultimate standard was the feeling of pleasure, *in reality* their ideal of character and of social good has determined what kind of pleasure they should consider preferable for themselves and others" (my italics).[29] Once utilitarians, like Mill, began appreciating that pleasures differed qualitatively, utilitarianism was positioned to transform itself into something less mathematically pretentious, into something more realistic and yet sublime. Once the "distinction of qualities [of pleasure] is introduced, the standard of 'perfection of character' or of 'the good of the community' has to be brought in to determine the qualities of pleasures."[30] In short, the problem of qualitative pleasures points utilitarianism beyond itself by leading it deeper. Lest we forget, pleasure is symptomatic of self-realization. Attend to, and puzzle about, symptoms long enough and you will invariably discover causes. Wrestle with, anguish about, the perplexities of utilitarian good obsessively enough and you will eventually see your way to maximizing self-realization as the finally unmasked criterion of right.

Of course, self-realization can come in many varieties. Claiming that good is self-realization and that it ought to be promoted leaves untouched what kind of self-realization we mean. Ritchie never provides a systematic

---

[26] Ritchie, "Evolution and Democracy," 15.   [27] Ritchie, "Note C, Utilitarianism," 169.
[28] Ritchie, "Evolution and Democracy," 16.
[29] Ritchie, "Moral Philosophy: On the Methods and Scope of Ethics," 322.
[30] *Ibid.*, 322. The "perfection of character" and the "good of the community" are identical principles because, like other new liberals, Ritchie deemed all forms of genuine self-realization to be mutually reinforcing, common goods.

and substantive account of self-realization though it is possible to reconstruct his meaning to some extent.

By self-realization, Ritchie plainly did not mean just any kind of life. A self-realizing life is not, for Ritchie, merely a successful life. Success does not establish worth. Indeed, success, individual or collective, in the struggle for existence says nothing about whether such success is, in fact, good. A murderer is always a murderer. And relatedly, for Ritchie, historical accounts of success prove nothing about good either. Contrary to what Spencer supposedly believed, "Origin does not determine validity (worth)."[31] A "law of nature is a statement of what as a fact *is*" and not an "expression of what *ought to be*."[32] So the substantive content of good is not discoverable through the study of facts, through description and explanation. Like many of his philosophical peers, Ritchie was often (but not always) attentive to the logical dangers of ethical naturalism.

Self-realization derives some of its content, according to Ritchie, from our "experience of and contact with actual life."[33] In actual life, anyone who acts without regard for others, becomes an enemy to society. Society must therefore instill a moral conscience in its members if it is to survive and to survive well. It must instill a sense of mutual respect in them: "Thus the good to be aimed at must be, in some sense, a common good. The self to be realized must be a self in *harmony* with other selves" (my italics).[34] So, self-realization means, at least partially, living harmoniously with others. It means treating them with respect by honouring, as we shall shortly see, their basic rights. And self-realization is *a* common good as it is for both Green and Hobhouse, for, when each acts respectfully towards others, all flourish. Self-realization is in everyone's common interest.

Ritchie also drew extensively from Hegel. May we not, he asks, "looking back now from the standpoint of the Ideal, regard all the blind struggle of

---

[31] *Ibid.*, 268. Also see D. G. Ritchie, "Mr. Newman on 'The Politics' of Aristotle," *The Quarterly Review*, 146 (July, 1902), 148, where Ritchie says approvingly that Aristotle "as a man of science, has an interest in purely historical questions of origin; but he never assumes that the history of how an institution came to be decides the question what is its proper function now."

[32] Ritchie, "Moral Philosophy: On the Methods and Scope of Ethics," 270. But see D. G. Ritchie, "The Rationality of History" in *Essays in Philosophical Criticism*, ed. Seth Pringle-Pattison and R. B. Haldane (London: Longmans, Green and Co., 1883), 140, where Ritchie says: "'If you justify the conduct of individuals or nations by results, is not that to confuse might and right?' In a sense it is – and, in a sense, might is right. If individuals or nations are able *permanently* to succeed in influencing the world, we must regard their conduct as justified by their success."

[33] Ritchie, "Moral Philosophy: On the Methods and Scope of Ethics," 295.

[34] *Ibid.*, 296. Even more than Ritchie, Hobhouse stressed the centrality of harmony as a constituent feature of self-realizing personality. See, for instance, Hobhouse, *Rational Good*, 115 and 124.

Nature as the lower and unconscious phases of this process of the realisation of the eternal Self?"[35] Moreover:

That "the real is the rational" is a doctrine which is implied in, and may be well
illustrated by, the theory of natural selection. All sorts of variations occur, i.e., they
exist but only those that prove to be of some value persist. Whatever maintains
itself must do so because of some rationality that it has or had.[36]

In short, there is rationality in all natural selection insofar as what happens
to survive, survives for a reason. If so, then there is a *telos* in the struggle
for existence. Wherever natural selection predominates, as among early
humans, this rationality remains concealed. The "non-rationality (indefinite variability)" of nature has always "ha[d] its reason."[37] The theory of
natural selection therefore corroborates, according to Ritchie, Hegel's
conviction that the "seeming non-rationality of nature" has always been
"itself a form of the rational."[38] Hence, it is a "mistake to speak as if they
[Darwinian and Hegelian evolution] were in conflict with one another – a
mistake which is responsible for much of the commonplace and 'scientific'
contempt for Hegel and those he has influenced."[39]

But with the emergence of utilitarian practical reasoning, rational
selection replaces natural selection and social evolution becomes self-
conscious. No longer furtive, reason declares itself though, at first, wearing
a hedonic mask. But as reason begins probing more deeply into the
meaning of good, seeing past its hedonic disguise, history begins seeming
much less an unfocused mystery, revealing its purpose, namely, everyone's
self-realization.

Teleologizing natural selection in this fashion may, as Ritchie often says
reassuringly, rescue us from pessimism about the meaning of natural, and
even of rational, selection. But in Ritchie's hands, self-realization, even
teleologized, remains overly formal and abstract. How can we possibly do

---

[35] Ritchie, *Darwin and Hegel*, 23.   [36] *Ibid.*, 70.   [37] *Ibid.*, 58.

[38] *Ibid.*, 70. For Ritchie's neo-Hegelian teleologizing of natural selection, see especially Sandra M. Den
Otter, *British Idealism and Social Explanation* (Oxford: Oxford University Press, 1996), 101–9. Also
see Boucher, "Introduction," *The British Idealists*, xiv–xx. And see Nicholson, "Introduction,"
xviii–xix. Note, especially, Nicholson's remark that Ritchie's "strategy, however, was to use Hegel
to turn Darwinism into a philosophical theory."

[39] D.G. Ritchie, "Bonar's 'Philosophy and Political Economy,'" *Economic Review*, 3 (1893), 554.
Ritchie concludes his review of Bonar remarking: "It is true that Natural Selection, as it operates
among plants and animals, means the perpetual destruction of the less fit; but I do not find in Hegel
any attempt to deny the prodigal wastefulness (*as it seems to us*) of nature's processes. The elimination
of the less fit in the merely natural struggle for existence is the necessary element of negativity in the
lowest form." (554–5). For the view that Green and his followers failed to reconcile Hegel and
Darwin, see Colin Tyler, "The Evolution of the Epistemic Self," *Bradley Studies*, 5 (1998).

what we ought when that which we are supposed to aim for is so substantively pale? Fortunately for us, whatever it is, it is co-extensive with pleasure. So if we just stick to promoting pleasure, then we shall do pretty well in promoting self-realization too.

SPENCERIAN OBSESSIONS

Ritchie was deeply indebted to Spencer for stimulating his thinking about the political and ethical import of Darwinism, though he sharply disagreed with Spencer on what this import was. Spencer always seems to be hovering in the background in Ritchie's writings like a shadowy obsession.[40] Beginning with the early *The Principles of State Interference*, which is primarily a spirited criticism of Spencer's polemic against state interference in *The Man Versus the State* (1884), Ritchie returns often in his later writings to Spencer's purported errors.

For instance, Ritchie accuses Spencer of succumbing to the metaphysical disease of abstract individualism in *The Man Versus the State*, according to which an individual supposedly has "meaning and significance apart" from his "relations to the community of which he is a member." Consequently, Spencer conceives society merely as an aggregation rather than an association of thickly situated selves. In addition, according to Ritchie, Spencer views the relationship between the state and individuals as a zero-sum game in which the liberty and power of individuals is inversely related to the liberty and power of the state.[41] Moreover, Spencer's abstract individualism conflicts with his contention that society is an evolving organism. His political theory is therefore fundamentally incompatible with his sociology. Though claiming to base his political theory on evolutionary theory, he has, in truth, "not got beyond Hobbes."[42] And even more seriously for Ritchie, Spencer misuses evolutionary theory to justify unrestricted laissez-faire.[43] Spencer, in effect, has not got beyond Adam Smith either.

In "Law and Liberty: The Question of State Interference," published the same year (1891) as *The Principles of State Interference*, Ritchie also

---

[40] For Spencer's influence on the development of Ritchie's thinking, see Den Boucher, *The British Idealists*, 93–8.

[41] Ritchie, *Principles of State Interference*, 11–13.

[42] *Ibid.*, 23. Many interpreters of Spencer have echoed Ritchie's accusation that Spencer's political and sociological theories are inconsistent. For a recent example of this view, see David Wiltshire, *The Social and Political Thought of Herbert Spencer* (Oxford: Oxford University Press, 1978), ch. 9.

[43] Ritchie, *Darwinism and Politics*, 10.

sharply criticizes Spencer's principle of equal freedom, which states, "Every man is free to do that which he wills, provided he infringes not the equal freedom of any other man."[44] If this principle, Ritchie says, means the liberty to do the very *same* act, then "I cannot occupy this spot of earth, on which at this moment I am standing, without interfering with the equal liberty of every one else to occupy this same spot at this same moment."[45] If equal liberty means the liberty to do *similar* acts, then, "No one has liberty to stand up and speak in his place [at a public meeting], unless every one else may stand up and speak in his place at the same time."[46] In truth, the "opportunity of speaking is dependent on the existence of the belief that there is some desirableness, some gain for the society as a whole, in hearing what people have to say." Equal liberty, then, "is not an absolute and primary, but a derivative principle, dependent on some idea of common good or advantage."[47] Thus, Ritchie concludes: "We are driven back, then, on 'Utilitarian' considerations; . . . that being understood to mean the highest development of individual capacities compatible with the coherence and continuance of the society as a whole."[48]

Ritchie also reproves Spencer's theory of rights. According to Ritchie, Spencer is a typical, wayward intuitionist proponent of natural rights despite his countervailing enthusiasm for evolutionary theorizing. In Ritchie's view, among "our leading writers only Mr. Herbert Spencer, in strange inconsistency with his conception of society as an organism, is to be found defending the theory of natural rights, the social contract, and what Huxley called 'administrative nihilism.'"[49] Spencer, moreover, mistakenly thinks that natural rights are proven to exist just because different societies uniformly recognize the same menu of basic rights. Rather, such uniformity of recognition suggests nothing more than that certain "conditions" are necessary to the stability and flourishing of any society. Societies have simply found themselves "compelled to observe these conditions"

---

44 Herbert Spencer [1891], "Justice," *The Principles of Ethics*, 2 vols. (Indianapolis: Liberty Press, 1978), Vol. II. 62. "Law and Liberty: The Question of State Interference" was first published in 1891 in *The Journal of the Society for the Study of Social Ethics*.

45 D. G. Ritchie [1902], "Law and Liberty: The Question of State Interference," *Studies in Political and Social Ethics, Collected Works of D. G. Ritchie*, Vol. IV, 58–9.

46 *Ibid.*, 59. Recall, too, Hobhouse's similar criticisms of Spencer's equal freedom principle in Hobhouse, *Elements of Social Justice*, 60 and Hobhouse, *Liberalism*, 36.

47 Ritchie, "Law and Liberty: The Question of State Interference," 59–60.

48 *Ibid.*, 62. Spencer's equal liberty principle is likewise ultimately grounded in utilitarian considerations which Ritchie seems not to appreciate. See my *Equal Freedom and Utility*, ch. II.

49 Ritchie, "Mr. Newman on 'The Politics' of Aristotle," 151.

sanctifying them as basic rights in order to flourish.[50] Hence, natural rights are really just universally successful strategies for promoting common good that all societies eventually adopt as rational selection relentlessly replaces natural selection in human affairs.

NATURAL RIGHTS

Ritchie exaggerates the differences between himself and Spencer on the question of natural rights perhaps because Ritchie held intuitionism in such ill repute and because he was overly eager to brand Spencer with its hot iron. Let us first analyze Ritchie's theory of rights in greater detail and then return to his overstated differences with Spencer.

In his brief but revealing contribution to a symposium on "Is Human Law the Basis of Morality, or Morality of Human Law?," in *Proceedings of the Aristotelian Society* (1894), Ritchie observes:

But, ... we may regard the Law of Nature as a statement of those *essential principles* [my italics] on which the stability and welfare of all societies ultimately depend. The Law of Nature may be taken to represent an ideal code which we gradually, as the result both of unconscious evolution and of conscious reflection, came to apprehend more and more, so that, though not in time yet in idea, it is prior to and, in this other sense, the 'basis' of particular laws and customs. Understood in this way the idea of a Law of Nature is unassailable on historical grounds. And even evolutionist ethics might accept the idea of the Law of Nature as a statement of the *essential conditions* [my italics] of social cohesion and growth – these conditions coming gradually to light in the course of evolution ... Similarly, when at a more advanced and reflective stage of social existence anyone can apply "Utilitarian" criteria, and maintain that such and such principles of conduct are right (although not yet adopted anywhere) because likely to promote the well-being of human society, we may allow him to express this by saying that those principles are in accordance with the Law of Nature, as that can be discovered by the use of Reason ... The *Jus Naturale* of the Roman jurists and the *Naturrecht* of the Germans are practically (as has been pointed out by Sir Henry Maine and Sir F. Pollock) the equivalent of Bentham's Theory of Legislation, though in appearance the very opposite.[51]

---

[50] Ritchie, *Principles of State Interfence*, 39. Also see Taylor's *Men Versus the State: Herbert Spencer and Late Victorian Individualism*, 241, which endorses Ritchie's assessment that Spencer defended traditional natural rights.

[51] D. G. Ritchie, "Symposium – Is Human Law the Basis of Morality, or Morality of Human Law?", *Proceedings of the Aristotelian Society*, Part II (1894), 126–7. Ritchie warns, however: "But the appeal to 'Nature' is so very ambiguous, and is so apt to mean an appeal away from Reason to unanalysed instincts or sentiments, that it would be better if those who use the term as just explained were to avoid it" (127). Also see Ritchie, *Principles of State Interference*, 33, where Ritchie says: "Sir F. Pollock

In other words, when properly understood in terms of evolutionary theory, the principles of natural law are really just fundamental, universally valid conditions of human flourishing whose efficacy gradually becomes apparent. They are neither *a priori* intuitions nor transcendent metaphysical moral truths. Instead, they are universally valid, hypothetical imperatives, which instruct us how to act given our increasingly overriding interest in general happiness. They are unrivalled empirical strategies for promoting well-being. Whereas natural selection favors societies that fortuitously institutionalize these conditions as custom and habit, rational selection accelerates well-being by making humans consciously aware of the utility of these conditions. Utilitarianism, in particular, marks a decisive sea change in practical reasoning for, with utilitarianism, humans not only recognize the utility of these conditions but also begin reformulating them as universal principles of right. And once utilitarianism becomes fortified by evolutionary theory and by a non-hedonic conception of good qua self-realization, rational selection finally supersedes natural selection in human normative affairs. The owl of Minerva takes flight on improved utilitarian wings.

By "essential conditions" of well-being, Ritchie means, moreover, basic rights. Evolutionary utilitarianism reveals that these "essential conditions" of natural law are not really genuine natural rights. So-called natural rights are simply those moral rights which ought to be recognized by society as being socially useful:

It is becoming clear that, when people speak of natural rights of liberty, property, etc., they really mean, not rights which once existed, and have been lost, but rights which they believe *ought* to exist, and which would be produced by a condition of society and an ordering of the State such as they think desirable. There is an *eidolon* which leads men to put their golden age in the past, and to claim reforms under the guise of restoring ancient rights.[52]

Evolutionary utilitarianism, by reinterpreting and rescuing natural rights theory, "makes what one may call a 'Copernican' change in our way of considering the question of rights."[53] Furthermore:

If it is argued that such an appeal [to the socially useful] is at least as ambiguous as a mere reference to natural rights, I answer, No; for in appealing to social utility, we

---

has rightly pointed out that *Naturrecht* is much the same sort of thing as Bentham's theory of legislation. It is an ideal code, 'purporting to be justified by the universal nature of human relations, and qualified by no respect of time and place.'"

[52] Ritchie, *Principles of State Interference*, 43–4. See, in addition, Ritchie, *Darwin and Hegel*, 282.
[53] Ritchie, *Natural Rights*, 101.

are appealing to something that can be tested, not merely by the intuitions of an individual mind, but by experience. History is the laboratory of politics.[54]

Evolutionary utilitarianism, moreover, regards rights as natural much in the same, unconventional way that Green conceded that they were natural. And once again, we have reason to doubt the received view which has over-inflated differences between the new liberalism and utilitarianism:

All appeals to "natural rights" *either* mean an assertion of the individual's infalli-bility and a refusal to submit to any further test than instinctive sentiment, *or* they must be interpreted by reference to the 'utilitarian' test of the common good, and "nature" is then no longer the final court of appeal. Now Green allows the phrase "natural rights" only in the carefully guarded sense of such an appeal to the common good. The ethical end, though described by Green to begin with as 'self-realization,' is always interpreted by him as the common good: and therefore in *political* philosophy he has far more in common with Utilitarians, such as Bentham and J. S. Mill, than with Intuitionists of any school whatever. The ethical hedonism of the Utilitarians he has, indeed, severely criticized; but he has himself recognized his affinity with the practical political principles which the utilitarians have (inconsistently) based on their individualistic hedonism.[55]

Now one reason, according to Ritchie, why we have misjudged the nature of rights prior to the advent of evolutionary utilitarianism has been our antiquated tendency of mistaking a "thought-process" for a "time-process." In recognizing certain conditions as necessary for well-being, we have wrongly pictured these conditions as existing prior to the existence of society, labeling them not just rights but natural rights. We confuse recognition with discovery, reifying the concept of a right as if rights have always somehow literally existed waiting to be unearthed as our intuitions become sufficiently honed. In short, we confuse what is really our formative, consequentialist reasoning with what seems a kind of intuitive archeological discovery of objective moral truth, rebuking the former as philistine, mechanical and immoral.[56] As suggested previously, Ritchie exaggerated his differences with Spencer regarding rights. Like Ritchie, Spencer was an evolutionary utilitarian who viewed fundamental rights as natural only in the sense of developing out of time-honored

---

[54] *Ibid.*, 103. See, as well, *ibid.*, 270. There, Ritchie says: "We can only allow natural rights to be talked about in the sense in which natural rights mean those legal or customary rights which we have come to think or may come to think it most advantageous to recognise." Also note that, for Ritchie, insofar as rights to life and liberty have proven to be our most advantageous of all rights, we have come to recognize them as our most fundamental ones. See Part II of *Natural Rights* for Ritchie's detailed discussion of these two basic rights as well as other important ones.

[55] Ritchie, "Bonar's 'Philosophy and Political Economy,'" 549.   [56] Ritchie, *Darwin and Hegel*, 50–1.

"customs" and "usages" that were gradually revealing themselves as necessary conditions to human well-being. Like Ritchie, Spencer also held that societies that institutionalized these essential "customs" and "usages" as basic rights were advantaged in being more harmonious and therefore more likely to thrive.[57]

Despite these similarities, Ritchie misinterpreted Spencer as a proponent of traditional natural rights.[58] He did so because he wrongly pegged Spencer as just another moral intuitionist dressing up a politically conservative intuitionism in the garb of evolutionary theory in order better to justify laissez-faire. But Spencer was no typical intuitionist. For Spencer, early humans naturally tended to approve or disapprove of actions that generated either pleasure or pain. Because of the purported biological mechanism of Lamarckian use-inheritance, this natural tendency to approve pleasure-producing actions and disapprove pain-producing ones eventually congealed into our present moral intuitions justifying certain "customs" and "usages" as morally right.[59] Indeed, traditional natural rights theory simply sanctifies the most important of our utility-generated moral intuitions. Other things being equal, societies where such intuitions have become sanctified as basic rights comparatively quickly have tended be more stable, happier and therefore comparatively more successful. In other words, Lamarckian use-inheritance channels and strengthens our acquired moral sentiments from generation to generation, transforming some into intuitive claims about rights and favoring those societies where this occurs. Sooner or later, according to Spencer, we become consciously aware of the utility-producing power of basic rights and the customs they protect and justify. And though we stop thinking of them as natural in the outmoded Lockean sense, we nevertheless reaffirm our respect for them as zealously as ever.

Ritchie, by contrast, rejected Lamarckianism as unproved and frequently criticized Spencer for embracing it.[60] In Ritchie's view, our moral sentiments

---

[57] Spencer, *Principles of Ethics*, II, 43.

[58] Ritchie admits that Spencer sometimes understands rights properly, especially where Spencer says that belief in natural rights constitutes the realization that certain conditions are essential to successful social life. See Ritchie, *Principles of State Interference*, 39. Also note Ritchie's comment in "'Bonar's 'Philosophy and Political Economy,'" 549, that "practically, however, the appeal to natural rights means with Mr. Spencer simply an appeal to those customs, usages, and ideas about property, etc., which approved themselves to the "philosophical radicals" of a by-gone generation."

[59] For Spencer's defense of Lamarckian use-inheritance, see his "The Inadequacy of 'Natural Selection,'" *The Contemporary Review*, 43 (1893) and his subsequent controversy with August Weismann about use-inheritance also published as a series of exchanges in *The Contemporary Review* between 1893 and 1895.

[60] According to Boucher, the British Idealists generally rejected Lamarckianism as unscientific. See Boucher, *The British Idealists* (Cambridge: Cambridge University Press, 1997), xvi.

have not been evolving via the unsubstantiated, biological mechanism of use-inheritance. Rather, the evolution of our utility-producing moral code is best explained by the mechanism of "objectified mind." "Objectified mind" includes language, tradition and all the other "definite institutions" of civilization.[61] As we begin rationally selecting our moral principles, instead of leaving their formation to the vicissitudes of natural selection, "objectified mind" works like a conduit simultaneously refining and propelling our moral principles forward from generation to generation. Language, culture, our political institutions and, indeed, utilitarian practical reasoning itself *qua* philosophical tradition, now become the vehicles of moral progress.[62]

But whether we opt for use-inheritance or for "objectified mind" to carry our normative heavy freight, it may make less substantive difference than meets the eye in terms of our theories of the good and the right. As Ritchie concedes, "Whether our ideals of goodness are due entirely to natural selection (of individuals and societies and usages) or partly to natural selection and partly to use-inheritance may be an interesting historical problem; but it has no direct bearing on the problem of what meaning there is in calling anything 'good' at all."[63] In short, the question of use-inheritance may be irrelevant to the important normative and political differences (and there are several) separating Spencer and Ritchie.

In brief, both Spencer and Ritchie were evolutionary utilitarians who viewed utilitarian practical reasoning as the rationalization of social evolution. Whereas Ritchie held that "rational" selection replaced natural selection as intuitionism gave way to more sophisticated utilitarian reasoning, Spencer held that moral progress was characterized by "empirical" utilitarianism replacing intuitionism followed by "rational" utilitarianism gradually superseding "empirical" utilitarianism in turn. For Spencer, as we begin deliberately promoting general happiness for its own sake, we learn to sanctify our most essential, utility-promoting moral conventions

---

[61] D.G. Ritchie, "Has the Hereditability or Non-Hereditability of Acquired Characteristics Any Direct Bearing on Ethical Theory?", *Proceedings of the Aristotelian Society*, III (1895–6), 145.

[62] Recent interdisciplinary studies in biology, psychology and anthropology come to similar conclusions. See, for instance, Matt Ridley, *The Origins of Virtue* (New York: Viking, 1997) especially where Ridley concludes: "What makes human beings different [from other species] is culture. Because of the human capacity of passing on traditions, customs, knowledge and beliefs by direct infection from one person to another, there is a whole new kind of evolution going on in human beings – a competition not between genetically different individuals or groups, but between culturally different individuals and groups. One person may thrive at the expense of another not because he has better genes, but because he knows or believes something of practical value" (179–80).

[63] Ritchie, "Has the Hereditability or Non-Hereditability of Acquired Characteristics Any Direct Bearing on Ethical Theory?," 147.

in the language of rights. Once we begin recognizing that certain classes of actions invariably promote general happiness and clothe them in the normative armor of indefeasible rights, our utilitarian thinking finally becomes self-consciously rigorous, scientific and rational. So for Spencer as for Ritchie, practical reasoning evolved following a similar sequence culminating in rational consequentialist reasoning triumphing over and replacing the haphazard impetuousness of moral intuitionism.[64]

Ritchie, however, was as much a socialist as he was a liberal utilitarian whereas Spencer was not.[65] Hence, like Green and Hobhouse, he favored a more enriched, indirect strategy of empowering welfare rights. Probably thinking of Spencer in comparison with himself, he observes: "How far this end [happiness] can be attained by leaving people alone, and how far it can be attained by interference – on this the great practical differences of opinion would begin. Where some [presumably new liberals like himself] would lay more stress on the need of directly removing obstacles to physical health, to intelligence and moral development, others [presumably Spencer] would lay more stress on the need for 'freedom', – on the need of letting people learn even by mistakes and failures, in order that their ultimate progress may be more secure."[66]

HUME, RITCHIE, MACKIE AND THE INVENTION OF MORALITY

In a suggestive passage at the end of Section I, Part II of Book III of *A Treatise of Human Nature*, Hume concludes:

---

[64] For both Ritchie and Spencer, then, our moral intuitions are rough-and-ready evolutionary adaptions to social life that utilitarian practical reasoning later refines. In a recent and similar vein, see James Wood Bailey, "Is it Rational to Maximize?", *Utilitas*, 10 (1998), 220, where Bailey writes: "One need not be a global moral sceptic to question the probative value of specific moral intuitions. Our moral intuitions may be a guide to some kind of strategic reality just as our physical intuitions are a guide to the physical universe. Such intuitions may be cognitive adaptions to the conditions of ordinary life."

[65] Ritchie's liberal socialism was shared by new liberals and Idealists alike, which Boucher calls a "true or right kind of socialism, which uses the state to advance freedom of choice by removing obstacles to the development of individual freedom." See Boucher, *The British Idealists*, xxiv–xxv. Spencer's liberal utilitarianism was closer to Bosanquet's liberalism in placing more emphasis on individual self-reliance and much less emphasis on state interference. Also see Nicholson, "Introduction,"xxiv–xxviii, which discusses Ritchie's relationship to Fabianism.

[66] Ritchie, *Natural Rights*, 274. Spencer and Ritchie also differed about whether or not rights were indefeasible. Ritchie suggests that basic rights, though stringent, are always open to refinement. Nonetheless, there was a legislative time and place for critical, second-level thinking about revising rights. Most of the time, we should diligently stick to respecting them as everyday decision procedures. Ritchie observes: "Accepted rules need revision and correction, not of course in the moment when they have to be applied – the battlefield is not the place for examining bayonets, though it certainly does test them." Ritchie, "Note C: Utilitarianism," 171. For an analysis of Spencer's view that rights were indefeasible as well as conventional, see my *Equal Freedom and Utility*, ch. III.

To avoid giving offence, I must here observe, that when I deny justice to be a natural virtue, I make use of the word *natural* only as oppos'd to *artificial*. In another sense of the word; as no principle of the human mind is more natural than a sense of virtue; so no virtue is more natural than justice. Mankind is an inventive species; and where an invention is obvious and absolutely necessary, it may as properly be said to be natural as any thing that proceeds immediately from original principles, without the intervention of thought or reflexion. Tho' the rules of justice be *artificial*, they are not *arbitrary*. Nor is the expression improper to call them *Laws of Nature*, if by natural we understand what is common to any species, or even if we confine it to mean what is inseparable from the species.[67]

For Hume, then, justice is an artificial virtue in the sense that it is conventional. Yet the rules of justice are natural insofar as they are such "obvious and absolutely necessary" conventions. Being so "obvious and absolutely necessary," these rules inevitably and gradually emerge albeit not necessarily by conscious design. Moreover, being so "obvious and necessary," a determinate unchanging set of basic rules invariably emerges which is why they are "not arbitrary."[68]

With respect to the institution of property, in particular, "public utility requires that" it "should be regulated by general inflexible rules." These rules are conventional "if by convention be meant a sense of common interest, which sense each man feels in his own breast, which he remarks in his fellows, and which carries him, in concurrence with others, into a general plan or system of actions which tends to public utility . . ."[69] The emergence of fixed rules regulating the acquisition and exchange of property is not unlike the informal understanding which two rowers achieve to row in unison: "Two men, who pull the oars of a boat, do it by an agreement or convention, tho' they have never given promises to each other. Nor is the rule concerning the stability of possession the less deriv'd from human conventions, that it arises gradually and acquires force by a slow progression, and by our repeated experience of the inconveniences of

---

[67] David Hume [1739–1740], *A Treatise of Human Nature*, ed. L. A. Selby-Bigge, rev. P. Nidditch (Oxford: Oxford University Press, 1978), 484.

[68] See, in addition, Hume, *A Treatise of Human Nature*, 620, where Hume says emphatically: "The interest, on which justice is founded, is the greatest imaginable and extends to all times and places . . . It is obvious, and discovers itself on the very first formation of society. All these causes render the rules of justice stedfast and immutable; at least as immutable as human nature." Likewise, see Green, *Lectures on the Principles of Political Obligation* 2, Sect. 30 where Green insists, not unlike both Hume and Ritchie, that though they are not "antecedent to society," rights are nevertheless "not arbitrary creations."

[69] David Hume [1751], Appendix III, "Some Further Considerations with Regard to Justice," *An Inquiry Concerning the Principles of Morals*, ed. Charles W. Hendel (New York: Liberal Arts Press, 1957), 122.

transgressing it."[70] Like the rules of ownership, the rules of efficient rowing are fairly specific. They are equally "not arbitrary." For Hume, there is one best general scheme of property ownership for promoting public utility just as there is a single best method of enjoyable and effective rowing.

In *The Treatise of Human Nature*, Hume furthermore says that we initially and gradually invent the rules of justice out of individual self-interest, even though public utility is simultaneously and unintentionally served by these same rules. Eventually, we come to forget why we originally invented these rules, believing instead that we did so to promote public utility.[71] "Consequently," according to Knud Haakonssen, "individuals are inclined to approve of the behavior that brings about the public good, for it appears as though this behavior were aimed at this outcome, and contrariwise, to disapprove of behavior having contrary effects."[72]

---

[70] Hume, *Treatise on Human Nature*, 490. Hume deploys this fitting and memorable example again in "Some Further Considerations with Regard to Justice," 123. Leah Hochman has suggested to me that Hume's two rowers' example does not do the work Hume wants especially if Hume has in mind two novice rowers. Being novices, they would surely discuss and agree to a plan of action before getting in their row boat. Although each might not go so far as to promise explicitly to the other that he or she will pull his or her oar in a particular way as long as the other promises to do the same, nonetheless both would undoubtedly start off by agreeing to some kind of rowing strategy, which they also would agree to try to improve as they went along.

[71] Hume, *Treatise on Human Nature*, 529. Hume scholars are divided about the purity of Hume's utilitarian credentials. For two recent critical readings of Hume as a utilitarian, see Roger Crisp, "Self-love and the General Interest: Hume on Impartiality" (unpublished) and F. Rosen, *Classical Utilitarianism from Hume to Mill* (London: Routledge, 2003), ch. 3. Crisp's essay also cites important utilitarian and non-utilitarian interpretations of Hume in two helpful footnotes (13). Crisp's Hume exemplifies what Robert Adams calls "motive utilitarianism" (though Crisp would reject this characterization of his view of Hume). For Hume, in Crisp's view, moral praise and blame are "directed at intention, and intentions emerge from character, the 'external signs' of which are actions." Hume asks not, "'Which actions are right and wrong?', but, 'Which aspects of character should we praise, and why?'" (19). In support of his interpretation, Crisp quotes the *Treatise on Human Nature*, 477, where Hume writes that in evaluating actions, "we regard only the motives that produced them, and consider the actions as signs or indications of certain principles in the mind and temper." In addition, see Hume, *Inquiry Concerning the Principles of Morals*, 55, n. 7, where Hume says by analogy: "Why is this peach tree said to be better than that other, but because it produces more or better fruit? And would not the same praise be given it, though snails or vermin had destroyed the peaches before they came to full maturity? In morals, too, is not *the tree known by the fruit?*" By contrast, recall Ritchie's nearly identical claim from "On the Meaning of the Term 'Motive,' and on the Ethical Significance of Motives" and cited in Chapter 4, Note 113, that the happiness one produces in the world mirrors the purity of one's motives or, in other words, the extent to which one is self-realizing. Thus, like Hume, Ritchie is arguably a virtue utilitarian for whom promoting happiness is a substitute strategy testifying to the existence of self-realizing virtue. And characterizing Ritchie as a virtue utilitarian is simply an alternative way of capturing the way in which he was an extensional perfectionist albeit not in Green's double sense. To be morally self-realizing, for Ritchie, was not explicitly and simultaneously a matter of promoting moral self-realization in others as it was for Green.

[72] Knud Haakonssen, "The Structure of Hume's Political Theory," *The Cambridge Companion to Hume*, ed. David Fate Norton (Cambridge: Cambridge University Press, 1993), 191.

Likewise, according to Antony Flew, Hume held that the rules of justice slowly emerged in the service of self-love though they unintentionally promoted public utility as well. Accordingly, Hume's "approach to the origin of social institutions is thus evolutionary" insofar as a "main insight of any such sophisticated understanding is that social institutions" often exhibit "functions and consequences which are not the fulfillments of anyone's intentions."[73] Moreover, in Flew's assessment, Hume and other Scottish Enlightenment figures, "prepared the way" for Darwin: "Whereas they [Hume and his compatriots] had shown that various social institutions which looked to be products of deliberate design might or even must have evolved rather than been consciously created, Darwin was to go on to apply the same ideas to all species of organisms."[74]

In Section VI of Part III, Book III, which concludes *A Treatise of Human Nature*, Hume reiterates his important claim that our sense of morals, including our sentiment of justice, is "inherent in the soul" and gains "new force" once it begins "*reflecting*" on itself, discovering "what is great and good in its rise and origin" (my italics).[75] And what is "great and good," particularly with respect to justice, is its public utility. Reflection, in short, enlivens and fortifies our commitment to justice by enabling us to appreciate consciously its utility-promoting power. Though justice emerges naturally, it does not begin to realize its utility-generating potential until we become self-conscious utilitarians capable of acknowledging just how critical the rules of justice are for our individual and collective well-being.[76]

Hume, then, like Ritchie after him, held that the rules of justice arise gradually and naturally and without conscious design though with a specific purpose. In Ritchie's case, natural selection favors those societies in which the rules of justice just happen to become firmly established because of their compelling utilitarian fecundity. Ultimately, for Ritchie, natural selection begins giving way to rational selection as members of developed societies begin consciously to appreciate the utility-promoting powers of these rules. And once utilitarian practical reasoning emerges as a

---

[73] Antony Flew, *David Hume* (Oxford: Oxford University Press, 1986), 159.

[74] *Ibid.*, 160. For Flew, Hume's proto-Darwinism was also the source of his political conservatism. (174). Also see Terence Penelhum, "Hume's Moral Psychology," *The Cambridge Companion to Hume*, 124. There, Penelhum says that, for Hume, our fundamental beliefs are products of instinct and that they are "useful" and "adaptive." Consequently, his "view of our beliefs is essentially a Darwinian view." T. H. Huxley likewise seems to have seen in Hume anticipations of his own version of evolutionary utilitarianism. See especially ch. XI, "The Principles of Morals" of his *Hume* (London: Macmillan, 1887).

[75] Hume, *Treatise On Human Nature*, 619.

[76] See, as well, Hume, *Inquiry Concerning the Principles of Morals*, 25.

public philosophy, rational selection finally trumps natural selection as the
engine of moral progress.

Likewise for Hume, justice arises spontaneously, naturally and unsystem-
atically in the service of public utility though, initially, self-interest alone
drives its haphazard invention. Sooner or later, just as with Ritchie,
reflection unmasks its public utility-producing power, leading good citizens, politicians and philosophers alike, to champion deliberately and self-
consciously the principle of public utility as their indisputable standard of
right and wrong. Like Ritchie, then, unsystematic utilitarianism gradually
and unavoidably gives way to deliberative rational utilitarianism. Of
course, in Hume's case, modern evolutionary theory plays no role in
justice's formative emergence.[77] Indeed, Hume not only "prepared the
way" for Darwin as Flew maintains, but, more poignantly, he "prepared
the way" for Ritchie too.[78]

And in preparing the way for Ritchie, Hume also prepared the way for
J. L. Mackie more recently. Mackie follows Hume explicitly in defending a
form of consequentialist moral subjectivism that nevertheless eschews
moral relativism.[79] For Mackie, morality is "made" rather than "discovered." It is a "device" that we have invented, though slowly and not by
deliberate design, in order to cope with the double challenge of limited
resources and our limited natural sympathies. Moreover, for Mackie,
"ordinary evolutionary pressures" combined with the "differential survival
of groups" in which moral sentiments flourish, "either as inherited psychological tendencies or as socially maintained traditions, will help to explain
why such sentiments become strong and widespread."[80] Not surprisingly,
then, Mackie also follows both Hume and Ritchie in denying the existence
of natural absolute rights. According to Mackie, we "recognize" fundamental moral rights as opposed to discovering them as much as we make,

---

[77] Hume's rational utilitarianism is similarly unlike Spencer's rational utilitarianism insofar as
Spencer, like Ritchie, espoused modern evolutionary theory. And it is also unlike Ritchie's in that
it is non-perfectionist. Furthermore, though Hume seems to hold, like Spencer and Ritchie, that
humans are prone to invent the same set of "non-arbitrary" fundamental rules of justice, he does not
clothe these rules in language of stringent rights as they do.

[78] Ritchie was clearly familiar with Hume's writings though it is impossible to tell just how much
Hume influenced his thinking particularly with respect to moral theory. For an example of Ritchie's
assessment of Hume, see Ritchie, "Bonar's 'Philosophy and Political Economy,'" 545.

[79] In Mackie's words, "my approach could be called in a very broad sense, a rule utilitarian one, since
any specific development of it would be based on some conception of the flourishing of human life,
but it would be utilitarianism without its characteristic [objectivist] fictions, and it would be not just
a rule-utilitarianism but a rule-right-duty-disposition utilitarianism." Mackie, *Ethics: Inventing
Right and Wrong*, 199–200.

[80] *Ibid.*, 113.

rather than discover, any other aspect of morality. And in keeping with typically utilitarian anxieties, he condemns natural rights theorizing as disastrously polarizing. Natural rights discourage negotiation and compromise and enflame passions. Hence, they undermine, instead of promote, flourishing and well-being.

Mackie echoes Ritchie in vehemently rejecting moral intuitionism, which he likewise sees as following from moral objectivism. For Mackie, if there were objective values such as natural rights, then their metaphysical status would be very queer as they would be unlike anything else in the universe. And being so queer, it is unsurprising that we would posit knowing them via some special and equally queer intuitive faculty. For example, we should expect moral objectivists like Locke to succumb to some form of intuitionism. Intuitionism makes "unpalatably plain what other forms of objectivism wrap up."[81]

Moral objectivism and moral intuitionism, then, go hand-in-hand. "Error theory" exposes both as errors that lazy thinking succumbs to all too readily. Consequently, it is "not surprising that widespread socially diffuse, and not obviously artificial institutions [like promising and natural rights] ... should have helped to produce the notions of what is intrinsically fitting or required by the nature of things."[82] For Ritchie, too, moral objectivism and moral intuitionism naturally go together. As we previously saw, Ritchie argues that moral progress consists in recognizing how certain basic rights are necessary conditions for human flourishing. Unfortunately, we tend to confound recognition with discovery. That is, we tend to confuse a "thought-process" for a "time-process" wrongly insisting on the queer metaphysical reality of natural rights, which we purportedly discover by equally queer, special intuitive insight. Recognition is a "thought-process" and not a gradual "time-process" of improving intuitive insight into objective moral truth. Recognition is, as Mackie would say, thinking through our need for certain artificial institutions like moral rights rather than discovering ready-made, moral absolutes. Moreover, for Mackie just as for Ritchie, we can ill afford to leave this thinking to sluggish tradition. As with Ritchie, we must deploy consequentialist practical reasoning diligently, systematically and vigorously in order to refine and improve common-sense morality more expeditiously: "But what is not disputable is that for the changes and political extensions that are now necessary we cannot rely on the past achievements of evolution and social tradition, nor

---

[81] *Ibid.*, 38.   [82] *Ibid.*, 82.

have we time to let them grow by a future process of natural selection."[83] As Ritchie quoted earlier says, we need to substitute rational selection for natural selection otherwise we risk unnecessarily prolonging considerable human suffering.

Hume anticipates Ritchie who, in turn, anticipates Mackie even more. Or perhaps we should say that in drawing on Hume in the way he does, Mackie would have benefited greatly had he read a little of Ritchie. At least, he might have appreciated that his central claim that we invent right and wrong for ultimately consequentialist reasons has a richer pedigree than he imagined.

CONCLUSION

Compared with other versions of the new liberalism, Ritchie's version was easily the most eclectic weave of diverse philosophical traditions. Part Humean utilitarian, part ethical Darwinist and part idealist, Ritchie nevertheless succeeded in constructing a bona fide liberalism that featured both the cultivation of individuality and stringent basic rights.

Like Green before him and Hobhouse after him, Ritchie made promoting everyone's self-realization the criterion of the morally right. And just like both Green and Hobhouse, he was an extensional perfectionist for whom pleasure was symptomatic of self-realization making the pursuit of the former a convenient surrogate, or marker, for pursuing the latter. Ritchie, then, was theoretically a perfectionist consequentialist. But for *practical* purposes, improved liberal utilitarianism would do just fine. Perhaps this substitute practicality is why he preferred calling himself a utilitarian.

Ritchie was equally an *evolutionary* utilitarian. He was convinced that the theory of evolution vindicated utilitarianism, making it more scientific by showing how sophisticated moral theorizing, particularly utilitarian practical reasoning, constituted the triumph of rational selection over the haphazard inefficiency and grinding sluggishness of natural selection in human normative development. But, of course, providing a scientific

---

[83] *Ibid.*, 239. Also see 148 where Mackie similarly recalls Ritchie: "What the individual can do is to remember that there are, in the different circles of relationship with which he is concerned, various fragments of a moral system which already contributes very considerably to countering specifiable evils which he, like others, will see as evils; that he can at once take advantage of this system and contribute to its upkeep; but that he may be able, with others, to put pressure on some fragment of the system, so that they come gradually to be more favourable to what he sees as valuable or worthwhile."

account of the emergence of utilitarian practical reasoning is not equivalent to justifying its conception of good, let alone justifying self-realization as the subterranean, true good.

But whatever his difficulties in trying to vindicate utilitarianism by Darwinism, Ritchie's evolutionary utilitarianism is nevertheless an authentic new liberalism. More than Green, and at least as much as Hobhouse, Ritchie's new liberalism powerfully highlights just how thoroughly utilitarian the new liberalism was.

CHAPTER 6

Utilitarian socialism: J. A. Hobson

INTRODUCTION

English new liberals, as I have been suggesting, are traditionally viewed as having been largely unsympathetic, if not hostile, to utilitarianism. My study rejects this view, which, no doubt, largely stems from nineteenth-century English idealism's legacy to the new liberalism. Hegelian idealists like Bradley criticized utilitarians like Mill and Sidgwick on many accounts including the futility of trying to maximize happiness. However, though new liberals endorsed many such criticisms, they nonetheless never abandoned utilitarianism entirely. They modified Millian utilitarianism, making all of them at least consequentialists if not full-blooded, conventional utilitarians.

This chapter focuses on Hobson's utilitarian inheritance by, first, examining his criticisms of "old" or "narrow" utilitarianism. Hobson conceded that classical utilitarianism was plagued by many of the shortcomings identified by idealists. Yet, he insisted that it could be compellingly renovated. Next, I examine Hobson's efforts to refurbish utilitarianism. In particular, I try to assess what he means by "organic welfare" and what he means by "social utility" as the ultimate criterion of right. I also address Hobson's theory of moral rights, hoping to demonstrate how Hobson followed other new liberals in defending robust moral rights as utility-maximizing conditions. This chapter, then, completes my endeavor to show that the new liberalism was fundamentally a form of consequentialism. Notwithstanding Green's consequentialism, the new liberalism was, more specifically, a variety of liberal utilitarianism. However, unlike previous chapters, this one eschews treating concepts like self-realization in sustained detail because Hobson was much less a moral philosopher than Green, Hobhouse or Ritchie. Though self-realization constituted ultimate good for Hobson in some sense, he was much less preoccupied than the others with its psychological intricacies especially with regard to will and good will and their relationship to happiness. Hobson's liberal utilitarianism was, in short, less patently perfectionist.

The history of utilitarianism is considerably richer and more nuanced than its contemporary critics wish to allow and its contemporary proponents might be surprised to know. I want to correct this misimpression not merely in the name of improving intellectual history but also for the sake of defending contemporary utilitarianism. Recent analytical maneuvers to render utilitarianism more ethically appealing by making it more authentically liberal can benefit from greater sensitivity to utilitarianism's own history including especially its new liberal history. Insofar as Hobson was not only a new liberal but also a self-confessed "new utilitarian" to boot, liberal utilitarians can benefit from studying Hobson as much as from devotedly studying Mill.[1]

"OLD" AND "NEW" UTILITARIANISM

In the "Preface" to *The Social Problem*, Hobson declares boldly that he aims to repair political economy by transforming it into a new, more nuanced "science and art of social utility":

This science and art of social utility is clearly sundered from the *old utilitarianism* which was individualistic and hedonist in its standard, and purely quantitative in its method or calculus. To this *new utilitarianism*, so ordered as to give due recognition and rightful supremacy to the higher needs and satisfactions of man in society, the rights of individual property are referred for delimitation, and are set upon a rational basis. The part played by social cooperation, in the production of all forms of wealth and the germination of all forms of value, is investigated; and upon the results of this analysis the rights of society to possess and administer property for the commonwealth are established. The primary antithesis of Work and Life, function and nutrition, is examined in its physical, economic, and moral aspects, and is applied alike to the individual and the social organism, so as to yield a scientific harmony of the claims of Socialism and Individualism. Especial attention is given to marking clearly the operation of those industrial and social forces which make for the larger and more various activities of the State in politics and industry, and those which, on the other hand, directly tend to enlarge the bounds of individual liberty and enterprise. [my italics][2]

---

[1] H. C. G. Matthew therefore correctly insists that the new liberals were "created by the century they eschewed" though he doesn't fully appreciate just how much they were "created" by Millian utilitarianism. See H. C. G. Matthew, "Hobson, Ruskin and Cobden" in *Reappraising J. A. Hobson*, ed. Michael Freeden (London: Unwin Hyman, 1990), 11.

[2] J. A. Hobson [1902], *The Social Problem* (Bristol: Thoemmes, 1996), v–vi. Also see Hobson's "Preface," *The Crisis of Liberalism*, xii where Hobson says that although his liberalism is not socialism "in any accredited meaning of the term," it nevertheless implies considerably "increased public

Hobson was thus a self-professed "new" utilitarian for whom the "premature abandonment" of utilitarianism by its critics "has not been justified."[3] "Old" utilitarians failed in being excessively individualistic, hedonistic and quantitative. They were excessively individualist insofar as they celebrated enlightened self-interest at the expense of beneficence and sympathy. Hence, they were less scientifically neutral than they appeared: "Approval was not the aim, but approval was conveyed; and the whole tone of the teaching regarded ruthless self-assertion of individuals and nations as wholesome energy, which made for the greatest good of the greatest number."[4] Utilitarianism could nevertheless be rescued by reformulating goodness more expansively as "higher needs and satisfactions" and by delimiting property rights more aggressively. Still, rescuing and repairing "old" utilitarianism did not necessarily entail rescuing and repairing Bentham primarily since its failures weren't fully applicable to Bentham, making him, in effect, a precursor to Hobson's more sophisticated "new" utilitarianism. Hobson concedes,

The particular vices of some special form of utilitarianism, the insistence that desirability was entirely to be measured by quantity and never by quality, the stress upon physical enjoyment, and the short range of measurement, which were somewhat incorrectly attributed to Bentham's system, are not inherent in utilitarianism, and need not deter us from using its convenient language.[5]

But if Bentham doesn't epitomize traditional utilitarianism for Hobson, then who does?

"Old" utilitarianism was also too narrow for having become too closely associated with the "old political economy" of Smith, Ricardo, Senior and James Mill. The latter was too specialized and utterly failed to take account of the great complexity involved in solving the "social problem" of how best to maximize "social satisfaction." The scientific pretensions of the "old political economy" prevented it from taking account of the full breadth of factors constituting social satisfaction. Contrary to what "old" utilitarians and political economists held, welfare included more than mathematically

---

ownership and control of industry." Moreover, "from the standpoint which best presents its continuity with earlier Liberalism, it appears as a fuller appreciation and realisation of individual liberty contained in the provision of equal opportunities for self-development." In addition, "to this individual standpoint must be joined a just apprehension of the social, viz., the insistence that these claims or rights of self-development be adjusted to the sovereignty of social welfare." According to P. F. Clarke, "Introduction," *The Social Problem*, xvii, is "in many ways the direct precursor" to *The Crisis of Liberalism*.

[3] Hobson, *Social Problem*, 4.   [4] *Ibid.*, 29.   [5] *Ibid.*, 5.

quantifiable marketable goods but also included "higher human goods" such as knowledge, freedom and mental and physical health.[6]

Moreover, "old" utilitarianism failed by following traditional "Manchester" political economy in being too materially productivist and mechanical. It overemphasized the "getting" of marketable wealth at the expense of using it. By making the production and accumulation of material goods the cornerstone of welfare, it wrongly devalued the importance of consumption, particularly so-called unproductive consumption, to well-being. It especially ignored the consumption of the "conveniences and comforts of life" such as "books, music, entertainment, education" as well as the "supply of all intellectual and moral needs." The wealth of nations was as much a function of how well societies satisfied these needs as it was a function of how many material commodities and how much industrial capital they produced. Finally, the "old" utilitarianism was too mechanical or "statical" because it ignored the implications for moral and political theory of recent discoveries in evolutionary theory. "Old" utilitarians consequently wrongly assumed that a single pattern of political and economic reform mechanically fits at least all modern societies.[7]

Many of Hobson's criticisms of traditional utilitarianism, and his firm conviction that it could be suitably repaired, were shared by Hobhouse and Ritchie. (Again, even Green was much more favorably disposed to utilitarianism, when improved as Hobson envisioned, than the received view of him concedes.[8]) By and large, as we have seen, all new liberals criticized older utilitarianism for being mechanically quantitative and narrowly hedonistic. Regarding its narrow hedonism, for instance, recall how Ritchie and Hobhouse followed Green in denying that good was pleasure and that maximizing pleasure was therefore a coherent criterion of right. For all three, traditional utilitarians were deluded in believing that the greatest sum of pleasure constituted an intelligible normative goal. We only experience pleasures serially, making aggregate greatest pleasure an experiential fiction. As we shall shortly see, Hobson too endorsed this criticism of older utilitarianism.

---

[6] *Ibid.*, 17–21. Presumably, then, Ricardo, Senior and James Mill epitomize traditional utilitarianism for Hobson though, as we saw previously, Bentham apparently does not.

[7] See especially *ibid.*, 26–32.

[8] In this regard, see Hobson's claim that "even the philosophers, like the late Professor Green, who are stoutest in repudiating Utilitarianism, invariably return to that terminology to express their final judgment on a concrete moral issue" *ibid.*, 4–5. See too J. A. Hobson, *Confessions of an Economic Heretic* (London: George Allen and Unwin, 1938) 26, where Hobson acknowledges Green's influence in liberating his thinking from the narrow materialism of traditional utilitarianism.

Hobson likewise agreed with his fellow new liberals that Mill repaired utilitarianism though inadequately. He followed other new liberals who concurred with Hobhouse that Mill implicitly conceded that good was self-realization, and not pleasure, insofar as he admitted that pleasures differed qualitatively. By conceding the existence and superior worth of higher pleasures, Mill raised "the question what sort of experience it is that will yield pleasure of the most desirable quality," thus implying that some lifestyles were more valuable than others.[9] But, according to Hobson, it was "precisely on this rock that J. S. Mill's Utilitarianism split." Mill never succeeded in "furnishing any method of reducing" quantitative and qualitative distinctions about pleasure to "common terms," thereby compromising his utilitarian calculus.[10]

Now Hobson never entirely succeeds where Mill fails. As we shall shortly see, Hobson's "new" utilitarianism arguably splits apart on the same methodological rock that he says vitiated Mill's utilitarianism. Still, Hobson insists that improved utilitarianism remains roughly serviceable insofar as we substitute "welfare" in place of pleasure or happiness as our ultimate standard of value.[11] For Hobson, welfare is "larg[er]" and more elastic in that it properly takes account, unlike older utilitarianism, of the psychological complexities of human motivation. Our activities are motivated by instinctive urges as much as they are by the conscious and deliberate pursuit of happiness.[12]

---

[9] Hobhouse, *The Rational Good*, 196.

[10] J. A. Hobson [1912–13], "How is Wealth to Be Valued?", *Writings on Distribution and Welfare*, ed. Roger E. Backhouse (London: Routledge/Thoemmes, 1992), 594, n1. Also, see John Allett, "The Moral Philosophy of J. A. Hobson" in *J. A. Hobson after Fifty Years*, ed. John Pheby (New York: St. Martin's, 1994), 5–7 and John Allett, *The New Liberalism: The Political Economy of J. A. Hobson* (Toronto: University of Toronto Press, 1981), 52–7 and 182–8 for Hobson's critical assessment of utilitarianism in general and Mill's version of it in particular. Though Allett notes that Hobson described his own position as "broadly utilitarian," Allett nevertheless reads him as much less sympathetic to utilitarianism than I do. For an account of Hobson more in keeping with my own, see Michael Freeden, "J. A. Hobson as a Political Theorist" in *J. A. Hobson after Fifty Years*, 24. For Freeden, Hobson "favoured a constrained version [of utilitarianism] that wishes to maximise or optimise only a liberal-humanitarian conception of human nature." I think that "optimise," rather than "maximize," captures more accurately the kind of operationalizing of good that Hobson defended. Throughout this study, I have argued that the new liberals were not so much *good-maximizing* consequentialists as they were *good-promoting* consequentialists. Optimizing seems closer to what I mean by promoting.

[11] See especially, J. A. Hobson, *Free-Thought in the Social Sciences* (London: George Allen and Unwin, 1926), 172 where Hobson says, "Though no exact comparison and measurement of pleasures and pains, or of satisfaction treated in terms of personality, is possible in dealing with different persons, the admittedly common character of mankind will suffice to furnish some very serviceable rules for the betterment of economic life, i.e. for the enlargement of economic welfare."

[12] Allett claims that Hobson's stress on instinctive motivation reinforces his claim that "our natural mode is an activist one" contrary to what traditional utilitarianism holds. And in undervaluing activity, traditional utilitarianism overvalued consumption as a source of pleasure because consumption is purportedly passive rather than active. Now Allett may be right that traditional utilitarianism undervalues activity and overvalues consumption. But the passage from Hobson he alludes to does not obviously suggest that because we are, in part, instinctively motivated, we are

ORGANIC WELFARE

The "new" utilitarianism, in contrast with its older version, was more nuanced art than mathematical science. Like its less sophisticated predecessor, it held that industrial society's socio-economic problems could only be solved by reforms guided by "some single standard of the humanly desirable." But unlike its predecessor, the "new" utilitarianism substituted in place of "old" utilitarianism's impoverished "monetary standard of wealth" a richer, more complex "standard of human well-being." The goal of reform should be, following Ruskin, "the multiplication of human life at its highest standard."[13]

Hobson sometimes refers to his criterion of right as "organic welfare" and sometimes as "social utility." For the moment, it is best to set aside what he means by the latter and instead concentrate on the meaning he gives to "organic welfare." The former designation is meant to highlight several advantages that his "new" utilitarian, normative standard possesses over "old" utilitarianism's mechanical standard. First, "organic welfare" underscores the extent to which the satisfaction of *physical* needs constitutes the foundation of human happiness.

Second, welfare understood organically testifies to the mistake of regarding production merely as cost and consumption merely as satisfaction in the way that "old" utilitarian political economy typically does. "Old" utilitarianism, that is, wrongly treats each person inorganically as two separate persons, namely as producer and consumer. In treating each as a producer, it treats each person's life as painful effort only. In treating each as consumer, it treats each person's life as exclusively pleasurable. For "old" utilitarianism, production is exclusively painful and consumption always pleasurable. Hence, "old" utilitarian economic policy amounts to little more than discovering strategies minimizing time spent producing and maximizing time spent consuming. However, production and consumption must be viewed in terms of their "total bearing upon the life of the producer or consumer." Welfare organically understood "obliges us to value every act of production or consumption with regard to its aggregate effect upon the life and character of the agent." In other words, producing is often satisfying and consuming often very unsatisfying. Hence, maximizing welfare requires taking account of how different kinds of production and consumption generate different

---

therefore naturally active whatever that means precisely. See Allett, "The Moral Philosophy of J. A. Hobson," 6. For the passage from Hobson that Allett draws on, see Hobson, *Free-Thought in the Social Sciences*, 168–9.

[13] J. A. Hobson [1914], *Work and Wealth* (London: George Allen and Unwin, 1933), 1–11.

combinations of utility and disutility respectively. *How* we produce and consume matters as much as *how much* we produce and *how much* we consume.[14]

Hobson was especially distressed by the deadening and degrading nature of capitalist production for workers. Wage labor rendered work degrading and joyless by routinizing it and by fragmenting workers and making them indifferent to the social nature of production:

No one acquainted widely with the facts of industry can seriously question the statement that the conditions of much modern work tend to crush out all human interest in it. A man can get no pleasure from his work when it imposes a constant strain upon the same muscles and nerves, and can be most easily done so far as the actions become automatic; when the tedium of constantly repeating the same narrow movements compels the cultivation of indifference; when strict confinement to a single process hides from him the true purposes and utility of his work, and he cannot claim any single whole commodity as the product of his labour.[15]

Moreover, wage labor eviscerated spontaneity, substituting another's will for the worker's own. It reduced workers to instruments of production thus treating labor power as just another commodity.[16] Instead of being what artists refer to as their *work*, wage labor is never more than mere debilitating *labor* for the hapless worker. Instead of realizing myself by "paint[ing] myself" on the "canvas of time," in laboring for a wage I mechanically duplicate myself endlessly.[17]

Finally, "organic welfare" reminds us that societies are not merely aggregations of individual men and women. Every society possesses a "group-life with a collective body, a collective consciousness and will" and is "capable of realising a collective vital end," making "recognition of the independent value of the good life of a society" absolutely "essential to any science or art of Society."[18] Therefore, in evaluating public policies as

---

[14] *Ibid.*, 12–14.　[15] Hobson, *The Social Problem*, 227–8.　[16] Hobson, *Work and Wealth*, 195.
[17] Hobson, "How is Wealth to Be Valued?," 602.
[18] Hobson, *Work and Wealth*, 15. Hobson continues, "Society may then be conceived, not as a set of social relations, but as a collective organism, with life, will, purpose, meaning of its own, as distinguished from the life, will, purpose, meaning, of the individual members of it." And on 17, Hobson adds that "in feeling and action," each person "is both an individual and a member of a number of social groups, expanding in a series of concentric circles from family and city to humanity and in dimmer outline to some larger cosmic organism." But he also cautions that the "concept 'organism' as applied to the life of animals and vegetables, is not wholly appropriate to describe the life of a society, but it is more appropriate than any other concept, and some concept must be applied." Some term is needed "to assist the mind in realising clearly that all life proceeds by the cooperation of units working, not each for its separate self, but for a whole, and attaining their separate well-being in the proper functioning of that whole" (15–16). See, as well, *The Social Problem*, 224, where Hobson says: "Society exists, not, as is sometimes maintained, in order consciously to

well as individual actions, we must consider their consequences not just for individuals separately or in the aggregate but for societies as organic wholes to which they belong. We must weigh consequences "not only upon the individuals who produce and consume the goods, but upon the city, nation, or other society to which they belong."[19]

Hobson's organicism threatens his political theory's liberal credentials though commentators have disagreed about how literally Hobson intended the analogy to be taken. Michael Freeden insists that Hobson never abandoned organicism though he gradually came to construe it in an increasingly psychological rather than biological fashion.[20] But whatever he meant by organicism, we shouldn't see it as vitiating all forms of utilitarianism though robust organicism unquestionably fits poorly with its liberal form in particular.

secure the separate welfare of its individual members, but to secure the health and progress of society always realized as a spiritual organism; but this end, interpreted at any given time in terms of 'social utility,' has been seen to involve the care and promotion of individual health and progress. It can never be the interest of society to attempt to dominate or enslave the individual, sucking his energies for the supposed nutriment of the State; any such endeavour would be futile, for, as we have seen, an attempt to exploit those energies, or to take away that 'property' which nature has set aside for individual support and progress, would defeat its end by drying up the sources of such energy and 'property.' Neither is it to the real advantage of the 'individuality' of any individual to retain a churlish isolation, and by an excessive pride of self-sufficiency to refuse a due acknowledgment of those external and internal social bonds which nature has likewise furnished to enable each 'individuality' to be enlarged and enriched form social sources." See, in addition, 223. According to John Allett, "The Conservative Aspect of Hobson's New Liberalism" in, ed. M. Freeden *Reappraising J. A. Hobson*, (London: Unwin Hyman), 84 and 85, *Work and Wealth* was the "high-point of Hobson's enthusiasm for organicist doctrine," which he deployed to suppress older utilitarianism's excessive individualism and hedonism.

[19] Hobson, *Work and Wealth*, 17.

[20] Michael Freeden, *Liberalism Divided* (Oxford: Oxford University Press, 1986), 233. According to Freeden, moreover, Hobson vacillated between physical vs. non-physical accounts of social organicism before WWI though, by the late 1920s, he tended to emphasize its "mental and cultural" attributes. Also, see Freeden, *The New Liberalism*, 105–9. Hobson was not so much vacillating between understanding societies as physical vs. non-physical organisms prior to WWI. Rather, he regarded them as having both physical and non-physical attributes. In the *Crisis of Liberalism*, 73, Hobson says that he considers societies physical and psychical organisms. Every society is "rightly regarded as a moral rational organism in the sense that it has a common psychic life, character, and purpose, which are not to be resolved into the life, character, and purpose of its individual members." Each "individual's feeling, his will, his ends, and interests, are not entirely merged in or sacrificed to the public feeling, will and ends, but over a certain area they are fused and identified, and the common social life thus formed has conscious interests and ends of its own which are not merely instruments in forwarding the progress of the separate individuals lives, but are directed primarily to secure the survival and psychical progress of the community regarded as a spiritual whole" (76). Note, nevertheless, that Hobson says that speaking of societies as physical organisms is a "convenience in language" (71). For Hobson's disagreement with Hobhouse regarding the existence of group mind, see especially J. A. Hobson, "The Theory of the State," *Manchester Guardian*, 23/11/1918. Also, see Hobson, *Confessions of an Economic Heretic*, 76–9. For Hobhouse, see *Social Development*, 178–87. And for Hobson's acknowledgment of the similarities between his organicism and Rousseau's conception of general will, see Hobson, *The Crisis of Liberalism*, 76.

THE POLITICAL ECONOMY OF "NEW" UTILITARIANISM

"Old" utilitarianism's mechanical political economy must be transformed into a "science of human wealth" if it is to be repaired and humanized as "new" utilitarianism. Three steps are required in order to "reduce" old to new utilitarianism: first, monetary wealth must always be converted into subjective pleasures or utilities because the former is a very crude measure of real well-being. Though England's annual income was steadily increasing, we shouldn't conclude that its citizens were necessarily becoming better off. Indeed, it was quite likely that they were making themselves into "greater drudges," working harder and chasing after phantom satisfaction via greater material consumption. With respect to unskilled wage labor in particular, no cost parity exists "between such work and the labour of the skilled craftsman working under wholesome conditions upon material whose handling evokes his genuine interest and skill – work which is in its nature educating and humanizing."[21] Second, insofar as subjective pleasures nevertheless fall short of completely capturing well-being, we must "adjust" them by "reference to the *real* good or worth of the individual life considered as a whole" (my italics). Third, we must "harmonize" individual and social good, making "social utility" our "*final* criterion" (my italics).[22]

Hobson devotes more detailed attention to the first transformatory step, particularly in *The Social Problem* and *Work and Wealth*. In order to measure the true utility contained in material production, Hobson recommends first that we take account of the character and conditions of work. Different types of work yield different combinations and net sums of pleasure and pain. For instance, landscape painting as a means of livelihood, being creative, is mostly highly satisfying and ennobling while sweated labor is almost entirely painful drudgery and dehumanizing. This is why, contrary to "old" utilitarian political economy, production isn't necessarily all pain and cost though, under unreformed capitalism, it appears to be. Hobson also recommends that we pay attention to the distribution of work in converting production to utility. Shared equally among a sufficiently large workforce over a modest workday, work is much less painful than when it is sweated out of an undersized workforce from dawn to dusk. Finally, Hobson insists that we consider the differing

---

[21] Hobson, *The Social Problem*, 46.
[22] *Ibid.*, 39. Hobson adds that since the realization of individual good coincides with the realization of social good, the second and third steps are practically identical.

capacities of workers when measuring the real utility of production. Their strength, skill, age, sex and race must be taken into account as otherwise potential well-being is wasted. Although Hobson does not say so explicitly, his inherent view is that most industrial labor is presumably less taxing and therefore more gratifying for healthy, adult, white males.

In sum, the cost of production must be "reduced to terms of life" in order to obtain a "truly scientific grasp" of the amount and kind of utility generated in industrial societies:

> If a manufacturer shows you a quantity of goods, and tells you how much they cost to produce, he gives you no information of human interest; even if he told you how many hours of labour were represented in the cost, you would still know nothing. You would want to know how heavily the burden actually fell upon each of those who contributed, how many men, women, and children worked, what the hours of labour and other conditions were in each case.[23]

Hobson also applies the same three-fold analysis to consumption, or what he calls "economic utility," as part of his first step of humanizing "old" utilitarian political economy. No less than its production, the consumption of wealth must likewise be converted or reduced to subjective pleasures in order to measure general happiness accurately and effectively. First, the monetary value of goods and services consumed must be converted into what Ruskin refers to as their "life-sustaining" and "life-improving" qualities.[24] Traditional political economy fails to penetrate beneath the superficial, monetary value of consumption, taking such superficial value as a genuine measure of well-being. It wrongly ranks the sale price of "large masses of adulterated foods, shoddy clothing, bad books, pernicious art, [and] snobbish personal services" as components of actual wealth.[25] Second, the true utility of consumption is also a function of how consumption is distributed. For instance, in calculating the real utility of the bread supply, "it is evident that, while the first portion of the supply has an infinite value, the last portion has no value, since servants throw it into the dustbin."[26] Or in the terminology of contemporary analytical utilitarianism, the utility of consumption tends to decline marginally as consumption increases. Satiated consumers derive declining satisfaction from continued consumption. One more of Dworkin's plover's egg adds next to nothing to one's happiness when one has already stuffed oneself with a half dozen. Moreover, so long as consumption is maldistributed with some citizens doing without necessities while others gorge themselves consuming

[23] *Ibid.*, 47. [24] *Ibid.*, 48. [25] *Ibid.*, 47. [26] *Ibid.*, 49.

marginally satisfying luxuries, considerable general happiness is wasted. Governments are accordingly justified in regulating consumption in the name of minimizing such waste. Third, in measuring the utility of consumption, we must finally take account of the character and education of consumers for the "higher or more refined kinds of modern commodities" would possess little value for a "barbarous race, however rightly distributed."[27] Hence, governments can also do much to foster general utility by educating the tastes and refining the character of consumers. But whatever they should do in the name of promoting well-being, they clearly ought not to equalize incomes since even well-educated consumers will experience differential consumption utilities depending upon their talents and abilities. Hence, "equality of opportunity does not imply equality but some inequality of incomes."[28]

No doubt, someone like Berlin would view such justification of government responsibility with trepidation, seeing, for instance, the education of consumer tastes as freedom-denying reeducation. And even if Hobson is merely implying that government ought to restrict itself to providing consumers with new opportunities for refining their tastes and character, Berlin might still worry that government would then be encouraging citizens to retreat to some officially favored inner citadel of consumer satisfaction. Perhaps Hobson means only to suggest that general welfare might improve if everyone had an equal chance to train their palates in the exquisite delights of plover's eggs. Yet government might succeed in improving general welfare even more dramatically simply by subsidizing everyone's opportunity to *retrain* their palates to crave something more readily available like cheap mush.

Notwithstanding Berlin's likely anxieties, Hobson nevertheless anticipates similar anxieties of those who would later condemn modern capitalism for surreptitiously promoting "new wasteful modes of conventional consumption."[29] Much like the Frankfurt School afterwards, Hobson reproves modern commercial society for the way that producers and advertisers manipulate consumers by persuading them to want things that they don't need.[30] Consumption is determined not by real "organic

---

[27] *Ibid.*, 49.   [28] Hobson, *Work and Wealth*, 165.   [29] *Ibid.*, 139.

[30] "A new line of drapery is 'pushed' into use by the repeated statement, false at the beginning, that 'it is worn'. . . In a word, the arts of the manufacturer and of the vendor, which have no direct relation whatever to intrinsic utility, overcome and subjugate the uncertain, untrained or 'artificially' perverted taste of the consumer. Thus it arises that in commercial society every standard of class comfort is certain to contain large ingredients of useless or noxious consumption, articles, not only bad in themselves, but often poisoning or distorting the whole standard. The arts of adulteration and of advertising are of course responsible for many of the worst instances." *Ibid.*, 133.

needs, but by imitation of the conventional consumption of the class immediately above in income or in social esteem."[31] Conventional consumption thoroughly fails as a source of "organic utility."

In sum, like production, consumption must be converted into real utility. That is, in calculating the satisfaction generated by consumption, we need to know the quality of the goods and services consumed, who consumes how much of them and the character and education of consumers.

THE AUTHORITY OF RUSKIN

In *Confessions of an Economic Heretic*, Hobson affirmed that from Ruskin, he drew the "basic thought for my subsequent economic writings, viz. the necessity of going behind the current monetary estimates of wealth, cost, and utility, to reach the body of human benefits and satisfactions which gave them a real meaning."[32] The extent to which Ruskin informed Hobson's subsequent efforts to repair utilitarianism is nowhere clearer than in Hobson's 1898 *John Ruskin, Social Reformer* where he extolled Ruskin's criticisms of traditional political economy's thin conception of wealth. There Hobson praises Ruskin for helping him appreciate that "human utility" was a function of (1) the nature of both work itself and the goods produced, (2) the capacities of workers and consumers to express themselves in production and consumption and (3) the distribution of work and consumption.

For instance, regarding the impact of the nature of work on well-being, Hobson says that Ruskin properly understood that insofar as work was challenging and educative, it was not really toil but instead satisfying. Whenever work is undertaken for a wage and becomes overspecialized, dull and rote, it degrades workers, alienating them from what should be a fulfilling activity by reducing work to labor. It divides workers into fragments of human beings, sapping them of their dignity. Moreover, it severs product from process, causing workers to no longer identify with, and take pride in, whatever they produce. In sum, Ruskin understood better than most that the "distinctive conditions of industrial work are, first, narrowness, the confinement to a single set of actions; second, monotony, the

---

[31] *Ibid.*, 140.
[32] Hobson, *Confessions of an Economic Heretic*, 42. For Ruskin's comparable influence on Collingwood, see David Boucher, "R. G. Collingwood: The Enemy Within and the Crisis of Civilisation" in Boucher and Vincent, *British Idealism and Political Theory*, esp. 185–6.

assimilation of the man-worker to a mechanism; third, irrationality of labour, by dissociating the work of each worker from the conscious attainment of any complete end."[33] Likewise, consumption was satisfying only insofar as it met wholesome wants. Consumption "for life" is genuine wealth whereas consumption of "noxious" commodities makes "for death" and therefore constitutes "illth."[34]

For Hobson, in sum, traditional utilitarians had much to learn from Ruskin, including his understanding of well-being, which he articulated so eloquently in *Unto This Last*: "THERE IS NO WEALTH BUT LIFE. Life, including all its powers of love, of joy, and of admiration. That country is the richest which nourishes the greatest number of noble and happy human beings; that man is richest who, having perfected the functions of his own life to the utmost, has also the widest influence, both personal and by means of his possessions, over the lives of others."[35] And utilitarians could learn so much from him because he was a utilitarian in the end, albeit an unconventional one. Though Ruskin rejected Benthamite utilitarianism for its apparent hedonism, he "may not unaptly be classed as a utilitarian." Though he denounced the principle of the greatest happiness of the greatest number because it grounded happiness in "fleeting pleasures and pains," he nevertheless held that morally right action was action in accord with "conditions of abiding

---

[33] J. A. Hobson [1898], *John Ruskin: Social Reformer* in William Smart and John Hobson, *John Ruskin*, ed. Peter Cain (London: Routledge/Thoemmes, 1994), 118. Also see 214 where Hobson praises Ruskin for comprehending how modern division of labor "subdivides the man, makes him less than a man – a mere servant of a machine in one narrow routine process . . . This is a mortal injury: it denotes the difference between a man who uses a tool and a tool that uses a man." And see 226 where Ruskin properly understood how Manchester and Leeds had become "typical machine-made products; they exist primarily not as 'cities,' for wholesome social life of citizens, but as workshops for the most economical production and distribution of machine-made goods." Finally, see J. A. Hobson [1909], *The Industrial System*, ed. Peter Cain (London: Routledge/Thoemmes, 1992), 334 where Hobson says: "The final harmony of industry is reached when we see a worker who lives in and for his work, who expresses himself freely and joyfully in it, and who is at one and the same time producer and consumer."

[34] *Ibid.*, 95. Also see J. A. Hobson [1896], "Human Cost and Utility" in R. E. Backhouse (ed.), *Writings on Distribution and Welfare* (London: Routledge/Thoemmes Press, 1992). See especially 13 where Hobson says: "Would the statement that the income of England had risen from £120,000,000 in 1770 to 1,500,000,000 in 1895 convey any information of what would rightly be described as a 'human' character . . . Would it even mean that his [the average man] balance of pleasure over pain was greater? Of course it would mean nothing of the sort. It might mean that he was making more of a drudge of himself, looking harder after money under conditions which sapped his vitality and disabled him from making a pleasant and a profitable use of his larger income."

[35] Hobson, *John Ruskin: Social Reformer*, 78. For this passage in Ruskin, see John Ruskin [1862], *Unto This Last* in *The Genius of John Ruskin*, ed. John D. Rosenburg (London: Routledge and Kegan Paul, 1979), 270. Hobson cites this passage again in *Confessions of an Economic Heretic*, 39.

happiness."[36] So, following Hobson and other new liberals, Ruskin purportedly thought that trying to maximize pleasure was incoherent because pleasures were so ephemeral whereas maximizing "abiding" happiness was not. And since maximizing happiness properly understood was entirely plausible, we are fully entitled to make it our ultimate criterion of right. Thus, Hegel wasn't the only avenue by which new liberals learned to reject Benthamism for adopting such a narrowly hedonic, and therefore problematic, conception of good as our maximizing goal (unless Ruskin, in turn, borrowed his criticism of hedonistic utilitarianism from Hegel). New liberal consequentialism drew from diverse philosophical sources in repairing traditional utilitarianism.

Ruskin, of course, was a conservative in many respects. Consequently, Hobson parted company with him on several accounts. For Hobson, Ruskin's solutions for nineteenth-century capitalism's ills were too backward-looking and feudalistic. Though the state would nominally own all agricultural land, real control of it would lie with the traditional aristocracy as would control of the professions and state bureaucracy. Moreover, Ruskin was neither an egalitarian nor a democrat. He was unenthusiastic about trade unionism and industrial cooperation, favoring traditional paternalistic remedies for alleviating poverty and working-class hardship.[37] For Hobson, then, Ruskin was simultaneously a fellow-traveling, radical critic and a reactionary reformer. But however much he dreamed the dream of *noblesse oblige* as modern industrial society's curative, he nevertheless followed Hobson and other new liberals in dreaming mostly consequentially.

FACT AND VALUE

As noted previously, Hobson devotes much less attention to the second and third steps for transforming "old" utilitarian political economy into a genuine and humanized science of well-being. With respect to the second step requiring that subjective pleasures be adjusted in accordance to the worth of individual lives considered as a "whole," Hobson says, for

---

[36] Ibid., 85. Hobson quotes *Unto This Last* (254) where Ruskin says that the "final outcome and consummation of all wealth is in the producing as many as possible full-breathed, bright-eyed, and happy-hearted human creatures." Hobson cites a similar passage from Ruskin in *The Social Problem*, 7. He then cites, and concurs with, Ritchie whom he interprets as claiming that morally right entails not just maximizing happiness appropriately understood but also minimizing pain understood as human "waste."

[37] See especially *The Social Problem*, chs VII–VIII, for Hobson's criticisms of Ruskin.

instance, that a "rational treatment of the wants and satisfactions in a completely ordered life will assign an infinite – i.e. an unquantitative – value to each of them, because it will regard each as a vitally necessary part of an infinitely valuable whole."[38] Now this is a deeply problematic claim for any self-professed utilitarian, "new" or otherwise, to make. How can we ascertain which actions are morally right when the wants and satisfactions we are called upon to promote are infinitely, and therefore, incalculably valuable? Hobson's doesn't make his position clearer where he adds that more valuable lives are "better, fuller, and more complex."[39] On the other hand, Hobson simply may be implying that certain wants are so basic, so "vitally necessary," that their satisfaction must be universally guaranteed if everyone is to enjoy real equal opportunity to flourish and thereby maximize general well-being indirectly.[40]

Finally, regarding the third transformatory step, Hobson says that making "social utility" our "final criterion" of right amounts to reducing the "current feelings of individuals" to a "standard of true or absolute utility regarded from the social standpoint."[41] It is "absolutely essential to our purpose to abandon the fleeting and often mistaken, estimates which individuals set upon efforts and satisfactions, regarded as passing separate phenomena, and to firmly establish, as an *objective* standard of reference, social utility" (my italics). Hobson thus *appears* to follow fellow new liberals in rejecting pleasure as an intelligible standard of right because pleasurable sensations are so ephemeral, making maximum pleasure an

---

[38] Hobson, *The Social Problem*, 78.   [39] *Ibid.*, 81.

[40] Notwithstanding the difficulties in measuring and promoting infinitely valuable, "vitally necessary" wants and satisfactions, Hobson further insists that no sharp distinction exists between vitally necessary wants and luxuries. Not only do life's necessities evolve and expand as industrialism develops, but the meaning of necessity at any point in time in any particular society is always contested in any case. (But as we shall shortly see, Hobson generally holds that our basic wants and desires appear stable though they evolve imperceptibly.) Nevertheless, according to Hobson, the satisfaction of lower material needs generally takes precedence over the satisfaction of higher moral and intellectual needs. Hence, philanthropists who concentrate on helping the poor meet their higher needs first promote considerable waste and disutility. Moreover, to those (presumably Bosanquet among others) who might reply that he mistakenly advocates enslaving the poor to their circumstances ignoring how external moral stimulus can encourage the poor to pull themselves up by their own bootstraps, Hobson replies with false-consciousness smashing sarcasm: "To such I would reply, firstly, that such cases constitute the 'moral miracles' to which reference is already made, and their rare existence abates but slightly the waste of reform energy; and, secondly, that the ability of one, or any, individual to get out of his class no more implies the ability of a whole class, or of any considerable proportion of a class, to get out of its condition than the fact that any boy in America is able to become President of the United States implies the ability of all the boys living at any given time to attain this position. To impute this power to a class involves a total misunderstanding of the nature of individual and class competition in industrial society" (*ibid.*, 84).

[41] *Ibid.*, 51.

incoherent normative target. And he substitutes in its place what *appears* to be an objective standard. Moreover, he happily accepts "organic welfare" and even sometimes the "self-realization of society" as alternative formulations of good though he nonetheless prefers "social utility" because "political philosophers, to whatever school or phraseology they profess allegiance, inevitably drift into language of 'utility,' whenever they are confronted with a practical issue of conduct the desirability of which is the subject of consideration."[42] Even "philosophers, like the late Professor Green, who are stoutest in repudiating Utilitarianism, invariably return to that terminology to express their final judgment on a concrete moral issue."[43]

So, for Hobson, humanizing utilitarianism also entails fortifying it with an improved, objective standard of right, namely social utility or "organic welfare" as he sometimes prefers to call it. Taking social utility as our ultimate normative criterion salvages "old" utilitarianism from the mechanical vulgarity of traditional political economy. Now Hobson acknowledges, responding to the emotivist anxieties of his times, that some (such as Keynes in particular) may accuse him of illicitly importing "*a priori* ethics" into political economic science. Some may object that he is confusing "a science of *what is* with a science of *what ought to be*."[44] But Hobson replies, joining idealistic epistemology and ontology with pragmatic political theory, that no ordering of facts is possible without appealing to outside ordering principles embodying the "objects or ends of the process of investigation in a hypothetical way." Social scientific investigation always presupposes "some clear *motive* for investigation, and this motive will be related to a wider motive, which will eventually relate to some large speculative idea."[45] In short, doing social science properly means drawing on Hegel along with some Dewey.

Social scientists, then, must avoid emasculating themselves morally.[46] They must avoid artificially separating ought from is:

The "ought" is not something separable and distinct from the "is;" on the contrary, an "ought" is everywhere the highest aspect or relation of an 'is.' If a "fact" has a moral *import* (as, in strictness, every fact of human significance must have, though,

---

[42] *Ibid.*, 64.   [43] *Ibid.*, 5.   [44] *Ibid.*, 66.

[45] Ibid., 65. Also see 65–6 where Hobson says, "Driven far back, the whole series of investigations and reasonings at different foci will be found to relate to and to be dependent on some hypothesis of political or social good, which is the 'end,' hidden, doubtless, as a conscious motive for the detailed student buried in his tiny group of facts, but none the less permeating the whole process with 'teleology.'"

[46] "The knowledge of 'positive facts' is not forwarded by a policy of moral emasculation" (*ibid.*, 67).

for convenience, we may often ignore it), that moral *import* is part of the nature of the fact, and the fact cannot be fully known as fact without taking it into consideration. We may, of course, institute an inquiry which ignores the "ought," and which so leaves out of view the net social *consequences* for good and evil of any fact; it may often be convenient to pursue this course; but do not let us deceive ourselves into believing that we are investigating all the fact and excluding something which is not fact. This is only another instance of the protean fallacy of individualism, which feigns the existence of separate individuals by abstracting and neglecting the social relations which belong to them and make them what they are ... No fact can be fully known as such without regarding it as belonging to a system of facts ordered by a principle which, by common acceptance, is regarded as ethical. There is nothing whatever "mystical" in this; it simply means you do not know a fact until and unless you know how it is *affected by* and *affects* other facts, and have applied some standard of valuation to these influences. [my italics][47]

Now contemporary non-cognitivists would surely brand Hobson's claims so much metaphysical gibberish and confused logic. Cognitivists, however, might be more sympathetic. They might agree with Hobson that Moore's account of the naturalistic fallacy is itself grounded in a deeper fallacy, namely the individualist fallacy. Avoid methodological individualism and the naturalistic fallacy disappears. Ontology and meta-ethics are ineluctably intertwined. When the former goes astray, the latter follows suit.[48] In other words, Hobson seems to hold that because positive facts only make sense in relation to other positive facts that they affect and are effected by, truth is therefore pragmatic. Truth is always oriented by motives about consequences, about how we want facts to affect each other. One can't make sense of the world, or put it together meaningfully, without understanding our motives about how we prefer the world to go. Different sets of motives put the world together differently and different ways of putting the world together, in turn, inform our motives. In sum, for Hobson, truth as coherence leads straight away to consequentialist ethics.

Though I confess to interpreting him sympathetically, I would not want to defend him uncritically. No doubt, analytical neo-Kantians would nevertheless continue insisting that Hobson confuses is and ought by confusing the fact that phenomena are causally related with the human evaluation of causal relationships. Just because phenomena have consequences, just because facts can be manipulated into different causal sequences, it doesn't follow logically that "moral import is part" of their nature.

---

[47] *Ibid.*, 66–7.
[48] Hobson presumably has Moore in mind as much as Keynes. Both Moore and Keynes were members of the Bloomsbury Circle. Like fellow Bloomsburians, Keynes looked to Moore for his moral philosophy.

Because scientific laws are causal and have consequences for humans, we shouldn't conclude that social science is necessarily moral science. At the very least, we certainly shouldn't conclude that natural science is equally moral science. Morality is not a constitutive feature of positive science.[49] Notwithstanding these likely criticisms, let us turn to Hobson's communitarianism for assistance.

COMMUNITY AND INFORMED PREFERENCES

In taking Social Utility for a standard of reference for the values of effort and satisfaction, we labour under no illusion as to definiteness or permanency. As a working hypothesis for the regulation of conduct, Social Utility is an *ever-changing* standard, nor is it precisely the same for any two individuals. It will be the function of ethics constantly to re-form and re-state the substance of Social Utility, and to readjust the standard to accord with a rising and more rational interpretation of "the essential needs or ultimate demands of our nature." But, though Social Utility may not mean precisely the same for any two persons, and may differ widely for two societies, or for one society in two ages, this is no valid objection to its adoption. Some *agreement* as to the meaning of Social Utility exists in every society, for otherwise the "general will" could not operate. In so far as the members of a society own the same nature, habits, education, institutions, and range of vision, they possess a *common* grasp of what is for the *good* of society, and growing experience and wisdom render it a more practically serviceable rule [my italics].[50]

Plainly, Hobson holds that social utility, as a criterion of right, is communally *situated*. Its meaning, in other words, is a matter of convention and *consensus*. Members of any vibrant society will always share a core understanding of what social utility means *for them* though they may disagree about its meaning around the edges.[51] Without this consensus, societies would disintegrate though they wouldn't progress either unless their consensus about social utility was not continually being reassessed.

---

[49] In *Free-Thought in the Social Sciences*, Hobson conflates is with ought differently. Rather than saying that facts are normative because they often have normative consequences, he says instead that, since norms can be studied scientifically, ethics is about what is as much as it is about what ought to be. "For an 'ought', i.e. some fact weighted with a 'moral' value, is none the less an 'is' (222–3). But, of course, describing and explaining normative claims sociologically and anthropologically doesn't necessarily establish anything at all about their validity. Emotivists have never denied that we can say much sociologically about the development of norms. For instance, see A. J. Ayer [1946], *Language, Truth and Logic* (New York: Dover, 1952), 112.

[50] *Ibid.*, 69.

[51] Also see *Work and Wealth*, viii where Hobson says: "Moreover, though idiosyncrasies will everywhere affect this operative ideal, there will be found among persons of widely different minds and dispositions a substantial body of agreement in their meaning of human welfare. The common social environment partly evokes, partly imposes, this agreement."

As early as 1901 in *The Social Problem*, then, Hobson was beginning to regard social utility as culturally conventional rather than universal and objective. Adjusting subjective pleasures to a "true" standard of utility (the second step for converting old into new utilitarianism) really meant adjusting them to dominant standards of utility varying from culture to culture.[52] Moreover, for Hobson, ethics' special task is to "re-form and re-state" continually our consensus about social utility, "readjust[ing]" this consensus according to our improved dexterity in interpreting our "essential needs" rationally. Ethics constantly prods and questions what we take social utility to mean, reshaping it relentlessly though carefully. The meaning of social utility is always unstable like all human conventions and must be constantly refortified and rearticulated philosophically if consensus about it is not only to hold firm but is to stimulate genuine social and political improvement as well.

In his intellectual biography, *Confessions of an Economic Heretic*, published in 1938 shortly before his death, Hobson raises the issue of whether we should take as our standard of right our *actual* desires about goodness (social utility) or those desires we *ought* to have about it. In his words, "Are we to take the existing estimate of the desirable and undesirable which each person holds, or some higher estimate of what is 'good' for them, what they ought to and would desire if they had a more intelligent view of their *real* interests?"[53] (We would now characterize such worries in terms of whether the *preferences we happen to have* about goodness or whether our *informed preferences* about goodness best capture its identity or meaning.) Hobson's response is a compromise. He says that in earlier works such as *Work and Wealth*, he maintained that actual preferences about goodness tended to coincide with preferences about goodness people would hold if they were properly informed. He then adds that in his later *Wealth and Life: A Human Valuation*, he modified this assumption, laying greater stress on informed preferences.[54] Informed preferences about goodness correct our

---

[52] Also see Hobson's 1910 *The Industrial System*, 327, where Hobson says, regarding transforming industrial production into real utility, that it must first be translated into the net balance of pleasure over pain (first step) and "secondly, into a balance of social welfare as indicated by the ideal standard which every society must *set before itself* [my italics]." See, as well, Hobson's 1914 *Work and Wealth*, 33, where Hobson similarly remarks that new utilitarianism requires that we reduce monetary values to "terms of that desirability corrected so as to conform to the best-approved standard of the desirable." By "best-approved," I take it that Hobson means "best-approved" within the confines of one's particular society.

[53] Hobson, *Confessions of an Economic Heretic*, 203.

[54] Meadowcroft claims that Hobson never satisfactorily reconciled the tension between subjective and objective goodness. See James Meadowcroft, "Introduction," Hobson, *The Social Problem*, xiv–xv.

actual preferences which are too often distorted by self-interest and personal taste. Informed preferences are "further-sighted" and, more importantly for our purposes, are grounded in a "more social interpretation" of utility. That is, they are *socially* informed though, of course, their being socially informed does not mean we should accept them uncritically. Moreover, improved recognition of the socially informed nature of informed preferences justifies greater public responsibility for providing public services: "As a larger and larger share of the control of industry and expenditure of income passes into public hands, this imposition of a more informed and further-sighted public choice upon the less informed shorter-sighted individual choice alters our attitude towards cost and utility, the human character of which is endowed with less of the casual personal estimate and more of a longer-sighted social estimate."[55] In sum, the more we appreciate the extent to which our preferences are socially informed, especially those pertaining to goodness itself, the more we should trust in the state not only to interpret and articulate those preferences but also to enforce their satisfaction.

In leaning more towards an informed preference over an actual preference account of good, *Wealth and Life* not surprisingly depicts more boldly what Hobson thinks informed goodness fundamentally is. Good is "personality in its widest sense" understood as a whole life rich in different kinds of conscious satisfactions. Actions were therefore right insofar as they contributed to "aggregate conscious satisfaction" grounded in the "organic harmonious cooperation of interrelated physical and mental activities."[56] And insofar as good consisted in conscious satisfaction, ethics was thus rescued "from vague conceptions of self-realization, in order to make of it a New Utilitarianism in which physical, intellectual, and moral satisfactions will rank in their due places."[57]

So Hobson now seems to be steering between Mill and other new liberals. On the one hand, he rejects self-realization as an impossibly ambiguous consequentialist standard. On the other hand, promoting conscious satisfaction is not necessarily equivalent to promoting the

---

[55] Hobson, *Confessions of an Economic Heretic*, 204–5. Also see *ibid.*, 74–5 where Hobson denies ever embracing "any absolute conception of 'the good life'" adding that the "substance of 'welfare' itself must shift with the changes that take place in economic and political institutions and activities." Such a "dynamic conception of welfare ... demands that economic activities shall be brought continually into conformity with the new and more enlightened conceptions of welfare." And see 141 where Hobson says that whether "'the good' be visualized in terms of utility, happiness, or any other form of welfare, its value is qualitative as well as quantitative, and the qualitative estimate is continually changing alike for the community and the individual."

[56] J. A. Hobson, *Wealth and Life* (London: Macmillan, 1930), 16 and 21.   [57] *Ibid.*, 16.

"greatest happiness of the greatest numbers, for quality must also count in satisfactions." Notwithstanding his efforts, however inelegant, to negotiate between fellow new liberals and Mill's conceptions of ultimate value, he nevertheless continues insisting, unlike either, that this standard, though fully objective, was always socially informed in the end.[58]

Hobson is fully alive to some of the criticisms his position is likely to generate. He recognizes that many traditional liberals and "old" utilitarians will worry that he is endorsing the view that the state knows better than its citizens what is best for them.[59] However, he insists that he is not assuming that the state generally knows what is best for its citizens. The state can never be normatively omniscient. Nor should it try to be an omnipotent moral enforcer and still hope to remain genuinely liberal. On the contrary, the state only knows what its citizens ought to prefer in the areas of its special expertise. State interference is only justified "by the economy of standardization, in the sense that the desires and needs of people are *similar* in character and can best be met by social regulation of the productive and consumptive processes which satisfy these desires and needs."[60] In other words, all humans have certain standard animal needs and desires (informed preferences in effect) like those for food, clothing and shelter. Their universal satisfaction is a *necessary* but *not sufficient* condition for maximizing social utility. And because these needs and desires are so fundamental and so ubiquitous, we can safely rely on the state to deliver them efficiently and effectively.[61] The unregulated capitalism of "old" utilitarianism has, in any case, proven itself wholly inadequate to the task. But insofar as the needs and desires of individuals are varied and unstandardized, their provision is not the state's responsibility. Wherever needs and interests vary, defying easy and obvious standardization, individuals should fend for themselves according to their own lights and

---

[58] See, for instance, *ibid.*, 53, where Hobson says that "taking any social group, we shall expect to find a general body of agreement upon the basic values, and a conception of social welfare in which these values form the chief factors." And see 60, where he also continues to insist that some are more expert than others in determining and "impos[ing]" these values.

[59] See J. A. Hobson [1926], "Economic Art and Human Welfare," in *Writings on Distribution and Welfare*, ed. Backhouse, 475 where Hobson says that determining general welfare is an art which should be left to society's "best qualified exponents." Hobson simply denies that these sentiments are dangerously elitist and authoritarian.

[60] Hobson, *Confessions of an Economic Heretic*, 207–8.

[61] Here, Hobson is unclear whether these needs and desires are absolutely unchanging or whether they evolve and expand as societies industrialize. We might conclude that he means to say that our threshold of standardized needs rises the more easily technology is able to meet them for everyone. Hence, consensus over basic needs invariably changes though often so slowly that they seem unchanging to most people at the time. And this would imply that the liberal state's responsibilities would slowly rise in tandem as well.

initiative. When it comes to what makes each of us unique rather than what makes us members of the same species, actual preferences always trump informed preferences, especially preferences informed by the state's illegitimate pretensions at expertise. In brief, "the assumption that 'equality' prevails along the plane of standardized goods and services remains valid, and the productive processes involved in their supply rightly tend to become 'socialized.'"[62]

For Hobson, social utility is a potent normative principle. Acting morally means promoting social utility first and foremost. But what makes Hobson's "new" utilitarianism more appealing as well as more problematic than its predecessors is the richer, more nuanced meaning that the term "utility" carries for him as well as the way in which its meaning is contextually or socially determined. Hobson's "new" utilitarianism, in short, is multi-textured, combining a thoroughly communitarian theory of informed, vital preferences with a consequentialist theory of right.[63]

REASON AND SOCIAL UTILITY

For Hobhouse and Ritchie, as we have seen, human social evolution qualitatively transforms haphazard biological evolution by directing it. According to Hobhouse, the emergence of "social mind" makes directionless, biological evolutionary struggle for survival "orthogenically" purposeful, converting it into our pursuit of general utility. Similarly for Ritchie, with the emergence of utilitarian "objectified mind," social evolution becomes self-conscious and purposeful as "rational" selection replaces "natural" selection. This is why the theory of natural selection "vindicate[s]" utilitarianism by investing it with "new meaning."

---

[62] Hobson, *Confessions of an Economic Heretic*, 208. As a category of legitimate, socially informed preferences subject to state regulation, Hobson also mentions the state's responsibility in protecting citizens from their own physically harmful and often fatal follies. For instance, in the name of maximizing social utility, the state must regulate road traffic. It is also entitled to protect ill-informed consumers from the unscrupulous practices of producers and advertisers who market unhealthy foods and injurious drugs. Finally, the state may justifiably regulate overtime in those industries in which long working hours risk harming the health of workers. Hobson does not explore how protecting citizens from themselves relates to securing the satisfaction of their fundamental needs and desires. Presumably, protecting them from serious self-harm is no less critical than protecting them from seriously harming each other because physical self-harm, even willful physical self-harm, undermines social utility just as critically as physical harm to others. For another later account of Hobson's rejection of "complete" in favor of "limited" or "practicable" socialism restricted to supplying standardized goods satisfying common needs, see J. A. Hobson, *From Capitalism to Socialism* (London: Hogarth Press, 1932), ch. XIII, "The Limits of Socialism."

[63] Allett, by contrast, interprets Hobson as a thoroughgoing ethical subjectivist, and therefore as an emotivist, because he holds that Hobson makes morality culturally relative. See Allett, "The Moral Philosophy of J. A. Hobson," 9.

Likewise for Hobson, nature was "reason gradually working itself out in the universe," insuring that "rational society" will become "natural society."[64] And for Hobson, following Ritchie especially, "natural selection" was gradually and relentlessly giving way to "rational selection" as human consciousness matured. Social evolution has thus far been mostly "unconscious" and consequently "slow, wasteful and dangerous." But happily, it was becoming the "conscious expression of the trained and organized will" of groups of people committed to "economy of action."[65] Happily, the "rule of reason" was slowly coordinating and harmonizing social interests, lifting social evolution from savage into reasoned moral struggle.[66] Fresh experiments in "collective self-consciousness" were "accelerating and directing the 'urge of the world' towards human enlightenment and well-being."[67] That is to say, social progress rested "more and more upon the capacity of societies for the conscious interpretation of social utility."[68]

Furthermore, for Hobson, "rational selection as the conscious pursuit of social utility was finally beginning to characterize even international relations, promising to transform, sooner or later, the League of Nations into a federated league of genuinely pacific federations. Imperialism was so reprehensible and disheartening because it reinfected international and national politics with irrational, savage emotions typifying "natural" selection. Imperialism reversed the evolutionary realization of "social utility."[69]

---

[64] Hobson, *The Social Problem*, 96. Also see J. A. Hobson, *Problems of a New World* (New York: Macmillan, 1921), 206 where he says that "all history exhibits progress in terms of the subjection of force to reason."

[65] Hobson, *The Crisis of Liberalism*, 132. Also see Hobson, *The Social Problem*, 215–16 where he deploys something like the "natural" vs. "rational" selection dichotomy in defending eugenics: "By putting down the wasteful and cruel methods of 'natural rejection' society is only performing half her duty; she must substitute methods of 'rational rejection.' In a word, it is all important to society that propagation should only take place from sound stock; only thus can she secure that the children, who are to be her future citizens and workers, shall be born. Our study of the necessary limits of efficient action by the State implies, and common sense readily endorses, the implication, that direct selection by society, or any full application of the arts of stirpiculture to the human race, would not be feasible or profitable. But a social policy of veto upon anti-social propagation, however difficult of enforcement it may seem, and whatever moral risks it may involve, is really essential." Such disturbing policies seem justified by Hobson's claim, noted earlier, that determining and promoting general welfare is an art best entrusted to society's most "qualified exponents." And they also seem compatible with his more robust formulations of social organicism. On the other hand, such a veto would seem to violate Hobson's principle that the state knows what is best for its citizens only in areas of its special expertise, namely those pertaining to food, clothing and shelter. The state should stick exclusively to directing the production and consumption of these basic needs since they are so standard and therefore so easily administered centrally. This particular example nevertheless nicely captures how Hobson's liberal utilitarianism was not consistently liberal.

[66] J. A. Hobson, *Rationalism and Humanism* (London: Watts, 1933), 17–18.

[67] Hobson, *The Crisis of Liberalism*, 275–6.   [68] Hobson, *The Social Problem*, 261.

[69] See especially J. A. Hobson [1902], *Imperialism* (Ann Arbor: The University of Michigan Press, 1965), 164 and 174. Also, see my "Consequentialist Cosmopolitanism" in *Victorian Visions of Global Order*, ed. Duncan Bell (Cambridge: Cambridge University Press, 2007).

Despite the received view, then, that Hobson followed Hobhouse in rejecting British idealism, we have seen that he followed Ritchie nearly as much in trying to accommodate Hegel to Darwin by investing evolution with mind and reason thus making "rational selection" continuous with "natural selection." And insofar as Hobhouse provided a similar evolutionary account of emerging mind, Hegelianism infused his thinking as well. And when we recall just how much Hobson, Hobhouse and Ritchie borrowed from Green and Bradley, particularly with respect to how hedonistic utilitarianism was psychologically incoherent, we have all the more reason to doubt the received view as oversimplistic. Though the new liberalism was, as I have been arguing, modified and improved utilitarianism, it appropriated much Hegelianism too.

RIGHTS, POSITIVE FREEDOM AND EQUAL OPPORTUNITIES

In the first chapter of Book II of *The Social Problem* entitled "The Rights of Man," Hobson chastises the critics (Bentham and his followers most probably) of natural rights theory for carrying their criticisms to excess. They fail to appreciate the utility of recognizing certain rights as fundamental. Though basic rights have "no natural or absolute validity," they nevertheless function as stringent constraints channeling social interaction. But social utility "must be paramount and absolute in marking the limits of such 'rights.'"[70] Rights, then, are necessary conditions for promoting social utility indirectly. Societies that zealously proclaim them and vigorously protect them are more likely to thrive because they give citizens real equality of opportunity to make the best of themselves on their own terms. Hence, for Hobson as for Mill, Hobhouse and Ritchie, rights constrain our duty to promote social utility by channeling its pursuit. They inoculate Hobson's utilitarianism from integrity-destroying impartiality and negative responsibility that contemporary critics of utilitarianism, such as Bernard Williams, find so unnerving. In short, by combining a utilitarian theory of good with a liberal theory of robust rights, Hobson provides another important example of liberal utilitarianism's rich heritage.

Hobson also follows other new liberals in denying that fundamental rights are natural, at least not in the traditional sense.[71] They are neither

---

[70] Hobson, *The Social Problem*, 89.
[71] See Chapters 3 and 5 for detailed discussions of Hobhouse and Ritchie's respective theories of utilitarian rights. But note Hobson's assertion in *The Social Problem*, 94, misguided in my view, that Ritchie regrettably abandons individual rights. Also see Meadowcroft's mistaken contention

history-transcending nor indefeasible. In the end, they are socially informed conventions, just like the meaning of social utility itself, that social consensus creates rather than discovers. And social consensus creates them precisely because of their formidable efficacy in promoting social utility indirectly.

For Hobson as well, respect for basic rights consists in much more than the absence of restraint. Hobson's version of new liberalism, like all versions, is no "narrow *laissez-faire* individualism." Like all new liberals, Hobson vigorously defends a positive conception of freedom though his conception features equal opportunity more prominently. Having the power to do what is worthwhile means, for him, having meaningful and effective equal opportunities to do what is worthwhile.

Furthermore, it means recognizing that, "as the area and nature of opportunities are continually shifting, so the old limited conception of the task of Liberalism must always advance." With each generation, liberals "will be required to translate a new set of needs and aspirations into facts."[72] Hence, as each society gradually reformulates the meaning it gives to basic needs, it implicitly reformulates the meaning it gives to equal opportunity and therefore to positive freedom too. Society determines these limits by stipulating which categories of actions are legitimately self-regarding and which are other-regarding violations of basic rights. Social consensus not only decides the meaning of social utility but also decides which actions are essential for promoting it. It then sanctifies the latter as self-regarding, enveloping them by the protective shield of fundamental rights.

Hobson's conception of positive freedom was as wooly as that of other new liberals, especially Green's. Even astute commentators, such as Freeden, have missed how new liberals sometimes confused positive freedom qua empowerment with positive freedom qua acting in worthwhile ways. For instance, Freeden suggests that Hobhouse and Hobson regarded an individual as free "when he *could* develop certain desirable

<hr/>

("Introduction," *The Social* Problem, xii) that Spencer, unlike Hobson, defended traditional natural rights long after they had gone out of fashion. See my *Equal Freedom and Utility*, especially chapters III–IV, for evidence to the contrary. Indeed, Spencer was no less a liberal utilitarian than Hobson. Of course, Spencer's liberal utilitarian differs significantly from Hobson's in that Hobson was a socialist and Spencer was not. For an account of Hobson's idiosyncratic conception of natural rights compatible with my own, see Freeden, "J. A. Hobson as a Political Theorist," 24–8. Freeden, however, sees Hobson as refining Ritchie's theory of natural rights. While I concur that both deployed remarkably similar theories, I don't see Hobson as at least *explicitly* improving Ritchie given his misunderstanding of Ritchie on this score.

[72] Hobson, *The Crisis of Liberalism*, 93.

characteristics and *willed* their attainment, whereas for [C. D.] Burns the individual was free when he *did* develop such characteristics."[73] In other words, for Hobhouse and Hobson according to Freeden, being positively free meant *merely* having the opportunities to engage in worthwhile actions as opposed to *actually* engaging in them. But Freeden also suggests that, for new liberals, positive freedom "was not a means to those ends [worthwhile activities]; it was tantamount to their attainment." Positive freedom "was vacuous unless linked to a specific set of desirable values, a cluster of ends that infused liberty with special meaning."[74] Here Freeden interprets new liberals as thoroughly moralizing the meaning of positive freedom. Positive freedom is not *merely* being positioned to act in worthwhile ways, but *actually* acting accordingly. Now insofar as Hobhouse and Hobson theorized positive freedom carelessly, if not sometimes inconsistently, they surely owe their confusion to Green. Green, too, held that positive freedom was simultaneously (1) merely being empowered to do what was worthwhile and (2) actually doing what was worthwhile in addition. (For discussion of this confusion in Green, see Chapter 2.)

Freeden is well known for arguing correctly that different kinds of liberalisms differently package core liberal values including the value of freedom. Compared to earlier liberals, new liberals repackaged freedom more robustly, generally regarding it not simply as a means to promoting other external values but as, in part, constituted by these values. Understanding full freedom as doing something worthwhile fits with this kind of consequentialism well. But to the extent that new liberals never resolved whether being fully free meant doing something worthwhile, in addition to having equal opportunities, their consequentialisms remained equivocal.

Notwithstanding the relationship between freedom, equal opportunity and worthwhile action for new liberals, all were keen to equalize opportunities more meaningfully. In Hobson's case, equality of opportunity meant, first and foremost, public education, which he often referred to as the "opportunity of opportunities."[75] In addition, it entailed giving each citizen "equal access to the use of his native land as a workplace and a home, such mobility as will enable him to dispose of his personal energies to the best advantages, easy access to that factor of capital or credit which modern industry recognizes as essential to economic independence, and to

---

[73] Freeden, *Liberalism Divided*, 278.   [74] *Ibid.*, 284.

[75] See, for instance, Hobson, *The Crisis of Liberalism*, 94. But see Hobson, *Work and Wealth*, 210 where he calls leisure the "opportunity of opportunities."

whatever new form of industrial power, electric or other, may be needed to co-operate with human efforts." In sum, "A man is not really free for purposes of self-development in life and work who is not adequately provided in all these respects, and no small part of constructive Liberalism must be devoted to the attainment of these equal opportunities."[76]

Insofar, then, as Hobson was not only a self-proclaimed "new" utilitarian but also a self-proclaimed new liberal who advocated juridically guaranteed equality of opportunity, improving and repairing utilitarianism meant reformulating liberalism. Improving the former entailed not just reformulating but also fully *accommodating* the latter. The "courage of an avowed utilitarianism" required equalizing opportunities for all so that many types of personality might flourish.[77] Hence, in Hobson's hands, "new" utilitarianism and new liberalism were one and the same.[78]

PROPERTY RIGHTS

Everyone, in order to be a free person, ought to have access to some share of the natural and developed resources of the world, and to the general stock of knowledge which will help him to realize his purposes with such materials. This right to property flows from the conception of a free personality in a world of equal opportunity ... property is good which is the instrument or the embodiment of the wholesome creative impulses of human beings.[79]

As with Hobhouse (see Chapter 3), then, self-realization requires equality of opportunity which, in turn, entails access to property. As necessary but insufficient conditions of self-realization, both equal opportunity and property are therefore rights. Indeed, for Hobson, we can consider them "natural" rights not because they are intuitive absolutes in the Lockean sense but simply because they are conditionally necessary for

---

[76] Hobson, *The Crisis of Liberalism*, 93–4. Also see ch. II, part II, "Equality of Opportunity," for a more complete account of the redistributive reforms constituting equal opportunity which includes employment security. See too J. A. Hobson, *Poverty in Plenty: The Ethics of Income* (New York: Macmillan, 1932), ch. III, for Hobson's defense of security of employment as a "right to work." Peter Nicholson has reminded me that Green also refers to himself as a "constructive liberal" in *Collected Works of T. H. Green*, Vol. V, 219. Also see Vol. V, 452.

[77] J. A. Hobson [1931], "Towards Social Equality," *Hobhouse Memorial Lectures: 1930–1940* (Oxford: Oxford University Press, 1948), 34. Not surprisingly, since he delivered this essay as the 1931 Hobhouse Memorial Lecture, Hobson invokes Hobhouse in accommodating liberal equal opportunity with utilitarianism.

[78] For an account of Hobson that views him as more socialist than authentic liberal, see Jules Townshend, "Hobson and the Socialist Tradition" in *J. A. Hobson after Fifty Years*.

[79] Hobson, *The Social Problem*, 173.

achieving self-realization and therefore happiness. Their instrumental importance, their conditional necessity, makes them naturally sensible strategies for us, in light of scarcity and preoccupied as we are with "social utility." For instance, property rights "may be described as 'natural' because certain laws of the physical universe and moral nature of man mark out the true limits of property in any given conditions of society."[80]

Individuals not only possess a "natural right" to subsistence property, but also a "natural right" to "any extra product" necessary to stimulate their best productive efforts, namely "the largest surplus of profit over pay."[81] Whereas the former is grounded in the "conservative demands" of our nature, the latter stems from our nature's "progressive demands," which are constantly evolving. Hence, while our right to subsistence tends to remain constant, our right to requisite "extra product" varies according to our changing needs and wants. Self-realization and "social utility" require not only guaranteed subsistence but also compensation sufficient to encourage workers to produce enough wealth capable of satisfying changing standards of well-being:

Rational man feels a continual impulse towards a fuller life; he will, therefore, not be content with a "property" just sufficient to maintain his present efficiency of work and life, but will require an ever-expanding margin wherewith to live a larger and better life. This "right" of property a community guided by "social utility" will also secure to the individual, for it is the essential of that growth of individual and of social character which is the most convincing aspect of "progress."[82]

Now these two natural rights to property correspond to Hobson's emphasis on both production and consumption as sources of well-being discussed earlier. As we saw then, a satisfying self-realizing life combined gratifying work as well as meaningful and genuinely satisfying consumption. Both the right kind of work and the right kind of consumption constitutes a happy life. But here Hobson emphasizes how the right kind of work must not only be gratifying but also simultaneously produces meaningfully satisfying commodities. Proper work inherently gratifies and maximizes proper consumption instrumentally. And in order to maximize proper consumption opportunities, workers must be properly motivated by having the opportunities to engage in meaningful work as well as opportunities to consume meaningfully, which, in turn, depends upon their being adequately compensated. Maximizing "social utility" requires optimally

---

[80] *Ibid.*, 98. [81] *Ibid.*, 104. Also see Hobson, *Poverty in Plenty*, 49.
[82] Hobson, *The Social Problem*, 105.

distributing meaningful work, fulfilling consumption in keeping with evolving needs and wants and adequate compensation.

The "natural" right to property, then, is simply a social utility-maximizing strategy of the first order. It stimulates citizens to do their best in doing what they are best suited to do.[83] Property is a "special sphere of activity, a scope of work and life, which is apportioned to the individual, and which may not be invaded by another." It is "that domain in which he may freely express himself" in work and consumption. And though the "presence of opportunity for self-expression, which is the essence of true 'property,' does not always imply the exclusive possession of some objective good, it does imply exclusive *use*" (my italics).[84] The "natural" right to property, in short, is fundamentally, when all is said and done, just a "natural" right to use.

Hobson qualifies "natural" property rights insisting that society, too, has a "natural claim" to property because society creates value along with individuals. Once more following Hobhouse (see again Chapter 3), Hobson contends that socially created value is "unearned" (by individuals) and arises from "public work and public wants." For example, by working together in building a boat, "Brown, Smith and Jones" create value in excess of aggregating their individual contributions. "Organized coopera-tion is productive power." And insofar as this excess socially created value is not returned to society via taxation principally, society is effectively sweated.[85]

In *The Crisis of Liberalism*, Hobson reinforces his defense of socially created value, claiming that it also follows from the fact that societies are

---

[83] But see *ibid.*, 108–9 where Hobson clarifies: "The activity, or 'virtue,' of an artist is in a large degree his own reward ... Where the process contains within itself no balance of satisfaction to yield sufficient motive to production, adequate 'property' in the product must be secured; when the process yields full measure of satisfaction, no such property in the product is essential."

[84] *Ibid.*, 96–7.

[85] *Ibid.*, 146–53. Contrary to Spencer's mistaken insistence, taxation is not mostly theft because society is more than a mere aggregation of individuals. Rather, the "tax imposed on A is simply the most convenient way of taking the results of social work which commingle with the work done by A: the joint product is not in itself directly divisible, so that society takes her share in a tax" (153). Chapter VI, in which much of the preceding analysis occurs and entitled "Society as Maker of 'Values,' is a refutation of Spencer in large part. For Hobson, Spencer exemplified "false individualism" (153). Even Spencer's concession that undeveloped land possessed social value belonging to the community presupposed confused individualistic assumptions according to Hobson. But Spencer's theory of unearned land values and related land nationalization scheme was much more complicated and fitful than Hobson appreciates. See my *Equal Freedom and Utility*, ch. 7. John Allett has argued, correctly it seems to me, that his doctrine of unearned sweated surplus lies behind his theories of under-consumption and imperialism thus giving his economic and political thought greater coherence than commonly realized. See Allett, *The New Liberalism: The Political Economy of J. A. Hobson*, ch. 8 especially.

organic. Because societies are sophisticated economic organisms which create value through cooperation primarily, property was not an inalienable right though it was, as we have seen, a "natural" right in Hobson and other new liberals' unconventional sense.[86]

Moreover, society's "natural" claim to property follows from the fact, that like individuals, societies require social property in order to self-realize. Because societies are organisms with their own interests above and beyond the summed interests of their members, they must have property as a means of expressing those interests. Just as individual self-expression depends on using property, collective self-expression necessitates collective access to property. Though individualists like Spencer not surprisingly fail to grasp this equivalent necessity, idealists like Bosanquet should have grasped it given their organicism and given their deep appreciation of property's importance to self-expression: "It is strange that a logician like Dr. Bosanquet, who so strongly builds his philosophic support of private property, should ignore the corresponding need of social property."[87] And individualists and idealists alike need not fear that social property and collective self-realization would somehow threaten individual self-realization because the latter flourishes only in healthy educated societies devoid of penury and want. Only such societies offer meaningful equal opportunities and promote "social utility" effectively.

"Social utility," not surprisingly then, is our criterion for balancing individual vs. social self-realization and, consequently, natural individual vs. social property. But "social utility" is a rather clumsy criterion and we can do better by making needs our "direct practical standard."[88] And as we have seen, some needs are basic and fixed while others evolve according to society's changing circumstances. Individuals must be able to satisfy the first and have meaningful hopes of satisfying the latter in order to be motivated to do their best. Hence, the balance between an individual and social property will constantly shift though never so much that individual property is marginalized. Individuals will always require minimum personal property for survival and the prospect of getting more so that they will work hard.[89]

---

[86] Hobson, *The Crisis of Liberalism*, 77.   [87] Hobson, *The Social Problem*, 151.   [88] *Ibid.*, 162.

[89] *The Social Problem*, chs. IX and X especially, elaborate in considerable detail what Hobson takes to be the guaranteed minimum of personal property. These include: (1) a "healthy settled home" through "public ownership of towns and villages"; and (2) fair access to productive land by "establishing judicially 'fair' rents" or by "public ownership of agricultural land." Hobson also insists that all citizens possess rights to basic education and employment. Recall that in *The Social Problem* (cited in Note 79), Hobson viewed knowledge as a property right. See, as well, J. A. Hobson, *Property and Improperty* (London: Victor Gollancz, 1937), especially ch. V, "The Lines of a Constructive Policy."

CONCLUSION

Hobson's "new" utilitarianism is multi-faceted, combining utilitarianism, communitarianism and liberalism among other theoretical elements. But utilitarianism is always more fundamental. Hobson's new liberalism was essentially repaired and refurbished utilitarianism. So Hobson wants to have his utilitarian monism and eat his liberalism too. He wants his political theory to be systematic but not at the cost of losing its liberal ethical appeal.

My primary aim has been to interpret Hobson. But, in my view, interpretation is invariably surreptitious prescription and I readily confess to interpreting him sympathetically or at least wanting to. Michael Freeden calls Hobson's political theory "modified constrained consequentialism," implying that his political theory is indeed multi-faceted in ways I have explicitly tried to show in greater detail. Freeden also readily concedes that Hobson's political theory is problematic and, at the very least, suffers from confused terminology.[90] I also agree.[91] But however we prefer to label Hobson's political theory, and whatever its limitations, we should at least admire its ambitions even if some of us might regrettably conclude that, when it comes to political theory, systematic coherence and liberal ethical appeal are always and unfortunately inversely correlated.

---

[90] See Freeden, "A Non-Hypothetical Liberalism: The Utilitarian Communitarianism of J.A. Hobson," 17.

[91] I have alluded to other shortcomings plaguing Hobson's "new" utilitarian liberalism without examining them in detail. For instance, much more could be said about the ambiguity of the meaning of social utility. And granting this ambiguity, we might also wonder how we are supposed to measure it meaningfully and thus promote it. Hobson sometimes seems to concede as much. See, for example, ch. VII, "The Quantitative Method in Social Science," *Social Problem* and *Confessions*, 148.

CHAPTER 7

Conclusion: intellectual history and the idolatry of conceptual dichotomies

FORGETTING AND REDISCOVERY

Every intellectual history is a narrative. Insofar as this study is part intellectual history, it is no exception. My narrative approach to nineteenth- and twentieth-century English political theory privileges liberal utilitarianism and the new liberalism because I firmly believe that both constitute English political theory's most significant contribution to modern Anglo-American political theory as well as to modern political theory in general. In my view, contemporary American political theorists, for whom Anglo-American political theory begins with Rawls, haven't taken either seriously enough. But those who fetishize Rawls should at least read Sidgwick, since *A Theory of Justice* was written largely in response to him.

Contemporary English political theory is less historically myopic, not only because liberal utilitarianism has long been an English preoccupation, but also because English political theory largely avoided falling under the ideological spell of German émigré intellectuals, like Arendt, Strauss and Voegelin, who found refuge in the US academy in the 1930s and 1940s, and who read their anxieties about fascism into their depictions of liberalism, infusing American political theory with intoxicating fevers and fascinations. No wonder Rawls's analytical liberalism seemed so bracing and therefore proved so historically numbing in turn. And no wonder American political theory unwittingly reinvented communitarianism since it knew next to nothing about the new liberalism. English political theory has fared somewhat better. From Bentham on, it has simultaneously maintained its analytical rigor without losing quite so much of its historical memory.

Analytical philosophy continues to enchant Anglo-American moral and political theory. For the most part, this enchantment has inspired great achievements in nuanced precision. But enchantment is sometimes thralldom. Contemporary Anglo-American political theory has become handicapped by dichotomous conceptualizing, driven, in part, by indolent pedagogical habits reinforced by insensitivity to its own, richly textured history. Such dichotomized theorizing marginalizes thinkers, who can not easily be appropriated through the prism of our favorite dichotomies, as merely *eclectic* curiosities. Our philosophical canon consequently mirrors back to us our current, parochial theoretical preoccupations. The idolatry of conceptual dichotomies encourages bad intellectual history, which only reinforces our preferred conceptual dichotomies all over again.

Now according to Brink, "Sidgwick's failure to engage Green's *Prolegomena* sympathetically represents a missed opportunity within the [early] analytic tradition for fruitful dialogue about the merits of a metaphysical approach to ethics and an interesting form of perfectionism."[1] But if I am right, this missed opportunity is unsurprising because such missed opportunities characterize the analytical tradition. What makes any intellectual tradition a tradition in part, including especially the analytical tradition, are missed opportunities. Intellectual traditions are exclusionary histories that invariably telescope the practices they celebrate and recount. Telescoped intellectual histories therefore are typically canonical. Being compressed narratives, they forget whatever they do not enshrine. Or perhaps we should say that whatever they do not enshrine, they tend to forget. And whatever gets forgotten sometimes reappears after a while as spurious novelty. Discovery is sometimes just unknowing rediscovery.

Contemporary pedagogy regrettably reinforces these bad narrative habits and episodes of ersatz philosophical discovery. Contemporary philosophical pedagogy thrives on tales of ongoing polarizing contests steeped in uncompromising partisanship. In moral philosophy, utilitarians are depicted as forever doing battle with neo-Kantians. In political theory, liberals fight off communitarians heroically if not always persuasively.

While titanic philosophical clashes make engaging classroom theater that help keep our audiences attentive, they reduce philosophy to formulaic sloganeering. Invariably, pedagogic convenience rebounds on philosophical scholarship itself, infecting it with dichotomized thinking. Such thinking, in turn, skews how we read our philosophical past, tempting us to reconstruct it through the prisms of our contemporary dichotomized preoccupations. And insofar as we reconstruct our philosophical past accordingly, we further our bad pedagogical habits, which then surely encourage dichotomous theorizing even more.

---

[1] David O. Brink, *Perfectionism and the Common Good: Themes in the Philosophy of T. H. Green* (Oxford: Oxford University Press, 2003), 124.

For all its subtle powers of refinement, then, philosophical analysis has not been always kind to intellectual history in general and to the history of political thought in particular. Philosophical analysis has encouraged historians of political thought to rationally reconstruct political thought's past through the lens of its categories of analysis, compacting and streamlining this past, as I have been suggesting, into narrative oversimplification. Too many historians of *liberal* political thought have been uniquely prone to reifying their intellectual past because Anglo-American philosophical analysis has so thoroughly dominated the practice of liberal political theory since the 1960s at least. Therefore, contemporary liberal political theorists have forgotten more than enough of their past. For them, the liberal tradition has become a compressed reflection of their favored conceptual concerns.

Not surprisingly, then, forgetting their own past has caused too many contemporary analytical liberals to repeat some of it rather dramatically, all the while mistakenly believing that they were breaking fresh theoretical ground. For how could they not think otherwise given their historical amnesia? What we forget and then relearn inescapably seems like the novelty that it is not. It is not that we are somehow fated to repeat what we have forgotten but, rather, that whenever we do, we are liable to misconstrue our repetitions for discoveries when all we are doing is mostly rediscovery.

I certainly do not want to insist that renewed appreciation of liberalism's new liberal past makes various theoretical rediscoveries unnecessary and unimportant. But I do wish to urge that greater familiarity with the new liberals would at least save contemporary analytical liberals not insignificant time in their efforts to reconcile some of the conceptual dualisms polarizing them. Contemporary Anglo-American philosophical liberals need not waste quite so much precious time reinventing some of their prototypes when they already have new liberal prototypes readily at hand.

BETWEEN LIBERALISM AND CONSEQUENTIALISM

Amy Guttman has insisted that conceptual dualisms tyrannize too much contemporary political philosophical discourse.[2] While a partisan defender of Rawlsian liberalism against its legions of communitarian detractors, Guttman nevertheless worries that the liberal vs. communitarian debate

---

[2] Amy Guttman, "Communitarian Critics of Liberalism" in *Communitarianism and Individualism*, ed. Shlomo Avineri and Avner de-Shalit (Oxford: Oxford University Press, 1992), 130–1.

has degenerated into two dueling theoretical opposites each weighted down with its own family baggage of related, interlocking conceptualizations.

Guttman's worries now seem overstated as liberals and communitarians have begun discovering common ground, making those who continue perpetuating their older debate seem tiresome and pedantic. Still, her worries remain a lesson to those still locking philosophical horns over purportedly incompatible, moral philosophical opposites such as consequentialism vs. deontology. Guttmann's anxieties about liberalism vs. communitarianism may no longer be quite so warranted as liberals have discovered that they could be communitarians and communitarians have discovered that they were really liberals just the same. Moreover, as Simhony and I have elsewhere recently suggested, what contemporary liberals and communitarians have begun discovering simply repeats much of what new liberals previously worked so diligently to recommend.[3] Liberals and communitarians have been reinventing, albeit with greater analytical rigor and nuance, the new liberalism much more than they know.

The new liberalism also combined what *we* have come to view as another irreconcilable conceptual dichotomy, namely Kantianism vs. consequentialism, particularly utilitarian consequentialism. Whereas the liberal vs. communitarian debate, including recent moves towards reconciliation, has primarily preoccupied political theorists, the alleged opposition between deontology vs. consequentialism has become staple fare for analytical moral philosophers.

In all likelihood, our contemporary infatuation with the irreconcilability of deontological with consequentialist ethics stems, in part, from the nature of the analytical tradition and the demands of pedagogy alluded to previously. Our preoccupation with this opposition is also surely exacerbated for reasons offered by Cummiskey, who, like me, believes that potent conceptual dualisms have regrettably come to oppress too much of our philosophical discourse.

For Cummiskey, there are several "possible" explanations for the "widespread assumption that there is a fundamental opposition between Kantian and consequentialist ethics." First, Kantians and consequentialists typically deploy "strikingly different" types of arguments. Second, the "simplifying division of moral theories into deontological or teleological" stems from a "more general failure to distinguish foundational issues from normative principles." Third, and most importantly in my view, the "explanation surely also involves Rawls's rejection of utilitarianism and presentation of

[3] Simhony and Weinstein, "Introduction," *The New Liberalism: Reconciling Liberty and Community.*

Kantian ethics as the [only] deontological alternative." Consequently, we now "teach and read Kant *as if he set out* to refute contemporary utilitarianism" (my italics).[4]

Now Cummiskey's Kantian consequentialism constitutes a sustained and ingenious attempt to reconcile deontological ethics with teleological ethics as well as expose the wrong headedness of interpreting Kant as though he aimed primarily to contest utilitarianism. Clearly, Kant could not possibly have intended to refute modern utilitarianism for it had scarcely been invented. Reading Kant as if he meant to refute classical utilitarianism plainly rationally reconstructs Kant's moral theory, exemplifying once again how our fascination with dichotomizing thinking reductively informs and simplifies the history of moral and political thought.

But notwithstanding Cummiskey's success both in reconciling Kantianism with consequentialism and in exposing misjudgments about Kant's purported intentions, Cummiskey nevertheless overestimates the novelty of his achievement. That is, he at least overvalues the originality of his hybrid moral theory, making his Kantian consequentialism, to some degree, just another rediscovery of our forgotten philosophical past. For, as we have seen, new liberals, especially Green, were Kantian consequentialists in rather flimsy and, what now seems to us, eclectic disguise.

The new liberals are typically dismissed for their eclecticism, for their poor fit with the conceptual categories and dichotomies upon which we have come to rely in constructing the liberal tradition and its canon. Because new liberals were neither partisans of what we now call liberalism, communitarianism or utilitarianism, we have banished them to the margins of the canon. Because they were not much concerned with either defending liberalism from criticisms of communitarians or attacking utilitarianism as incompatible with liberal principles and values, we have tended to disregard them as curiosities at best and as deeply confused at worst. Only deeply confused political philosophers would naively mix an unstable brew of liberalism, a large dose of utilitarianism, and some communitarianism with an infusion of perfectionism.

Of course, from our perspective, the new liberals could hardly have avoided appearing confused. After all, they wrote political and moral

---

[4] Cummiskey, *Kantian Consequentialism*, 17. By contemporary moral philosophy's failure to distinguish sharply between "foundational issues" and "normative principles," Cummiskey means that contemporary moral philosophers too often confuse *justification* with its *results*. They confuse the *grounds* of normative principles with these principles themselves. In fact, deontology and consequentialism tend to generate the *same* basic normative principles, which ought to make us skeptical about the purported intuitive superiority of either.

philosophy mostly prior to the emergence of philosophical analysis. They were mostly pre-analytic, Sidgwick notwithstanding. For them, liberalism vs. communitarianism and Kantianism vs. consequentialism could scarcely have been the polarizing dualisms that they have become for us. In their historical and intellectual context, they lacked the kind of philosophical apparatus which we have learned to use so skillfully but sometimes at the cost of straitjacketing our conceptual universe and at the cost of how we have accordingly constructed the liberal tradition. Little wonder, then, that the new liberals seem so eclectic whenever we bother to consider them.

Green, Hobhouse, Ritchie and Hobson wrote in English and in Britain during the immediate aftermath of English classical utilitarianism's high tide. They were its heirs though often very critical heirs. All were inspired by, and drew considerably from Mill, while simultaneously disputing much in Bentham following Mill too. They criticized Bentham with the philosophical weaponry at hand, namely with Mill but also with infusions of Kant and Hegel from continental Europe and, of course, with evolutionary theory from Britain. Hence, though they were no longer conventional utilitarians, they remained consequentialists fundamentally all the same. Green was a perfectionist consequentialist for whom promoting good will happened to promote happiness contingently as well while Hobhouse, Ritchie and Hobson were all utilitarian consequentialists more or less. Whereas Green's consequentialism is harder to disentangle because (1) of how pleasure piggybacked contingently on good will and because (2) promoting good will constituted good willing in part, Hobhouse, Ritchie and Hobson's versions of consequentialism were much easier to see because they were much more conventionally utilitarian. The new liberalism was consequentialist through and through.

The liberal tradition, as I have been suggesting, invariably telescopes its past, consequently forgetting much of it. While any intellectual tradition is a forgetting, the liberal tradition's version of forgetting is especially shaped by the practice of Anglo-American philosophical analysis, which has so thoroughly informed post-war political theorizing in the English-speaking world. Analytical political theory has encouraged us to forget, and consequently ignore, the history of liberal utilitarianism after Mill especially. Perhaps this is also due, in part, to the rise and fall of British idealism, against which early twentieth-century philosophical analysis cut its teeth. Tainted by its kinship with idealism, the new liberalism went the way of idealism in the overly historically insensitive hands of philosophical analysis. The baby of new liberalism was thrown out with the bath water of English neo-Hegelianism. Notwithstanding whether or not this philosophical bathwater was really bathwater that needed discarding, the new liberalism, in my view, never should have been disposed of simultaneously principally because of its utilitarian heritage. The new liberalism, including Green's, was improved utilitarian practical reasoning fully grounded in the tradition of Mill's liberal utilitarianism. Though it eclectically drew from Kant and Hegel, it ultimately remained a form of liberal utilitarianism or, at least, a form of what we would now call liberal consequentialism. If Mill's liberal utilitarianism continues to be relevant to us insofar as liberal utilitarianism remains an ongoing, contemporary philosophical preoccupation, then the new liberals do not deserve our neglect. The history of Anglo-American, liberal political thought is much richer than our re-imagined, compressed narrative has made it.

TWO AIMS RESTATED

This study has argued two principal claims. First, I have tried to show that Green, Hobhouse, Ritchie and Hobson were considerably more indebted to Mill's liberal utilitarianism than the received view of them has maintained. All four were consequentialists if not necessarily utilitarian consequentialists although Hobson, and less obviously Hobhouse and Ritchie, were utilitarians primarily if they were anything. Moreover, all four were *liberal* consequentialists or, in the case of Hobson, Hobhouse and Ritchie, *liberal* utilitarians. And even though Green was certainly not a utilitarian consequentialist in the justificatory sense, he was indeed a utilitarian *practically speaking.*[5] For Green, though at the cost of some inconsistency, maximizing happiness generally substituted quite well in place of maximizing self-realization as an everyday normative guiding principle. The inconsistency stemmed, as we have seen, from Green's claim, shared by Bradley, that trying to maximize happiness was incoherent and therefore futile. And if it was futile, how could it possibly substitute for maximizing self-realization as a propitious, substitute

---

[5] The fact that Green and Mill's differing justificatory moral theories converge on similar practical moral rules and policies deepens our reasons for accepting these rules and policies. To the extent that different axiological maximizing criteria generate nearly identical practical rules, our grounds for endorsing these rules seems to be all the more compelling. I am thinking here of what Rawls has in mind by the legitimating results that constitute a robust and axiologically diverse, "justificatory conversation." For how differing conceptions of consequentialist well-being typically generate similar practical rules, see Brad Hooker, *Ideal Code, Real World: A Rule Consequentialist Theory of Morals* (Oxford: Oxford University Press, 2000), 42. And for the extent to which Kant and Mill purportedly arrive at the same "recommendations on different grounds," see Hill, "Happiness and Human Flourishing," 180–1.

practical strategy? How can anything futile effectively stand in for anything else? Here, more than anywhere, Green's consequentialism parts
ways with his liberalism.[6]

Second, my study has suggested that, notwithstanding certain incon-
sistencies such as that just noted, Green, Hobhouse, Ritchie and Hobson's
new liberal consequentialism remains remarkably instructive for us. Insofar
as we have marginalized the new liberalism thanks partly to our analytically
induced amnesia regarding the liberal tradition's richness, we are invariably
prone to repeat many of its theoretical discoveries and accommodations,
ignorantly and elatedly proclaiming them innovative. Just as recent efforts
by many contemporary liberals and communitarians to bridge their differences and achieve theoretical accommodation are less original than liberals
and communitarians realize, so much recent scholarship aimed at adjusting
utilitarianism to liberalism is less innovative than many contemporary
liberal utilitarians appreciate. Liberal utilitarians have as much unrecog-
nized and undervalued precedent in the new liberals as do liberal communitarians. It is not so much that new liberals saw themselves as accommodating
liberalism with utilitarianism *just as* contemporary liberal utilitarians see
themselves as trying to do. They could not possibly have since the contest
between liberalism vs. utilitarianism has now become sharply dichotomized
and prosecuted with the conceptual weaponry of philosophical analysis.
Neither of these features characterized new liberal thinking. Political philosophy was not the academic discipline then that it has since become. Rather,
insofar as new liberals combined liberal political theory with utilitarian moral
theory much after the fashion of Mill, they can stimulate us to think more
creatively through the challenge of determining whether utilitarianism is
logically compatible with liberalism.

Simon Caney has suggested that philosophical liberalism since the 1970s is
retracing the path it trod in the nineteenth century but without losing its way
as before. In the nineteenth century, according to Caney, utilitarianism was
superseded by Kantianism which, in turn, gave way to vagrant Hegelianism.
Likewise, twentieth-century philosophical liberalism has moved from utilitarianism to its neo-Kantian rejection championed by Rawls to refurbished
Hegelianism renamed as communitarianism. Fortunately, in Caney's view,
modern liberalism has "learned from" its "previous [Hegelian] mistakes" in
order to combine the "best in communitarianism with traditional liberal

---

[6] See my "Bradley's Rejection of Utilitarianism," unpublished, for the acuteness of this inconsistency
in Bradley.

commitments."[7] For Caney, perfectionist liberals like Raz have "learned" this lesson particularly well combining customary liberal enthusiasm for variegated forms of autonomy with a sober appreciation of how the values comprising an autonomous life are communally constituted.[8]

Perhaps, though, liberalism began learning from its mistakes much earlier than Caney thinks. Perhaps it never really committed the mistakes Caney insists that it did. In *Beyond Individualism*, Crittenden claims that his liberalism "beyond individualism," grounded upon a socially reconstituted liberal self, is a "continuation of the 'revisioning' of liberalism undertaken by T. H. Green and his [new liberal] disciples."[9] Just as Hurka momentarily looks back to new liberals as progenitors of consequentialist perfectionism, Crittenden likewise looks back to them in his endeavor to steer liberalism safely between the twin shoals of individualism and communitarianism. Thus, for precious few modern liberals who see themselves as rescuing a disoriented liberalism by infusing it with communitarianism and consequentialist perfectionism, the new liberalism was already pointing the way forward. But I would suggest that the new liberalism more than illumined the way. Rather, it had already completed much of the journey making retracing the path in this and the previous century a redundant rediscovery self-inflicted by our myopic estimation of the liberal tradition and by our infatuation with analytical conceptual dichotomies. Hopefully, liberals, and especially liberal utilitarians, have also learned not to forget the route liberalism is now retracing so that it won't have to be retraveled, and the new liberalism reinvented, yet again.

---

[7] Simon Caney, "Liberalism and Communitarianism: A Misconceived Debate," *Political Studies*, 40, 2 (June, 1992), 289.

[8] James Griffin, we should add, has likewise learned this lesson well though, contrary to Raz, his liberal perfectionism is blatantly consequentialist. See especially *Well-Being* (Oxford: Oxford University Press, 1986), 70–2.

[9] Crittenden, *Beyond Individualism*, 154.

Works cited

ARCHIVES

Bradley, F. H. *Red Notebook, Related to ETR.* In Bradley Collection, IIB2. Merton College, Oxford University.

"Utility as (1) an End or (2) Standard of Morality," *Multi-Colored Notebook.* In Bradley Collection, IA12. Merton College, Oxford University.

"Whether Pleasure is Good and in What Sense – Is Pain Evil?," *Black Notebook, Related Chiefly to ES.* In Bradley Collection, IB11. Merton College, Oxford University.

Green, T. H. "Lecture E. T. 78." Unnumbered MSS. In T. H. Green Papers, Balliol College, Oxford University.

"Note D on Pleasure and Kant's Moral Philosophy" in "Notes A–F." Unnumbered MSS. In T. H. Green Papers, Balliol College, Oxford University.

"Utility as a Principle of Art and Morality." Unnumbered MSS. In T. H. Green Papers, Balliol College, Oxford University.

BOOKS

Allett, John (1981). *The New Liberalism: The Political Economy of J. A. Hobson.* Toronto: University of Toronto Press.

Annas, Julia (1993). *The Morality of Happiness.* Oxford: Oxford University Press.

Aristotle (1954). *The Nicomachean Ethics,* W. D. Ross (trans.). Oxford: Oxford University Press.

Ayer, A. J. (1946), *Language, Truth and Logic.* New York: Dover.

Berlin, Isaiah (1999). *The Roots of Romanticism.* Princeton, NJ: Princeton University Press.

Bosanquet, Bernard (2001). *The Philosophical Theory of the State,* Gerald F. Gaus and William Sweet (eds.). South Bend, IN: St. Augustine's.

Boucher, David (1997). *The British Idealists.* Cambridge: Cambridge University Press.

Boucher, David and Andrew Vincent (2001), *British Idealism and Political Theory.* Edinburgh: Edinburgh University Press.

Bradley, F. H. (1988). *Ethical Studies* (1927). Oxford: Oxford University Press.
  (1999). *Red Notebook*. In *Collected Works of F. H. Bradley*, Carol A. Keene (ed.), Vol. III. Bristol: Thoemmes Press.
Brink, David (2003). *Perfectionism and the Common Good: Themes in the Philosophy of T. H. Green*. Oxford: Oxford University Press.
Clarke, Peter (1978). *Liberals and Social Democrats*. Cambridge: Cambridge University Press.
Clarke, P. F. (1996). Introduction. In J. A. Hobson, *The Social Problem (1902)*. Bristol: Thoemmes Press.
Collini, Stefan (1979). *Liberalism and Sociology*. Cambridge: Cambridge University Press.
Crittenden, Jack (1992). *Beyond Individualism*. Oxford: Oxford University Press.
Cummiskey, David (1996). *Kantian Consequentialism*. Oxford: Oxford University Press.
Darwall, S. (2003). *Consequentialism*. Oxford: Blackwell.
Den Otter, Sandra M. (1996). *British Idealism and Social Explanation*. Oxford: Oxford University Press.
Donner, Wendy (1992). *The Liberal Self*. Ithaca, NY: Cornell University Press.
Dunn, John (1996). *The History of Political Theory and Other Essays*. Cambridge: Cambridge University Press.
Feldman, Fred (2004). *Pleasure and The Good Life*. Oxford: Oxford University Press.
Flanagan, Owen (1991). *Varieties of Moral Personality*. Cambridge, MA: Harvard University Press.
Flew, Antony (1986). *David Hume*. Oxford: Oxford University Press.
Franco, Paul (1999). *Hegel's Philosophy of Freedom*. New Haven and London: Yale University Press.
Freeden, Michael (1986). *Liberalism Divided*. Oxford: Oxford University Press.
  (1978). *The New Liberalism*. Oxford: Oxford University Press.
  (1991). *Rights*. Minneapolis: University of Minnesota Press.
  (1996). *Ideologies and Political Theory*. Oxford: Oxford University Press.
Gewirth, Alan (1998). *Self-Fulfillment*. Princeton, NJ: Princeton University Press.
Gray, John (1989). *Liberalisms*. London: Routledge.
Green, T. H. (1997a). *Lectures on the Principles of Political Obligation* (1886). In *Collected Works of T. H. Green*, Peter P. Nicholson (ed.), Vol. II. Bristol: Thoemmes.
  (1997b). *Prolegomena to Ethics* (1883). In *Collected Works of T. H. Green*, Peter P. Nicholson (ed.). Vol. IV. Bristol: Thoemmes.
Griffin, James (1986). *Well-Being*. Oxford: Oxford University Press.
Harris, F. P. (1944). *The Neo-Idealist Political Theory*. New York: King's Crown Press.
Hegel, G. W. F (1952). *Philosophy of Right* (1821), T. M. Knox (trans.). Oxford: Oxford University Press.
Hobhouse, L. T. (1973). *Democracy and Reaction* (1904). New York: Barnes and Noble.

(1964). *Liberalism* (1911). Oxford: Oxford University Press.

(1968). *Social Evolution and Political Theory* (1911). Port Washington: Kennikat Press.

(1912). *The Labour Movement*. London: T. Fisher Unwin.

(1915). *Mind in Evolution*. London: Macmillan and Co.

(1918). *The Metaphysical Theory of the State: A Criticism*. London: Allen and Unwin.

(1919). *Morals in Evolution*. New York: Henry Holt.

(1921). *The Rational Good*. New York: Henry Holt.

(1949). *The Elements of Social Justice* (1922). London: Allen and Unwin.

(1924). *Social Development*. London: George Allen and Unwin.

(1927). *Development and Purpose*. London: Macmillan and Co.

Hobhouse, L. T. (1966). *Sociology and Philosophy*. Cambridge: Cambridge University Press.

Hobson, J. A. (1965). *Imperialism* (1902). Ann Arbor: The University of Michigan Press.

(1996), *The Social Problem* (1902). Bristol, Thoemmes.

(1974). *The Crisis of Liberalism* (1909), P. F. Clarke (ed.). Brighton: Barnes and Noble.

(1914). *Work and Wealth*. London: George Allen and Unwin.

(1921). *Problems of a New World*. New York: Macmillan.

(1926). *Free-Thought in the Social Sciences*. London: George Allen and Unwin.

(1930). *Wealth and Life*. London: Macmillan.

(1932). *From Capitalism to Socialism*. London: Hogarth Press.

Poverty in Plenty: The Ethics of Income. New York: Macmillan.

(1933). *Rationalism and Humanism*. London: Watts.

(1937). *Property and Improperty*. London: Victor Gollancz.

(1938). *Confessions of an Economic Heretic*. London: George Allen and Unwin.

(1992). *The Industrial System* (1909), Peter Cain (ed.). London: Routledge/Thoemmes.

(1994). *John Ruskin: Social Reformer*. In William Smart and John Hobson, *John Ruskin* (1898), Peter Cain (ed.). London: Routledge/Thoemmes.

Hooker, Brad (2000). *Ideal Code, Real World: A Rule Consequentialist Theory of Morals*. Oxford: Oxford University Press.

Hume, David (1978). *A Treatise of Human Nature* (1739–40), L. A. Selby-Bigge, Rev. P. Nidditch (eds.). Oxford: Oxford University Press.

Hurka, T. (1993). *Perfectionism*. Oxford: Oxford University Press.

Huxley, T. H. (1887). *Hume*. London: Macmillan.

Johnston, David (1994). *The Idea of a Liberal Theory*. Princeton, NJ: Princeton University Press.

Kant, Immanuel (1987). *Fundamental Principles of the Metaphysics of Morals* (1785), T. K. Abbott (trans.). Buffalo: Prometheus.

(1991). *The Metaphysics of Morals* (1797), Mary Gregor (ed.). Cambridge: Cambridge University Press.

Korsgaard, Christine (1996). *The Sources of Normativity*. Cambridge: Cambridge University Press.

Lamont, W. D. (1934). *Introduction to Green's Moral Philosophy*. London: George Allen and Unwin.

MacCunn, John (1907). *Six Radical Thinkers*. London: Edward Arnold.

Mackie, J. L. (1977). *Ethics: Inventing Right and Wrong*. London: Penguin.

Mill, J. S. (1977), *On Liberty* (1859). In *Collected Works of John Stuart Mill*, John M. Robson (ed.), Vol. XVIII. Toronto: University of Toronto Press.

Moore, G. E. (1986). *Principia Ethica*. Cambridge: Cambridge University Press.

Mulhall, Stephen and Adam Swift (1996). *Liberals and Communitarians*. Oxford: Blackwell.

Neuhouser, Frederick (2000). *Foundations of Hegel's Social Theory*. Cambridge, MA: Harvard University Press.

Nicholson, Peter (1990). *The Political Philosophy of the British Idealists*. Cambridge: Cambridge University Press.

Norman, Richard (1987). *Free and Equal*. Oxford: Oxford University Press.

Patten, Alan (1999). *Hegel's Idea of Freedom*. Oxford: Oxford University Press.

Plamenatz, John (1968). *Consent, Freedom and Political Obligation*. Oxford: Oxford University Press.

Raz, Joseph (1986). *The Morality of Freedom*. Oxford: Clarendon Press.

Ridley, Matt (1997). *The Origins of Virtue*. New York: Viking.

Riley, Jonathan (1988). *Liberal Utilitarianism: Social Choice Theory and J. S. Mill's Philosophy*. Cambridge: Cambridge University Press.

Ritchie, D. G. *Darwin and Hegel* [1893]. In *Collected Works of D. G. Ritchie*, Peter P. Nicholson (ed.), Vol. II. Bristol: Thoemmes.

   Natural Rights [1895]. In *The Collected Works of D. G. Ritchie*, Peter P. Nicholson (ed.), Vol. III. Bristol: Thoemmes.

   (1998). *The Principles of State Interference* [1902]. In *Collected Works of D. G. Ritchie*, Peter P. Nicholson (ed.), Vol. I. Bristol: Thoemmes.

Rosen, F. (2003). *Classical Utilitarianism from Hume to Mill*. London: Routledge.

Ross, W. D. (1930). *The Good and the Right*. Indianapolis: Hackett, 1988.

Ruskin, John (1979). *Unto This Last* (1862) In *The Genius of John Ruskin*, John D. Rosenburg (ed.). London: Routledge and Kegan Paul.

Ryan, Alan (1995). *John Dewey and the High Tide of American Liberalism*. New York: W. W. Norton.

Schneewind, J. B. (1977). *Sidgwick's Ethics and Victorian Moral Philosophy*. Oxford: Oxford University Press.

Sher, George (1997). *Beyond Neutrality*. Cambridge: Cambridge University Press.

Sidgwick, Henry (1902). *Lectures on the Ethics of T. H. Green, Mr. Herbert Spencer and J. Martineau*. London: Macmillan.

Spencer, Herbert (1970). *Social Statics* (1851). New York: Robert Schalkenbach Foundation.

Stephen, James Fitzjames (1991). *Liberty, Equality and Fraternity* (1874). Chicago: University of Chicago Press.

Sumner, Wayne (1987). *The Moral Foundations of Rights*. Oxford: Oxford University Press.

Skyrms, Brian (2004). *The Stag Hunt and the Evolution of Social Structure*. Cambridge: Cambridge University Press.

Taylor, M. W. (1992). *Men Versus the State*. Oxford: Oxford University Press.

Thomas, Geoffrey (1987). *The Moral Philosophy of T. H. Green*. Oxford: Oxford University Press.

Weinstein, David (1998). *Equal Freedom and Utility*. Cambridge: Cambridge University Press.

Wiltshire, David (1978). *The Social and Political Thought of Herbert Spencer*. Oxford: Oxford University Press.

Wollheim, Richard (1959). *F. H. Bradley*. London: Penguin.

ARTICLES AND ESSAYS

Allett, John (1994). "The Conservative Aspect of Hobson's New Liberalism." In *Reappraising J. A. Hobson*, Michael Freeden (ed.). London: Unwin Hyman.
    "The Moral Philosophy of J. A. Hobson." In *J. A. Hobson after Fifty Years*, John Pheby (ed.). New York: St. Martin's.

Anderson, Elizabeth S. (1991). "John Stuart Mill and Experiments in Living." *Ethics*, 102: 4–26.

Bailey, James Wood (1998). "Is it Rational to Maximize?" *Utilitas*, 10: 195–221.

Barker, Ernest (1929). "Leonard Trelawny Hobhouse 1864–1929." *Proceedings of the British Academy*, 15: 536–54.

Berlin, Isaiah (2002). "Two Concepts of Liberty." In Berlin, *Four Essays on Liberty*, Henry Hardy (ed.). Oxford: Oxford University Press.

Bosanquet, Bernard (1903). "Hedonism among the Idealists," *Mind*, n.s., 12: 202–24.

Boucher, David (1997). "Introduction." In David Boucher (ed.), *The British Idealists*. Cambridge: Cambridge University Press.

Bradley, F. H. (1999). "Utility as (1) and End or (2) Standard of Morality." In F. H. Bradley, *Collected Works of F. H. Bradley*, Carol A. Keene (ed.), Vol. 1. Bristol: Thoemmes.

Brink, David (1992). "Mill's Deliberative Utilitarianism." *Philosophy and Public Affairs*, 21: 67–103.

Brink, David O. (2003). "Introduction." In T. H. Green, *Prolegomena to Ethics*, David O. Brink (ed.). Oxford: Oxford University Press.

Caney, Simon (1992). "Liberalism and Communitarianism: A Misconceived Debate." *Political Studies*, 40: 273–90.

Cohen, G. A. (1996). "Reason, Humanity and the Moral Law." In Korsgaard, *Sources of Normativity*. Cambridge: Cambridge University Press.

Condren, Conal (1997). "Political Theory and the Problem of Anachronism." In *Political Theory*, Andrew Vincent (ed). Cambridge: Cambridge University Press.

Crisp, Roger. "Self-love and the General Interest: Hume on Impartiality." Unpublished.

Cummiskey, David (1990). "Kantian Consequentialism." *Ethics*, 100: 586–615.

Dewey, John (1893). "Self-Realization as the Moral Ideal." *Philosophical Review*, 2: 652–64.

Frankfurt, Harry (1971). "Freedom of the Will and the Concept of a Person." *The Journal of Philosophy*, 68: 5–20.

(1988). "Identification and Wholeheartedness." In *The Importance of What We Care About*. Cambridge: Cambridge University Press.

Freeden, Michael (1993). "A Non-Hypothetical Liberalism: The Utilitarian Communitarianism of J. A. Hobson." Paper delivered at the 1993 Annual Meeting of the American Political Science Association.

(1994). "J. A. Hobson as a Political Theorist." In *J. A. Hobson after Fifty Years*, John Pheby (ed.). New York: St. Martin's.

Gewirth, Alan (1962). "Political Justice." In *Social Justice*, Richard B. Brandt (ed.). Englewood Cliffs, NJ: Prentice-Hall.

Ginsberg, Morris (1929). "The Contribution of Professor Hobhouse to Philosophy and Sociology." *Economica*, November: 251–66.

(1966). "Introduction." In L. T. Hobhouse, *Sociology and Philosophy*. Cambridge: Cambridge University Press.

Green, T. H. (1877). "Hedonism and Ultimate Good." *Mind*, o.s., 2: 266–69. Reprinted in *Collected Works of T. H. Green*, Peter P. Nicholson (ed.), Vol. IV. Bristol: Thoemmes Press.

(1997). "On the Different Senses of 'Freedom' as Applied to Will and the Moral Progress of Man" (1886). In *Collected Works of T. H. Green*, Peter P. Nicholson (ed.), Vol. II. Bristol: Thoemmes Press.

"Lecture on 'Liberal Legislation and Freedom of Contract'" (1881). In *Collected Works of T. H. Green*, Peter Nicholson (ed.), Vol. III. Bristol: Thoemmes Press.

"Lectures on the Philosophy of Kant" (1886). In *Collected Works of T. H. Green*, Peter Nicholson (ed.), Vol. II. Bristol: Thoemmes Press.

"Notes on Moral Philosophy". *Collected Works of T. H. Green*, Peter P. Nicholson (ed.), Vol. V. Bristol: Thoemmes Press.

"Utility as a Principle of Art and Morality." *Collected Works of T. H. Green*, Peter P. Nicholson (ed.), Vol. V. Bristol: Thoemmes.

Guttman, Amy (1992). "Communitarian Critics of Liberalism" (1985). In *Communitarianism and Individualism*, Shlomo Avineri and Avner de-Shalit (eds.). Oxford: Oxford University Press.

Guyer, Paul (2002). "Freedom as the Inner Value of the World." In *Kant on Freedom, Law and Happiness*. Cambridge: Cambridge University Press.

"Kantian Foundations of Liberalism." In Guyer, *Kant on Freedom, Law and Happiness*. Cambridge: Cambridge University Press.

"Kant's Morality of Law and Morality of Freedom." In *Kant on Freedom, Law, and Happiness*. Cambridge: Cambridge University Press.

"Nature, Freedom, and Happiness: The Third Proposition of Kant's *Idea for a Universal History*." In *Kant on Freedom, Law, and Happiness*. Cambridge: Cambridge University Press.

Haakonssen, Knud (1993). "The Structure of Hume's Political Theory." In *The Cambridge Companion to Hume*, David Fate Norton (ed.). Cambridge: Cambridge University Press.

Hare, R. M. (1993). "Could Kant Have Been a Utilitarian?" *Utilitas*, 5: 1–16.

Hill, Thomas E. Jr. (2002). "Happiness and Human Flourishing." In *Human Welfare and Moral Worth*. Oxford: Clarendon Press.

Hobhouse, L. T. (1913). "The Historical Evolution of Property, in Fact and in Idea." In *Property, Its Duties and Rights*, Charles Gore (ed.). London: Macmillan and Co.

　(1931). "The Problem." In *L. T. Hobhouse*, J. A. Hobson and Morris Ginsberg (eds.). London: George Allen and Unwin.

　"About Happiness." In *L. T. Hobhouse*, J. A. Hobson and Morris Ginsberg (eds.). London: George Allen and Unwin.

　(1966). "Industry and State" (1931). In L. T. Hobhouse, *Sociology and Philosophy*. Cambridge: Cambridge University Press.

Hobson, J. A. "The Theory of the State." *Manchester Guardian*, 23 November 1918.

　(1948). "Towards Social Equality" (1931). In *Hobhouse Memorial Lectures: 1930–1940*. Oxford: Oxford University Press.

　(1992). "Human Cost and Utility" (1896). In *Writings on Distribution and Welfare*, Roger E. Backhouse (ed.). London: Routledge/Thoemmes Press.

　"How is Wealth to Be Valued?" (1912–13). *Writings on Distribution and Welfare*, Roger E. Backhouse (ed.). London: Routledge/Thoemmes Press.

　"Economic Art and Human Welfare" (1926). In *Writings on Distribution and Welfare*, Roger E. Backhouse (ed.). London: Routledge/Thoemmes Press.

Hume, David (1957). Appendix III, "Some Further Considerations with Regard to Justice," *An Inquiry Concerning the Principles of Morals* (1751), Charles W. Hendel (ed.). New York: Liberal Arts Press.

Hurka, Thomas (1993). *Perfectionism*. Oxford: Oxford University Press.

　(1995). "Indirect Perfectionism: Kymlicka on Liberal Neutrality." *The Journal of Political Philosophy*, 3: 36–57.

Kymlicka, Will (1988). "Liberalism and Communitarianism." *Canadian Journal of Philosophy*, 18 (June): 181–203.

Lyons, David (1982). "Utility and Rights." In *Ethics, Economics and the Law*, Nomos 24, John W. Chapman and J. Roland Pennock (eds.). New York: New York University Press.

MacCallum, Gerald C. (1967). "Negative and Positive Freedom," *Philosophical Review*, 76: 312–34.

MacNiven, Don (1984). "Bradley's Critiques of Utilitarian and Kantian Ethics." *Idealist Studies*, 14(1): 67–83.

McCarthy, T. (1989–90). "The Politics of the Ineffable." *Philosophical Forum*, 21: 146–68.

Martin, Rex (2001). "T. H. Green on Individual Rights and the Common Good." In *The New Liberalism*, Avital Simhony and D. Weinstein (eds.). Cambridge: Cambridge University Press.

Matthew, H. C. G. (1990). "Hobson, Ruskin and Cobden." In *Reappraising J. A. Hobson*, Michael Freeden (ed.). London: Unwin Hyman.

Meadowcroft, James (1996). "Introduction." In J. A. Hobson, *The Social Problem* (1902). Bristol: Thoemmes.

Nesbitt, D. (2001). "Recognising Rights: Social Recognition in T. H. Green's System of Rights," *Polity*, 33.

Nicholson, Peter P. (1985). "T. H. Green and State Action: Liquor Legislation." *History of Political Thought*, 6: 517–50.

(1998). "Introduction." In *The Collected Works of D. G. Ritchie*, Peter P. Nicholson (ed.), Vol. I. Bristol: Thoemmes Press.

Panagakou, S. (2005). "Defending Bosanquet's Philosophical Theory of the State: A Reassessment of the 'Bosanquet-Hobhouse Controversy.'" *British Journal of Politics and International Relations*, 7: 29–47.

Penelhum, Terence (1993). "Hume's Moral Psychology." In *The Cambridge Companion to Hume*, David Fate Norton (ed.). Cambridge: Cambridge University Press.

Pettit, Philip (1993). "The Contribution of Analytical Political Philosophy." In Robert Goodin and Philip Pettit (eds.), *A Companion to Contemporary Political Philosophy*. Oxford: Blackwell.

Pippin, Robert (2000). "Hegel's Practical Philosophy: the Realization of Freedom." In Karl Ameriks (ed.), *The Cambridge Companion to German Idealism*. Cambridge: Cambridge University Press.

Railton, Peter (2002). "Alienation, Consequentialism, and the Demands of Morality" (1984). In *Consequentialism*, Stephen Darwall (ed.). Oxford: Blackwell.

Raz, Joseph (1999). "When We Are Ourselves: The Active and the Passive." In *Engaging Reason*. Oxford: Oxford University Press.

Ritchie, D. G. (1883). "The Rationality of History." In *Essays in Philosophical Criticism*, Seth Pringle-Pattison and R. B. Haldane (eds.). London: Longmans, Green and Co. Also in D. G. Ritchie (1998). *Collected Works of D. G. Ritchie*, Peter P. Nicholson (ed.), Vol. VI. Bristol: Thoemmes Press.

(1893). "Bonar's 'Philosophy and Political Economy'." *Economic Review*, 3: 541–55. In D. G. Ritchie (1998). *Collected Works of D. G. Ritchie*, Peter P. Nicholson (ed.), Vol. VI. Bristol: Thoemmes Press.

(1893–94). "On the Meaning of the Term 'Motive,' and on the Ethical Significance of Motives." *International Journal of Ethics*, 4: 89–104. In D. G. Ritchie (1998). *Collected Works of D. G. Ritchie*, Peter P. Nicholson (ed.), Vol VI. Bristol: Thoemmes Press.

(1998). "Locke's Theory of Property" (1893). In Ritchie, *Collected Works of D. G. Ritchie*, vol. II, *Darwin and Hegel*, Peter Nicholson (ed.). Bristol: Thoemmes Press.

(1998). "Review of T. H. Huxley, *Collected Essays*, Vol. I" (1893–4). *The International Journal of Ethics*, 4: 531–5.

(1894). "Symposium – Is Human Law the Basis of Morality, or Morality of Human Law?" *Proceedings of the Aristotelian Society*, Part II: 124–29. In

D. G. Ritchie (1998). *Collected Works of D. G. Ritchie*, Peter P. Nicholson (ed.), Vol. VI. Bristol: Thoemmes Press.

(1894–5). "Review of Benjamin Kidd, Social Evolution." *The International Journal of Ethics*, 5: 107–20. In D. G. Ritchie (1998). *Collected Works of D. G. Ritchie*, Peter P. Nicholson (ed.), Vol. VI. Bristol: Thoemmes.

(1895). "Free-Will and Responsibility." *International Journal of Ethics*, 5: 409–31. In D. G. Ritchie (1998). *Collected Works of D. G. Ritchie*, Peter P. Nicholson (ed.), Vol. IV. Bristol: Thoemmes.

(1895–6). "Has the Hereditability or Non-Hereditability of Acquired Characteristics Any Direct Bearing on Ethical Theory?" *Proceedings of the Aristotelian Society*, III: 144–8. In D. G. Ritchie (1998). *Collected Works of D. G. Ritchie*, Peter P. Nicholson (ed.), Vol. VI. Bristol: Thoemmes Press.

(1900). "Evolution and Democracy." In *Ethical Democracy: Essays in Dynamics*, S. Coit (ed.). London: G. Richards. In D. G. Ritchie (1998). *Collected Works of D. G. Ritchie*, Peter P. Nicholson (ed.), Vol. VI. Bristol: Thoemmes Press.

(1902). "Mr. Newman on 'The Politics' of Aristotle." *The Quarterly Review*, 196: 128–51.

(1998). "Moral Philosophy: On the Methods and Scope of Ethics" (1905). In *Philosophical Studies, Collected Works of D. G. Ritchie*, Peter P. Nicholson (ed.). Vol. V. Bristol: Thoemmes Press.

"Law and Liberty: The Question of State Interference" (1902). In *Studies in Political and Social Ethics, The Collected Works of D. G. Ritchie*, Peter P. Nicholson (ed.), Vol. IV. Bristol: Thoemmes Press.

"Natural Selection and the History of Institutions" (1901). In *Darwinism and Politics, The Collected Works of D. G. Ritchie*, Peter P. Nicholson (ed.), Vol. I. Bristol: Thoemmes Press.

"Natural Selection and the Spiritual World" (1901). In *Darwinism and Politics, The Collected Works of D. G. Ritchie*, Peter P. Nicholson (ed.), Vol. I. Bristol: Thoemmes Press.

"Confessio Fidei" (1905). In *Philosophical Studies, The Collected Works of D. G. Ritchie*, Peter P. Nicholson (ed.), Vol. V. Bristol: Thoemmes Press.

Rorty, Richard (1991). "Freud and Moral Reflection." In *Essays on Heidegger and Others, Philosophical Papers*, Vol. II. Cambridge: Cambridge University Press.

Sandel, Michael (1984). "Morality and the Liberal Ideal." *The New Republic*, 190, 18 (May 7, 1984): 15–17.

"The Procedural Republic and the Unencumbered Self." *Political Theory*, 12, 1 (February, 1984): 81–96.

Scarre, Geoffrey (1996). *Utilitarianism*. London and New York: Routledge.

Sen, Amartya (1982). "Rights and Agency." *Philosophy and Public Affairs*. 11 (1, Winter): 3–39.

Sidgwick, Henry (1884). "Green's Ethics." *Mind*, o.s., 9: 169–87.

Simhony, Avital (1989). "T. H. Green's Theory of the Morally Justified Society." *History of Political Thought*, 10: 481–98.

(1991). "On Forcing Individual's to Be Free: T. H. Green's Liberal Theory of Positive Freedom." *Political Studies*, 39: 303–20.

(1995). "Was T. H. Green a Utilitarian?" *Utilitas*, 7, 1: 121–44.

Simhony, Avital and D. Weinstein (2001). "Introduction." In Avital Simhony and D. Weinstein (eds.), *The New Liberalism: Reconciling Liberty and Community*. Cambridge: Cambridge University Press.

Simhony, Avital (2005). "A Liberalism of the Common Good: Some Recent Studies of T. H. Green's Moral and Political Theory." *The British Journal of Politics and International Relations*, 7: 126–44.

Skorupski, John (2006). "Green and the Idealist Conception of a Person's Good." In Maria Dimova-Cookson and William J. Mander (eds.), *T. H. Green: Ethics, Metaphysics, and Political Philosophy*. Oxford: Oxford University Press.

Spencer, Herbert (1978). "Justice" (1891). In *The Principles of Ethics*, Vol. II. Indianapolis: Liberty Press.

(1893). "The Inadequacy of 'Natural Selection'." *The Contemporary Review*, 43: 153–66.

Taylor, A. E. (1925). "F. H. Bradley." *Mind*, n.s., 34: 1–12.

Townshend, Jules (1994). "Hobson and the Socialist Tradition." In *J. A. Hobson after Fifty Years*, John Pheby (ed.). New York: St. Martin's.

Tuck, Richard (1993). "The Contribution of History." In Robert Goodin and Philip Pettit (eds.), *A Companion to Contemporary Political Philosophy*. Oxford: Blackwell.

Tyler, Colin (1998). "The Evolution of the Epistemic Self." *Bradley Studies*, 5: 175–94.

"The Metaethics of Pleasure: Jeremy Bentham and his Idealist Critics." *Contemporary Political Studies 1998*. A. Dobson and J. Stanyer (eds.), 1: 261–8.

Walton, A. S. (1983). "Hegel, Utilitarianism and the Common Good." *Ethics*, 93 (July): 753–71.

Watson, Gary (1982). "Free Agency." In *Free Will*, Gary Watson (ed.). Oxford: Oxford University Press.

Weiler, Peter (1972). "The New Liberalism of L. T. Hobhouse." *Victorian Studies*, 16: 141–61.

Weinstein, D. (1991). "The Discourse of Freedom, Rights and Good in Nineteenth Century English Liberalism." *Utilitas*, 3: 245–62.

(2000). "Deductive Hedonism and the Anxiety of Influence." *Utilitas*, 12, special symposium on Henry Sidgwick: 329–46.

(2001). "The New Liberalism and the Rejection of Utilitarianism." In *The New Liberalism*, Avital Simhony and D. Weinstein (eds.). Cambridge: Cambridge University Press.

(2002). "Herbert Spencer." In *Stanford Encyclopedia of Philosophy*. Center for the Study of Language and Information, Stanford University, online hypertext: plato.stanford.edu

(2004). "English Political Theory in the Nineteenth and Twentieth Centuries." In *Handbook of Political Theory*, Gerald Gaus and Chandran Kukathas (eds.). London: Sage.

(2005). "British Idealism and the Refutation of Utilitarianism." Conference on *Idealism Today*, Harris Manchester College, Oxford University: unpublished.

(2006). "Consequentialist Cosmopolitanism." In *Victorian Visions of Global Order*, Duncan Bell (ed.). Cambridge: Cambridge University Press, 2007.

Weinstein, W. L. (1965). "The Concept of Liberty in Nineteenth Century English Political Thought," *Political Studies*, 13.

Westphal, Kenneth (1993). "The Basic Context and Structure of Hegel's *Philosophy of Right*." In *The Cambridge Companion to Hegel*, Frederick C. Beiser (ed.). Cambridge: Cambridge University Press.

Wollheim, Richard (1962). "Introduction." In F. H. Bradley, *Ethical Studies* (1927), Richard Wollheim (ed.). Oxford: Clarendon Press.

Wright, Crispin (1984). "The Moral Organism." In Anthony Manser and Guy Stock (eds.), *The Philosophy of F. H. Bradley*. Oxford: Clarendon Press.

Index

IDEAS IN CONTEXT

Edited by Quentin Skinner and James Tully